U.S. SUPREME COURT OPINIONS
AND THEIR AUDIENCES

This book is the first study specifically to investigate the extent to which U.S. Supreme Court justices alter the clarity of their opinions based on expected reactions from their audiences. The authors examine this dynamic by creating a unique measure of opinion clarity and then testing whether the Court writes clearer opinions when it faces ideologically hostile and ideologically scattered lower federal courts; when it decides cases involving poorly performing federal agencies; when it decides cases involving states with less professionalized legislatures and governors; and when it rules against public opinion. The data shows the Court writes clearer opinions in every one of these contexts, and demonstrates that actors are more likely to comply with clearer Court opinions.

RYAN C. BLACK is Associate Professor of Political Science at Michigan State University.

RYAN J. OWENS is Professor of Political Science at the University of Wisconsin-Madison.

JUSTIN WEDEKING is Associate Professor of Political Science at the University of Kentucky.

PATRICK C. WOHLFARTH is Assistant Professor of Government and Politics at the University of Maryland, College Park.

U.S. SUPREME COURT OPINIONS AND THEIR AUDIENCES

RYAN C. BLACK

RYAN J. OWENS

JUSTIN WEDEKING

PATRICK C. WOHLFARTH

CAMBRIDGE
UNIVERSITY PRESS

University Printing House, Cambridge CB2 8BS, United Kingdom

Cambridge University Press is part of the University of Cambridge.

It furthers the University's mission by disseminating knowledge in the pursuit of
education, learning and research at the highest international levels of excellence.

www.cambridge.org
Information on this title: www.cambridge.org/9781107137141

© Ryan Black, Ryan Owens, Justin Wedeking and Patrick Wohlfarth 2016

First published 2016

A catalog record for this publication is available from the British Library

Library of Congress Cataloging-in-Publication Data
Names: Black, Ryan C., 1982- author. | Owens, Ryan J., 1976- author. |
Wedeking, Justin, author. | Wohlfarth, Patrick C., author.
Title: U.S. Supreme Court opinions and their audiences / Ryan C. Black
and Ryan J. Owens and Justin Wedeking and Patrick C. Wohlfarth.
Other titles: US Supreme Court opinions and their audiences |
United States Supreme court opinions and their audiences
Description: Cambridge, United Kingdom : Cambridge University Press, 2016. |
Includes bibliographical references and index.
Identifiers: LCCN 2015042012 | ISBN 978-1-107-13714-1 (Hardback)
Subjects: LCSH: United States. Supreme Court. | Judicial opinions–United
States–Language. | Judges–United States–Public opinion. | BISAC: LAW / General.
Classification: LCC KF8742 .B574 2016 | DDC 347.73/2602643–dc23 LC record
available at http://lccn.loc.gov/2015042012

ISBN 978-1-107-13714-1 Hardback

To Sarah – RCB
To Karen, Wyatt, and Henry – RJO
To Michelle – JPW
To Mom and Emily, for their steadfast support – PCW

CONTENTS

Acknowledgement   ix

1   **Introduction**   1
    1.1   Audiences and the Supreme Court   2
    1.2   Overcoming audience-based obstacles using opinion
          clarity   10
    1.3   Why care about strategic opinion writing?   12
    1.4   Structure of the book   14

2   **A theory: using opinion clarity to enhance compliance and manage
    public support**   17
    2.1   Literature on responsive compliance   19
    2.2   Theorizing how the Court uses opinion clarity to enhance compliance
          and manage public support   26
    2.3   Face validity for the theory   32

3   **Estimating the clarity of Supreme Court opinions**   40
    3.1   Previous efforts to measure opinion clarity   40
    3.2   Our approach: textual readability   46

4   **Supreme Court opinions and federal circuit courts**   60
    4.1   A theory of opinion clarity and federal circuit courts   61
    4.2   Lower court audiences and legal motivations   61
    4.3   Lower court audiences and ideological motivations   65
    4.4   Data and measures   67
    4.5   Methods and results   74
    4.6   Discussion   78

5   **Supreme Court opinions and federal agency implementors**   80
    5.1   A theory of opinion clarity and federal agencies   81
    5.2   The Supreme Court and federal agencies   83
    5.3   How past performance and agency characteristics influence Supreme Court
          opinion clarity   86

vii

5.4 Data and measures 88
5.5 Methods and results 93
5.6 Discussion 96

6 Supreme Court opinions and the states 97
6.1 A theory of opinion clarity and states 99
6.2 Legislative and gubernatorial professionalism 101
6.3 Data and measures 107
6.4 Methods and results 113
6.5 Discussion 118
6.6 Appendix to Chapter 6 120

7 Supreme Court opinions and the secondary population 122
7.1 A theory of opinion clarity and the mass public 123
7.2 An individual-level analysis of opinion clarity
and public opinion 125
7.3 An aggregate analysis of opinion clarity and public
opinion 132
7.4 Discussion 139
7.5 Appendix to Chapter 7 140

8 Establishing compliance as a function of clarity 141
8.1 Modeling lower court compliance as a function
of opinion clarity 141
8.2 A study of non-elite compliance as a function
of opinion clarity 149
8.3 Discussion 155

9 Conclusion 156

References 161
Index 178

ACKNOWLEDGEMENT

For helpful comments on portions of the manuscript, we thank Neal Allen, Barry Burden, David Canon, Michael Giles, Tim Johnson, Ken Mayer, Rich Pacelle, Alex Tahk, Joe Ura, and the participants at the American Politics Workshop at the University of Wisconsin and the University of Maryland, College Park. We thank Tom Marshall for sharing his data with us. We also thank our home institutions and colleagues. Each provided valuable support.

We could not have completed this book without the support of our families. Thank you for your patience and understanding as we worked on this book.

1

Introduction

In *Swann v. Charlotte-Mecklenburg Board of Education* (1971), the U.S. Supreme Court found itself embroiled in another desegregation dispute, this time over school busing. Nearly two decades earlier, in *Brown v. Board of Education* (1954), the Court prohibited segregation in public schools. Yet, racial integration still eluded much of the country's schools, partly because whites and blacks lived apart from one another. Federal judges and local school boards struggled (and evaded) for almost two decades to determine whether federal law compelled or even allowed school busing to achieve racial integration. After years of dodging the issue, the Supreme Court would finally decide whether court-ordered busing was constitutionally permissible. It was a case fraught with difficulties.

Since *Swann* would likely determine the extent of federal authority over state governments, it was poised to divide observers along racial and political lines. For some, allowing federal courts to force schools to bus students in an effort to achieve racial balance would be viewed as another High Court affront to states. Resistance threatened to expose the Court's institutional limitations. Indeed, earlier in the case's history, district court Judge James McMillan was hanged in effigy after he ordered the busing of more than 10,000 black students from inner-city schools to outlying white schools – and ordered some white students to be bused into the black inner-city schools. He received death threats. Crowds demonstrated at the courthouse, and politicians denounced his decision (Schwartz 1986, 21). Put plainly, opponents of a pro-busing decision would (and did) resist ferociously. So, if the Court wanted to allow busing, it would have to write a specially crafted opinion, and the justices knew it.

Not surprisingly, the fur began to fly after Chief Justice Burger circulated his draft majority opinion to his colleagues. Justices made numerous changes to Burger's draft opinions, all in an effort to make the final opinion clearer, with the hope that enhanced clarity would generate enhanced compliance. This endeavor was made more complicated because unlike the other justices in the majority, Burger did not fully support school busing. In response to some of Burger's language that sounded sympathetic to segregationists, Justice Brennan admonished Burger and the states' insignificant efforts. He demanded that the language of the Court's opinion not make them sound heroic and thereby indirectly validate them. He stated:

> We deal here with boards that were antagonistic to *Brown* from the outset and have been noteworthy for their ingenuity in finding ways to circumvent *Brown's* command, not to comply with it … I think any tone of sympathy with local boards having to grapple with problems of their own making can only encourage more intransigence … we might court a revival of opposition if we provide slogans around which die-hards might rally
>
> (Wahlbeck, Spriggs, and Maltzman 2009).

Brennan further noted the importance of staying the course and using clear and correct language in light of some nascent southern sympathy toward desegregation:

> For me, *the matter of approach* has assumed major significance in light of signs that opposition to *Brown* may at long last be crumbling in the South. The recent inaugural addresses of the new Governors of Georgia and South Carolina, and at least some of the newspaper surveys reported in the last month give concrete encouragement that this may be the case … I nevertheless suggest that *our opinion should avoid saying anything that might be seized upon as an excuse to arrest the trend. Some things said in your third circulation seem to me to present that hazard*
>
> (Wahlbeck, Spriggs, and Maltzman 2009) (Emphasis supplied).

As Brennan's comments highlight, Supreme Court justices care deeply about how their "audiences" will respond to their opinions – and with good reason. By constitutional design, justices rely on lower court judges to interpret their opinions, on executive and state officials to implement them, and on the general public to support them and the Court. Brennan knew this, of course, which is why he pushed Burger for clearer language that could limit noncompliance and strengthen the Court's decision. He understood the language of the Court's opinion is linked to compliance with its decisions – and often its institutional support – and that the Court might benefit from tailoring opinion clarity to its audience.

1.1   Audiences and the Supreme Court

Those responding to the Supreme Court's decisions – its audiences – have the ability to circumvent the Court's policies. Whether it is within the judicial hierarchy, in the administrative and regulatory apparatus of the federal government, across often politically diverse state governments, or among various groups or individuals in the general public, the Supreme Court's audiences can block or escape the Court's policies. Supreme Court decisions do not mark the beginning of the end for most legal controversies but, rather, the end of the beginning. Rarely does the Court have the last say or take the last action in a case. Instead, others must implement or apply its policies. And these actors can obstruct the Court. The question justices routinely face is: do I seek out my own goals without regard to the responses of my audiences, or do I try to anticipate and manage audience-based obstacles? We believe it is the latter.

The central effort of this book is to examine whether justices modify the clarity of their opinions to enhance compliance with their decisions and to manage support for the Court.

Of course, we are not the first to suggest audiences can influence how judges and justices behave – though we are the first to examine systematically how justices change the clarity of their opinions because of those audiences. In 2006, Baum published a book called *Judges and Their Audiences: A Perspective on Judicial Behavior*. Baum's argument was that judges and justices might alter their behavior for a number of reasons, chief of which were personal or instrumental.

On the personal level, some judges, he argued, might cast votes or take positions so as to improve their reputations and to maintain favor with key groups. For example, some justices appear to value the support of legal academics, and might therefore pay attention to the views of legal academia when deciding cases. Other justices have strong ties to philosophical groups like the ACLU or the Federalist Society and might behave so as to protect or enhance those relationships.

Additionally, and in line with the argument we propose in this book, Baum argued judges and justices might pay attention to their audiences for *instrumental* reasons. By currying favor with key audiences – or, less skeptically, by not offending them – judges are less likely to lose legitimacy. And when they maintain judicial legitimacy, judges maintain their own power. Accordingly, by anticipating audiences' responses, judges can protect their institutions and their power to make legal policy. Baum's ideas have spread. Ginsburg and Garoupa (2009) distinguish not only between individual and collective viewpoints, but also between internal versus external audiences. As they note, "[b]y internal, we mean audiences within the judiciary itself; by external, we mean audiences such as lawyers, the media or the general public" (Ginsburg and Garoupa 2009, 453). As they later explain (2009, 458–489):

> External incentives come from outside of the judiciary, reflecting the views of society or public opinion in general, but also the interests of the particular relevant constituencies with power over the courts. These constituencies might include the bar, academic commentators, other branches of government, as well as political parties and others, depending on the institutional environment of courts. How the judges respond to these external constituencies, individually and collectively, shapes the social and political influence of the judiciary as a whole.

We build upon this foundation of thought. We argue the Supreme Court wants to enhance compliance with its decisions and manage public support for the Court. Accomplishing those goals depends upon the behavior of actors within the judiciary and those external to it. That is, it depends on the Court's audiences.

In the next chapter, we provide more justification for our theoretical argument, but here we offer some brief foreshadowing to extoll the theory's plausibility. Consider the following comment by Justice Thomas. Thomas was asked why he wrote short and seemingly simple opinions. His response?

> There are simple ways to put important things in language that's accessible ... [t]he editing we do is for clarity and simplicity without losing meaning ... We're not there to win a literary award. We're there to write opinions that some busy person or somebody at their kitchen table can read and say, I don't agree with a word he said, but I understand what he said
>
> (Friedersdorf 2013).

Clearly, Thomas believes opinion clarity has consequences. And he is not alone. Justice Powell's office manual to his law clerks stated:

> Although all work for the Court is important, the substance and form of Court opinions have first priority with Justice Powell
>
> (Wahlbeck, Spriggs and Sigelman 2002, 175).

The link between opinion clarity and the Court's audiences is important because opinion language will influence how audiences comply with and respond to Supreme Court decisions. Thinking back to *Brown* and the phrase that schools should desegregate "with all deliberate speed" provides an easy example of how a lack of clarity corresponds with diminished compliance. Without knowing what "all deliberate speed" meant, it was difficult to tell whether courts and implementers met the Court's goals.

Murphy (1964) agrees with respect to the importance of opinion clarity. Clear opinions are among the conditions he says are necessary for the Court to make efficacious policy: "The first condition is an unambiguous commitment to a policy, an unambiguous commitment unambiguously stated" (93). This point becomes even more important when viewed from Murphy's framework that emphasized the Court's *outputs* and their *impacts* "may in turn generate *feedbacks* into the judicial process, creating fresh *demands* or altering old ones ..." (Murphy 1964, 35).[1] Similarly, Wheeler (2006) cites a lengthy list of legal scholars who have argued for the importance of clarity, and adds: "the clarity of a judicial opinion and the manner in which it is communicated can have an important effect on those responsible for implementing that opinion" (1187). Wheeler examines the well-known case, *INS v. Chadha* (1983), which deals with the constitutionality of the legislative veto, and asks a very basic question: did opinion clarity influence the implementation (or lack thereof) in *Chadha*? Through his in-depth case study, Wheeler highlights that while the opinion was clear in the sense that the legislative veto was unconstitutional, the opinion was far less clear on other crucial aspects (such as the severability issues) that were important for lower courts to know. In other words, this case illustrates the important policy consequences that a lack of opinion clarity can have. At the same time, it emphasizes how opinion clarity can be an important tool to manage audience concerns. While we go into greater detail about how and why the Court adapts to its audiences in later chapters, the bottom line is this: *if the Court wants to maximize the impact of its decisions, it must adapt to its audiences.* And one way it can adapt is to modify the clarity of its opinions in the process.

So, who are these audiences to whom the Court must adapt? Perhaps the most well-known classification of the Court's various audiences comes from Canon and Johnson (1999), who categorize the Court's audiences into four groups – the interpreting audience, the implementing audience, the consumer audience, and the secondary audience. Though we do not hew precisely to their categories in this book, we find their four groups

---

[1] Though, it should be noted Murphy also acknowledges when an opinion writer is sure about the goal but uncertain about the best means of achieving it, vagueness can be valued if it provides implementers discretion that provides the Court an empirical choice at a later date (93).

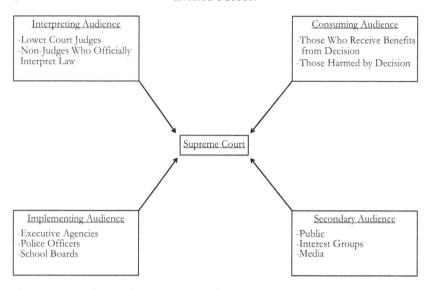

Figure 1.1: Audiences that can constrain the U.S. Supreme Court (Canon and Johnson 1999).

useful in a broad presentational sense.[2] Figure 1.1 displays Canon and Johnson's four groups.

Interpreting audience. The interpreting audience includes those who interpret and apply Supreme Court decisions – a group Canon and Johnson (1999) argue consists almost entirely of lower court judges. There are 13 circuit courts of appeals and 94 federal judicial districts (each with at least one district judge), comprising a total of 865 Article III judges.[3] Each of these judges interprets and applies Supreme Court precedent. In addition, there are a number of Article I courts that apply Supreme Court precedent. The states and territories also have courts that apply U.S. Supreme Court precedent.

Not surprisingly, the Court's interpreting audience is busy. A simple glance at caseload data confirms the importance and activity of the lower courts. During the Supreme Court's 2012 term (which ran from October

---

[2] Our hesitancy stems from the fact that there is considerable overlap among the four groups, where implementing audiences can be the same as interpreting audiences who can also be part of the consumer audience. For example, school boards in the *Swann* case are part of all three categories.

[3] Data from www.uscourts.gov/FederalCourts/UnderstandingtheFederalCourts/Courtof Appeals.aspx. Data current as of September 29, 2014.

2012 – October 2013), the High Court decided 74 cases.[4] In the 12 months preceding March 31, 2013, however, the federal circuit courts terminated just under 60,000 cases. And, the federal district courts terminated roughly 350,000 cases.[5] State court dockets, combined, dwarf these numbers. So, while the Supreme Court renders significant decisions, it is predominantly the lower courts who then interpret and apply them to new situations.

This interpreting audience can evade the Court's decisions. Given the sheer number of cases they decide, lower court judges have many opportunities to circumvent Court policies. And they sometimes do (see, e.g., Dolbeare and Hammond 1971; Milner 1971; Peltason 1971).[6] Consider Judge Stephen Reinhardt, a liberal judge on the Ninth Circuit Court of Appeals, who once stated lower court judges should not change their views "in order to please the Supreme Court" (*cited in* Cross 2005, 379). He claims to "follow the law the way it used to be, before the [conservative] Supreme Court began rolling back a lot of people's rights" (Carlsen 1996; *cited in* Baum 2006). Other judges have made similar comments. One judge remarked: "We follow [Supreme Court rulings] when we can't get around them" (Baum 1978, 212). And, District Court Judge Brevard Hart once wrote an opinion stating: "This Court's independent review of the relevant historical documents … convinces it that the U.S. Supreme Court has erred in its reading of history" (Caminker 1994*b*, 819).[7] Hart went on to ignore the Supreme Court's Establishment Clause precedents.[8]

Lower court judges have numerous ways to limit, or, "underrule" (Paulsen 1990) Supreme Court decisions (Murphy 1959). For example, judges can ignore the Court's decisions and cite one of their own instead (Manwaring, Reich, and Wasby 1972). They can criticize or question the Court's opinion in an effort to weaken that decision's perceived authority (Tarr 1977). They can distinguish the Court's previous decisions by

---

[4] These are signed opinions and per curiam opinions with oral argument.
[5] Data come from Tables B-1, C-1, and D-1 of the Federal Judicial Caseload Statistics, which are available at: www.uscourts.gov/Statistics/FederalJudicialCaseloadStatistics/caseload-statistics-2013.aspx.
[6] To be sure, while lower court judges often comply (e.g., Benesh 2002*b*; Benesh and Reddick 2002; Wahlbeck 1998; Songer and Sheehan 1990; Baum 1980; Gruhl 1980), their compliance is not guaranteed.
[7] *See Jaffree v. Board of School Commissioners*, 545 F. Supp. 1104, 1128 (S.D. AL 1983).
[8] *See also Stell v. Savannah-Chatham County Board of Education*, 220 F. Supp. 667 (S.D. GA 1963)(finding that social science data undercut *Brown v. Board's* factual findings).

claiming a particular decision does not apply because the facts are too different from the case currently before them. In a similar capacity, they can simply interpret the Supreme Court decision narrowly by stating the holding only applies in limited situations. And, not to be ignored, lower court judges can dismiss cases on procedural grounds rather than apply the Court's decisions at all. In short, lower court judges frequently interpret Supreme Court policies and have the opportunity to use their discretion to evade those policies. Justices, if they want to effectuate their goals, may need to adapt in anticipation of judges' likely responses to their decisions.

Implementing audience. Next, the implementing audience consists of the authorities who actually execute the Court's decisions. As Canon and Johnson (1999) state: "implementors apply the system's rules to persons subject to their authority" (19). For example, when the Court holds a practice in public schools is unconstitutional, local school boards, administration, and state education departments implement new policies to accommodate the decision. When the Court holds searches or seizures violate the Fourth Amendment to the U.S. Constitution, law enforcement officials must implement the decision. And, when the Court holds the federal government has (or does not have) certain specified regulatory powers, the executive branch, through administrative agencies, implements the decision.

Implementors, like interpreters, can use their discretion to advance or frustrate the Court's decisions. They, too, can evade a decision by finding the Court's policy irrelevant to the circumstances at hand. One study, focusing specifically on implementation after *Adarand Constructors, Inc. v. Peña* (1995)(limiting the power of federal agencies to use racial preferences in federal contracts), found little agency compliance (Gao 2012, 4). Another study found newer federal agencies, and those dedicated to certain programmatic dynamics, are less likely to implement Supreme Court policies faithfully (Spriggs 1996). Mountains of books on desegregation highlight how some school boards and education officials refused to implement the Court's decision in *Brown*. The take-home point from these studies and others we will discuss later is that implementers can obstruct justices' goals. So justices must adapt.

Consuming audience. The consuming audience consists of those who will receive benefits or suffer injuries because of the Court's decision (Canon and Johnson 1999, 20). For example, in a taxpayer suit against the federal government, the taxpayer involved in the dispute, all taxpayers similarly situated, and the federal government would be the consuming audiences. In a labor dispute case, the consuming audience would be employees, unions, employers, and possibly stockholders. And in an abortion case, the consuming audience would include, at a minimum, the unborn baby and the mother.

A common example of how the consumer audience can hinder the Court from achieving its policy goals is, again, the issue of school desegregation. While *Brown* had the goal of integrating schools, in many places desegregation did not occur because of "white flight" (whites leaving public schools for private or suburban schools). While this effect was more immediate in parts of southern states, white flight occurred in many places. For example, whereas in 1973, 55% of school children in the Boston public schools were white, that number plummeted to 13% by 2009 (Monahan and Walker 2009, 218).[9]

Secondary audience. Finally, the secondary audience refers to the general public (Canon and Johnson 1999). The public stands in a position to assist the Court by supporting its decisions or, alternatively, opposing them and the Court. The Court relies on public support to maintain its institutional legitimacy (Gibson, Caldeira, and Baird 1998). As Alexander Hamilton (1788) noted, the Court has "no influence over either the sword or the purse" and must instead rely on public respect for its opinions to have any force. Public support can provide the Court with considerable power to stand up to elected officials when necessary. Conversely, public opposition and diminished legitimacy can limit its power.[10]

Prevailing empirical evidence supports our theoretical claim and shows public opinion is an obstacle that can influence justices' decision making. For example, Casillas, Enns, and Wohlfarth (2011) find public opinion can directly influence justices' decisions. Knowing the Court lacks formal institutional power to coerce compliance with its decisions, justices seek to avoid widespread negative scrutiny and public opposition that could undermine the Court's legitimacy and jeopardize subsequent implementation. McGuire and Stimson (2004) also discover justices are highly responsive to changes in public mood. Flemming, Bohte, and Wood (1997) find a strong link between justices and public mood (see also, Enns and Wohlfarth 2013; Flemming and Wood 1997; Giles, Blackstone, and Vining 2008; Mishler and Sheehan 1993, 1994; Stimson,

---

[9] We do not examine the consuming audience in this book because they are so varied. It would be nigh impossible to make generalizations about them.

[10] See, e.g., *Ex Parte McCardle* (1869) (where the post-*Dred Scott* Court lost legitimacy and conceded Congress could strip the Court of jurisdiction).

Mackuen, and Erikson 1995). Indeed, as Hall (2014) notes, the popularity of the Court's decision is an important component for the Court's ability to enact social change.

In summary, the Court faces various audiences that can obstruct its policies. Lower court judges can use their discretion to evade High Court rulings. Implementers can dig in their heels to circumvent the Court's decisions. And the public's reaction to Court decisions can influence judicial legitimacy and power. Accordingly, if justices want to effectuate their goals – and we have every reason to believe they do – they must adapt to these audiences and manage the constraints they present.

The question, though, is *how* can justices navigate those potential obstacles? How can they best achieve their goals in the face of actors who can circumvent them? Our answer is simple: they anticipate and manage those obstacles *by writing clear opinions*.

1.2 Overcoming audience-based obstacles using opinion clarity

Clear opinions can help justices achieve their goals for four primary reasons, all of which we discuss more extensively in the next chapter. We point to Figure 1.2 as a useful way to understand the four primary reasons we discuss. It contains two main components – enhancing compliance and managing legitimacy. First, as Figure 1.2 shows, opinion clarity can *remove discretion* from actors opposed to the Court's decision. For example, when the Court renders a clear decision, a lower court judge's ability to evade it decreases. This was a key finding of Romans (1974) in his study on compliance with the Supreme Court's criminal procedure cases. Only after the Court's "clear and to the point" decision in *Miranda v. Arizona* (1966) did lower courts come around to accept the holding of *Escobedo v. Illinois* (1964) (criminal suspects have a right to counsel during police interrogations) (Romans 1974, 51). By writing a clear opinion, the Court removes ambiguity opponents can manipulate to evade it.

Second, opinion clarity can help whistle-blowers *monitor* and report on the behavior of actors who defy the Court (Cross and Tiller 1998). Literature suggests justices – and actors who are friendly to them – may have an easier time monitoring whether actors comply with their decisions when the decisions themselves are clear. For example, Staton and Vanberg (2008, 507) argue: "[t]he more clearly an opinion states the policy implications of the decision, the easier it is to verify whether policy makers have faithfully complied, making it more likely that external actors

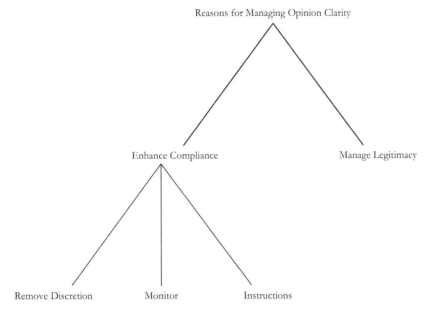

Figure 1.2:   Role of opinion clarity for the Supreme Court.

can monitor and impose costs for noncompliance." When they observe noncompliance, these actors (e.g., interest groups, the Solicitor General, state Attorneys General) can help parties litigate cases and appeal to the Supreme Court to seek reversal (Black and Owens 2011*b*; Brent 2003).

Third, clear opinions can serve as *instructions* that help guide actors who are inclined to follow the Court's decisions but might not have the resources to be able to do so. That is, clear opinions can help facilitate compliance among actors that may lack the resources to determine how best to comply. Like the dutiful but confused student who works hard for an "A" but simply does not fully understand the material taught by the professor, actors may want to comply with a Supreme Court opinion but find it hard to do so. By writing a clear opinion, the Court helps these actors to comply.

Fourth, the Court may *manage its legitimacy* by writing clear opinions. Those who read Court opinions expect them to be coherent and understandable, and when they are not, the Court might suffer. The rule of law supposes clarity (Owens and Wedeking 2011). So, when justices write unclear opinions, they fail to fulfill one of their key obligations. By writing clear opinions, they can maintain – and perhaps even improve – the Court's reputation.

To be sure, the Court's opinions vary in terms of clarity. As any Court watcher can attest, the Court does not always write clear opinions. Some opinions could win awards for incoherence. Yet, we believe much of the variation is systematic and explainable. And, more importantly, we think it is often intentional. Indeed, we have evidence to suggest as much. Consider the following concern by Justice Powell in *Pruneyard Shipping Center v. Robins* (1980). Powell displayed his concern about the need for clarity when he stated:

> In sum, Bill [Rehnquist], I think this is an extremely important case. It will prompt special interest groups of all shades of persuasion to go to work immediately on state legislatures to expand the opportunities for promoting causes. *We can be sure that every sentence in the opinion will be scrutinized ...*
>
> (Wahlbeck, Spriggs, and Maltzman 2009).

In some cases, the Court will write clearer opinions to remove discretion from opposed actors, to help whistle-blowers, to provide better instructions, and to manage the Court's support. What are these cases? Under what conditions will the Court write clearer opinions? We explain our hypotheses more fully in the next chapter, but for now, we suggest the Court will write clearer opinions under the following conditions:

- When it is ideologically distant from the lower federal courts – and when those courts are ideologically scattered;
- When it rules against poor performing federal agencies;
- When it rules against states with less professionalized legislatures; and
- When it rules against public opinion.

1.3   Why care about strategic opinion writing?

Before we proceed, we pause to address the consequence of all this: Why care about Supreme Court opinions, and, more specifically, why care whether justices strategically alter their opinions to adapt to audiences and their likely reactions? What does this matter in terms of our understanding of law and the Supreme Court? We offer four answers.

First, readers should care how justices write opinions because it is the *content* of the Supreme Court's opinions that guide behavior. As Spriggs and Hansford (2001) tell us: "Supreme Court opinions set up referents for behavior by providing actors with information necessary to anticipate the consequences of their actions" (1092). Actors within society look to those opinions to determine whether they can engage in particular behaviors. "[S]cholars, practitioners, lower court judges, bureaucrats, and the public closely analyze judicial opinions, dissecting their content in an endeavor to understand the doctrinal development of the law" (Corley, Collins, and Calvin 2011, 31). In other words, people must understand the content of opinions and, as such, scholars should understand the factors that influence the clarity of those opinions.

Second, our holistic approach expands knowledge of the Court by considering it as one institution in a larger political system where justices know they do not necessarily have the last word. We place justices in a broader framework than most existing studies. Instead of focusing solely on how *internal* Court dynamics influence opinions (which is, of course, important), we look more broadly at how the entire system can influence opinions. Our approach shows how the Court is tied into a larger network of actors and audiences in the American political and legal system. By examining how justices write opinions with the lower federal courts in mind, we shed new light on how lower courts can actually influence the U.S. Supreme Court. By analyzing how executive agencies influence the writing of opinions, we can better understand the separation of powers and its effects on the Court. By focusing on how state attributes affect judicial opinions, we underscore the importance of federalism to the Court. And, by examining the role of public opinion, we expand the literature on public opinion and the Court. In sum, this book reveals the Court in a holistic and interconnected environment.

Third, knowing justices intentionally alter the language of their opinions to overcome audience-based obstacles tells us something important about the strategic aggressiveness of justices. The results in this book show justices as actors with goals who do what they can to overcome obstacles. The approach falls squarely within a strategic conception of judging (Epstein and Knight 1998) and provides empirical support on opinion writing that, to date, has not yet been discovered.

Finally, understanding how the Court alters its opinions can inform us about how the Court acquires and maintains judicial legitimacy. Legitimacy allows judges to accomplish their broader goals and protect the Court's institutional authority (e.g., Casillas, Enns, and Wohlfarth 2011; Gibson and Caldeira 2011; Ura and Wohlfarth 2010). The Court lacks the capacity to execute its own opinions. Its reason and logic are the foundations of its support. Given the Court's power ultimately comes from its legitimacy – and that sustained negative attention and unpopular decisions can erode public support for the Court (Durr, Martin, and

Wolbrecht 2000) – justices should avoid repeatedly calling that legitimacy into question. By investigating whether justices modify their opinions to adapt to their audiences, we can – and do – make inferences about how they maintain and build their legitimacy.

1.4 Structure of the book

This book unfolds in nine chapters. In Chapter 2, we discuss the literature on compliance with Supreme Court decisions. We examine historical and recent scholarship on compliance. And, we draw on a growing body of scholarship that focuses on how extralegal factors motivate judges (see, e.g., Baum 2006). We take our cue from this literature and develop our central theory – that justices alter the clarity of their opinions to induce audiences to comply with them, and to manage audience responses to them.

In Chapter 3, we explain how we measure the clarity of the Court's opinions. Our measure of opinion clarity focuses on the readability of the Court's opinions. As we discuss in Chapter 3, readability scores offer "quantitative, objective estimates of the difficulty of reading selected prose" (Coleman 2001, 489). Researchers use readability scores to measure the degree of difficulty in reading a text (DuBay 2004). As other works have done (Black and Owens 2012b; Goelzhauser and Cann 2014; Owens, Wedeking, and Wohlfarth 2013), we use textual readability as a measure of opinion clarity. But, unlike existing studies, we use a sophisticated compound measurement approach that allows us to make much stronger inferences about opinion readability. What is more, using human coders, we also empirically validate this measure to verify it is a legitimate and useful indicator of text difficulty.

Chapter 4 is the first of five empirical analyses. In it, we examine the Supreme Court's relationship with lower federal courts. We consider whether justices craft clearer opinions when the federal circuits are ideologically scattered, and when they are ideologically distant from the Court. Justices have legal and policy goals. They want to reduce inter-circuit conflict. They also want to make favorable legal policy. When they write clearer opinions, they can help themselves satisfy both goals. The results of Chapter 4 suggest justices write clearer opinions when the circuit courts are ideologically scattered and are likely to create conflicts among themselves. Justices also write clearer opinions when they are increasingly distant from the circuits. In other words, the characteristics of lower courts lead justices to modify the clarity of their opinions.

Chapter 5 investigates whether justices alter the clarity of their opinions based on the characteristics of the federal agencies charged with executing them. We examine if justices alter the clarity of their opinions based on whether the federal agency whose decision they review have a poor track record of performance. We find justices enhance opinion clarity when ruling against poor performing federal agencies. Justices utilize clarity to constrain or perhaps simply better instruct such agencies – and they are increasingly likely to do so when the Court rules against the agency.

Chapter 6 analyzes a second implementing audience. It examines whether justices alter the clarity of their opinions based on the characteristics of the states that appear before them and who therefore will be expected to implement their decisions. We scrutinize whether the Court writes differently when it decides cases against states whose governments are more professionalized versus those that are less professionalized. Our results show the Court crafts clearer opinions in cases with part-time legislatures who lack resources and policy expertise. What is more, these results are magnified when those states are politically unified.

Chapter 7 examines whether justices alter the clarity of their opinions when they rule against prevailing public sentiment. We review what happens when justices anticipate a greater likelihood of public opposition to their decisions. The results show justices write increasingly clear opinions when they rule contrary to popular opinion than when they rule consistent with majority sentiment. In other words, when justices have greater reason to expect public opposition to their decisions – and believe external actors might use public opinion as a license to shirk the Court's decisions – justices enhance opinion clarity. They use clarity to manage the Court's public support.

Chapter 8 confirms our overarching assertion that opinion clarity *does in fact* influence whether audiences comply with the Court's decisions. There, we examine a large sample of federal circuit court decisions to determine whether the clarity of Supreme Court opinions affects how federal circuit court judges treat (i.e., apply) them. We also employ a survey experiment to determine whether clarity also affects non-elites. The results confirm that compliance is strongly correlated with opinion clarity. These results, then, support the validity of our measurement strategy and the approaches we take in the book: Not only do justices use opinion clarity strategically, opinion clarity has the actual effects we hypothesize.

In Chapter 9, we summarize our key findings and briefly discuss their broader importance for the Supreme Court's position in the American legal and political system. We discuss what our results mean in terms of the strategic behavior of justices and the constraints on justices' behavior. We review how our findings could apply to other political institutions, such as the bureaucracy, that are not elected but nevertheless might be subject to indirect electoral constraints.

***

We began this chapter by discussing *Swann*. Returning to it, we ask if Justice Brennan's concern in *Swann* was the exception or the rule. What can justices do, if anything, to enhance compliance with their decisions? Can they take affirmative steps to drive up support for those decisions and drive down the probability of non-compliance? How do the audiences who grapple with the Court's decisions influence the Court's opinions? In the next chapter, we lay out our theory. We examine what previous scholarship has to say about compliance and the Court's audiences. We then build on these studies and present our theory.

A theory: using opinion clarity to enhance compliance and manage public support

In *Cervantes v. Guerra* (1981),[1] the Fifth Circuit Court of Appeals examined whether a government-funded, nonprofit organization constitutionally could prohibit foreigners from serving on the organization's board. The Hildago County Community Action Agency received federal money (pursuant to the Economic Opportunity Act of 1964) to provide services to the poor. Federal law stated one-third of its board of governors had to be "chosen in accordance with democratic selection procedures adequate to assure that they are representative of the poor in the area served."[2] After the Agency adopted a bylaw declaring non-citizens could neither serve on the board nor vote to select its members, two non-citizens challenged it. They claimed the bylaw violated the Equal Protection Clause of the Constitution.

The judges on the Fifth Circuit panel that heard the case most certainly opposed the bylaw personally. Judge John Minor Wisdom, a moderate Eisenhower appointee, had been instrumental in pushing racial desegregation in the South (Bass 1981; Friedman 2009). John Robert Brown, another moderate Eisenhower appointee, also made his mark on desegregation, earning a spot (along with Wisdom) in the so-called Fifth Circuit Four – a group of judges who pushed for racial integration (Bell 1982). Rounding out the three-judge panel was Carol Dineen King, a Jimmy Carter appointee. Each of these judges' policy preferences seemed to oppose the bylaw. None seemed to have an interest in upholding it. Yet they did uphold it. As the panel put it: "when the Supreme Court speaks clearly, we are bound to obey."[3]

In contrast, the Fourth Circuit Court of Appeals disobeyed the Supreme Court in *Davis v. Davis* (1981).[4] At issue was whether a forty-year prison

---

[1] *Cervantes v. Guerra*, 651 F.2d 974 (5th Cir. 1981).
[2] *Cervantes* at 976.
[3] *Cervantes* at 981.
[4] See *Davis v. Davis*, 646 F.2d 123 (4th Cir. 1981).

sentence for the possession of nine ounces of marijuana violated the Eighth Amendment (i.e., the cruel and unusual punishment provision). The Fourth Circuit, in an *en banc* ruling, held it did. On review, the Supreme Court vacated that decision and sent the case back to the Circuit for reconsideration. The Circuit quickly reaffirmed its previous decision in a ruling many believe amounted to the liberal judges' repudiation of the increasingly conservative Supreme Court. And by "many," we include the Supreme Court. The High Court was not pleased. It reviewed the case a second time – and the justices showcased their displeasure with the Fourth Circuit's intransigence. The Court scolded the Circuit for "having ignored, consciously or unconsciously, the hierarchy of the federal court system," stating:

> [U]nless we wish anarchy to prevail within the federal judicial system, a precedent of this Court must be followed by the lower federal courts no matter how misguided the judges of those courts may think it to be.[5]

Why did the Fifth Circuit follow the Supreme Court in *Cervantes* while the Fourth Circuit ignored it in *Davis*? What can the Court do to enhance compliance with its decisions and manage public support? We believe justices can and do use opinion clarity instrumentally. They write clearer opinions to enhance compliance and to manage public support for the Court and its decisions.

Policymakers often seek to ensure that actors charged with interpreting and implementing their decisions actually do so. Because of bureaucratic hierarchies, the separation of powers, and federalism, no single governmental actor or institution has the power to create and execute its own policies. Between policy creation and policy application, victories can turn into defeats. As policies proceed from creation to interpretation and, later, implementation, initial losers can turn into subsequent winners. With so many hands in the policymaking "cookie jar," outcomes are never certain. Put simply, compliance – "behavior that is in some way consistent … with the behavioral requirements" of the policy decision (Canon and Johnson 1999, 17) – is not guaranteed.[6]

---

[5] *Hutto v. Davis*, 454 U.S. 370, 375 (1982).

[6] A host of scholars also examine anticipatory compliance, or whether lower courts and implementors fall in line with *current* Supreme Court preferences. Because this book focuses on what the Court can do to enhance compliance *after* it renders a specific decision, we do not discuss anticipatory compliance. For a good review of it, however, see Westerland et al. (2010); Caminker (1994a); Songer, Segal, and Cameron (1994); and Eskridge (1986).

The Supreme Court's unique reliance on other institutions leaves it especially vulnerable to noncompliance. Because the Court lacks an electoral connection to voters, it is bereft of conventional arguments for legitimacy based on popular sovereignty. So, its decisions are constantly scrutinized by the public and by actors who must execute those decisions – actors who *do* have an electoral connection. What is more, the Court lacks the power to raise its own revenue, which means it must rely on Congress for funding. Congress is not always charitable.[7] Further adding to the Court's woes, it relies on others to execute its decisions. And faithful policy implementation is no guarantee. Combined, these vulnerabilities mean justices must tread carefully, anticipate audience responses to their decisions, and minimize the threat of noncompliance.

What does the literature tell us about responsive compliance and how these limitations relate to compliance? When are audiences more or less likely to comply with Court decisions? We address these questions now.

2.1   Literature on responsive compliance

Scholarship on responsive compliance has deep roots, going back to the Warren Court era when scholars examined responses to the Court's desegregation (McKay 1956), religion (Birkby 1966; Dolbeare and Hammond 1971; McGuire 2009; William Ker Muir 1967), and criminal rights decisions (Milner 1971; Manwaring 1968). These and other studies (Murphy 1959; Vines 1963; Wood and Anderson 1993) suggest there are systematic conditions under which audiences (fail to) comply with Supreme Court decisions.[8] More specifically, research suggests responsive compliance is strongly correlated with four features: *ideological congruence* between the audience and the Supreme Court, *coalitional and case characteristics* of the Supreme Court's original decision, the *resources* of the audience, and the *clarity* of the Court's opinions. We explain each of these in turn.[9]

---

[7] The entire federal judiciary takes up just 0.02% of all federal outlays (Roberts 2013), and the Supreme Court itself accounts for only 0.0002% of total federal outlays (Kennedy 2013). The Court is not, in other words, a major budgetary priority for Congress.

[8] See Estreicher and Revesz (1989) for an interesting study on agency non-acquiescence with federal circuit court decisions.

[9] It is worth pointing out scholars believe lower courts frequently comply with High Court decisions (Hoekstra 2005; Benesh 2002b; Benesh and Reddick 2002; Wahlbeck 1998; Songer, Segal, and Cameron 1994; Johnson 1979; Benesh and Martinek 2002; Songer and Haire 1992; Songer and Sheehan 1990; Songer 1987; Stidham and Carp 1982; Gruhl 1980).

2.1.1   Responsive compliance as a function of ideological congruence with the Supreme Court

If compliance scholarship has coalesced around anything, it is that ideological congruence strongly influences positive and negative responses to Supreme Court decisions. Numerous studies have demonstrated that lower court judges and bureaucrats often exercise their ideological preferences when rendering decisions (e.g., Benesh 2002*a*; Clinton and Lewis 2008; Clinton et al. 2012; Hettinger, Lindquist, and Martinek 2003; Songer and Haire 1992; Songer, Segal, and Cameron 1994). These preferences, of course, sometimes conflict with the precedent articulated by the Supreme Court (McGuire 2009). And, when that happens, noncompliance becomes more likely.

For example, looking at lower court compliance with the Supreme Court, Romans (1974) examines criminal procedure cases in the aftermath of *Escobedo v. Illinois* (1963) (on the admissibility of confessions) and finds conservative state supreme courts evaded the Supreme Court's liberal decision. Liberal state courts, of course, eagerly complied. More systematically, Kassow, Songer, and Fix (2012) find that ideological agreement with U.S. Supreme Court precedent leads state supreme courts to treat that precedent positively: "a liberal court," they find, "is more likely to positively treat precedent when such a positive treatment will lead to a liberal outcome" (379). They also find conservative state supreme courts are more likely to treat conservative precedents positively. A similar study by Comparato and McClurg (2007) shows some state supreme courts drag their feet for ideological reasons when forced to apply Supreme Court precedent. Benesh (2002*b*) finds that while case facts influence lower court judges' decisions to overturn confessions, so too do their ideological predispositions. In her sample, a panel of liberal judges overturned confessions with a probability of 0.13 while a panel of conservative judges did so with a probability of 0.01.

After *Brown*, many Southern judges who were ideologically opposed to the decision dug in their heels and obstructed (Peltason 1971). Similarly, as Canon and Johnson (1999) state, "in one extreme case, a Birmingham, Alabama, municipal judge not only refused to follow Supreme

So the reader should be aware that noncompliance, while worthy of study because of its importance and uniqueness, may not be the modal response to Supreme Court decisions. Nevertheless, we believe the literature – at least regarding lower court responsiveness – has room to expand.

Court decisions desegregating municipal facilities, but also declared the Fourteenth Amendment unconstitutional" (38). Similarly, in *Stell v. Savannah-Chatham County Board of Education* (S.D. GA 1963), a judge in the Southern District of Georgia, opposed to desegregation, sought to use social scientific data to challenge the Supreme Court's reasoning in *Brown*. He held: "[t]he Court accordingly accepts the evidence given in the present case as having somewhat stronger indicia of truth than that on which the findings of potential injury were made in *Brown*." Rosenberg (1991) likewise points to Federal District Judge Harold Cox of Mississippi who called a group of African Americans "a bunch of niggers" and "chimpanzees" for registering to vote (90). These challenges, and others we could mention, involved actors who were ideologically predisposed against the High Court's decision.

At the agency implementation level, scholarship likewise shows bureaucrats want to craft policy consistent with their own ideological preferences, and might refuse to comply because of these policy differences. They also seek to promote their agencies' missions – even when their behavior goes against congressional or judicial preferences (e.g., Niskanen 1971; Wildavsky 1992; Wilson 1989). Indeed, numerous studies point to how agency self-interest – and the likelihood of noncompliance in particular – leads the elected branches to attempt to control agency implementation (e.g., Bawn 1995, 1997; Huber, Shipan, and Pfahler 2001; Lewis 2003, 2008; McCubbins, Noll, and Weingast 1987; Moe 1985; Shipan 2004; Weingast and Moran 1983; Wood and Waterman 1994). Agency policy preferences also affect compliance with Supreme Court decisions. Spriggs (1996), for instance, finds that agencies dedicated to certain programs are less likely to comply with Court decisions that undo or modify those programs (see also, Spriggs 1997). Other studies suggest an agency's organizational intent to protect its policy jurisdiction affects responsiveness to judicial decisions (Johnson 1979; Johnson and Canon 1984; Shapiro 1968). Bureaucrats are more likely to resist complying with judicial directives if the agency as a whole is firmly committed to a particular policy.

2.1.2 Responsive compliance as a function of opinion coalitions and case characteristics

Other scholars look beyond ideology and argue the makeup of the Court coalition that decides a case, and the contextual components of the case, can influence responsive compliance. Some have argued audiences are less likely to comply with, or respond favorably to, Supreme Court decisions rendered by small majority coalitions of justices. For instance, Murphy (1964) argues smaller majorities on the Court might signal weakness with the decision. Weakness, in turn, may lead lower court judges to avoid complying with the precedent. "The greater the majority," he claims, "the greater the appearance of certainty and the more likely a decision will be accepted and followed in similar cases" (66) (*cited in* Johnson 1979, 793). Judge Richard Posner makes a similar point, stating: "a dissenting opinion undermines the majority opinion not only by indicating a lack of unanimity but also by expressing criticisms of the outcome" (Posner 2008, 400).[10]

A number of studies show the size of the Court's coalition matters. Benesh and Reddick (2002) find lower courts comply more quickly with unanimous Supreme Court precedents than with non-unanimous precedents. Hansford and Spriggs (2006) find larger voting coalitions decrease the probability a future Supreme Court negatively interprets a precedent (see also, Corley and Wedeking 2014). In their study of state supreme court treatment of U.S. Supreme Court precedent, Kassow, Songer, and Fix (2012) find state supreme courts are more likely to treat Supreme Court precedents positively when large coalitions create them. And Zink, Spriggs, and Scott (2009) find through experiment that when the Court produces a unanimous opinion, the general public is more likely to agree with and accept a decision, even when they disagree with it ideologically. In short, the size of the Supreme Court's coalition seems to influence compliance, with audiences more likely to comply with decisions adopted by larger majority coalitions.

Audience responses may also turn on whether the Court overrules one of its precedents. For example, in their experiment, Zink, Spriggs, and Scott (2009) find respondents were more likely to agree with, and accept, a Supreme Court decision that followed precedent than one overruling precedent. And, this result held even after accounting for a respondent's general ideological proclivity to support or oppose the decision. Other studies concur. Corley and Wedeking (2014), for instance, find lower courts are more likely to treat a Supreme Court precedent negatively than positively when it overrules precedent. Thus, it appears audiences are

---

[10] Looking at the Supreme Court's treatment of its own precedent, Spriggs and Hansford (2001) find the Court is more likely to overrule one of its decisions when a minimum winning coalition created it.

sometimes more likely to comply with decisions that follow rather than overrule precedent.

Whether the Court exercises judicial review to strike a law also influences audience responses. Corley and Wedeking (2014) find lower courts are more likely to treat a precedent negatively when that precedent struck a federal statute as unconstitutional. When striking down a law, the Supreme Court places the judiciary in the crosshairs of political controversy and potential public ire, and lower court judges and policy implementors are not likely to be pleased.

Studies suggest the complexity of a Supreme Court decision might also influence audience responses to it. Consider the plight of busy lower court judges and bureaucrats who must interpret and apply the High Court's pronouncements. Given their workloads, they are often unable to spend vast amounts of time thinking through complex policies. As such, they must sometimes rely instead on heuristics to make decisions (Gigerenzer and Gaissmaier 2011). A heuristic is an informational shortcut used to facilitate decision making when receivers face large and complex amounts of information, making it cognitively demanding to process messages systematically. A busy lower court judge or implementor who does not have the time to determine whether and how a Supreme Court precedent fits within a case might simply apply the High Court precedent and move on. In other words, a complex precedent, applied in what is likely to be a complex dispute later, might influence compliance. Busy audiences will refer to what the Supreme Court has already sorted out. In fact, empirical evidence supports the claim that audiences are more likely to comply with complex precedent. Benesh and Reddick (2002) show lower court judges are more likely to follow complex Supreme Court decisions than less complex decisions.[11]

In short, the literature shows that when the Supreme Court's opinion is a narrow majority, overrules precedent, or invalidates a law, audience responses may more likely be negative.

2.1.3 Responsive compliance as a function of audience resources

Another factor that most certainly influences compliance with High Court decisions is audience resources. There is, for instance, a

---

[11] Though we should also note that the literature on heuristics suggests that while they increase efficiency in the decision making process, heuristics also introduce a fair amount of bias in decision making (Lau and Redlawsk 2001).

well-established literature on how resources improve litigant success in the judiciary. A party with resources can stack the deck in its favor (Songer, Kuersten, and Kaheny 2000, 540). Well-resourced parties tend to hire better lawyers who conduct extensive research. They can anticipate legal challenges to their actions and inoculate themselves against those challenges by creating "comprehensive litigation strategies" (Songer, Sheehan, and Haire 1999, 812). At the trial level, well-resourced parties engage the services of solid expert witnesses, who thereby create better trial court records. They take polls and hold mock trials, which allow them to test legal arguments in harmless venues (Galanter 1974). The same logic might also underscore the importance of resources for those who respond to Court rulings.

Scholars have also shown resources are important to state legislatures, as states with more resources appear to produce better policies. Policy in states with resource-poor legislatures tends to be simpler and of lesser quality (King, Zeckhauser, and Kim 2004). Thus, assuming an audience wants to follow a Supreme Court precedent, if it has more resources, the audience will be better able to comply with it. After all, compliance with Supreme Court decisions is not always easy. The issues in some decisions require considerable amount of policy expertise. Others require time and staff for research. Not all institutional actors possess such resources.

2.1.4   Responsive compliance as a function of opinion clarity

A number of prolific scholars argue the language of the Court's opinion can influence audience responses. Baum, for example, asserts compliance with Supreme Court decisions is a function of the clarity with which the Court writes its decision, and the effectiveness of the policy's communication (Baum 1978, 1976). Wasby (1993) states: "greater clarity is generally thought to produce greater compliance" (371). In her study on federal taxpayer standing, Staudt (2004) finds: "[w]hen the legal precedent is clear, unambiguous, and narrow (or is perceived to be such) ... judges adhere to it ... " (659). And to the extent that greater certainty correlates with enhanced clarity, Corley and Wedeking (2014) discover lower courts are more likely to treat a Supreme Court precedent positively when the precedent expresses more certainty in its language.

The problem for justices, of course, is they can control *only some* of the features shown to enhance compliance. Justices cannot control whether audiences agree with them ideologically. They cannot control the

Table 2.1: *The Supreme Court's control over audience-related features.*

Compliance Feature	Court Control
Audience Ideology	None
Audience Resources	None
Case Salience	Moderate
Case Complexity	Moderate
Case Coalition Size	Moderate
Ideological Coalition	Moderate
Overrule Precedent	Extensive
Exercise Judicial Review	Extensive
Opinion Language	Extensive

resources available to their audiences.[12] They do not have substantial control over the salience of their cases. They can, of course, grant review to highly salient cases or refuse to grant review to mundane cases. But, once granted, justices cannot directly control their salience (beyond the implications of the legal rule they craft).[13] They have only a moderate degree of control over the complexity of their case by instructing the issues to be briefed. Further, there is little a majority coalition can do to generate unanimity on the Court, or to meet some of the coalitional characteristics that lead to enhanced compliance. Certainly, justices can bargain and accommodate to reach unanimity (Johnson, Spriggs, and Wahlbeck 2005), but there is no guarantee that accommodating one's colleague will further one's goals. Sometimes accommodation would be detrimental to justices' goals.

What justices *can* control is whether they overrule a precedent, whether they strike a law, and, most importantly for us, the clarity of their opinions. Once they decide how they will vote and the rationale they will use to support their decision, they will want to strengthen their opinion. And here is where opinion clarity comes in to play. Justices can use clarity to support their decisions. They decide what language goes into an opinion.

---

[12] There may be instances in which the Court can use procedural rules to benefit some groups over others in the legislative or judicial process (see, e.g., McCubbins, Noll, and Weingast 1987), but by and large the Court's control over such matters is negligible.

[13] Of course, salience is multifaceted and can be captured both before and after the decisions (e.g., legal salience is typically measured by whether a decision makes Congressional Quarterly's list of influential precedents or whether *The New York Times* reports on it).

And, they can use opinion clarity to enhance compliance and manage public support.

2.2   Theorizing how the Court uses opinion clarity to enhance compliance and manage public support

Our theoretical starting point is that justices are strategic judicial decision makers who seek to pursue their policy goals but are constrained from so doing by a host of internal and external norms and actors. "Most justices, in most cases, pursue policy; that is, they want to move the substantive content of law as close as possible to their preferred position" (Epstein and Knight 1998, 23). But, justices pursue their goals in an interdependent environment in which their decisions are a function not only of their personal goals, but also the goals of those with whom they interact. What this means is justices must do the best they can to achieve their goals, given their audiences and the potential constraints they impose. They will write clearer opinions to enhance compliance with their decisions and to manage the Court's public support.[14]

2.2.1   Using clarity to enhance compliance

Clarity removes discretion. When the Court renders a clear decision, an actor's ability to evade decreases. Canon and Johnson (1999) make the point succinctly when they state: "the greater the ambiguity ... the wider the range of possible interpretations" (49). This was a key finding of Romans (1974) in his study on compliance with the Supreme Court's criminal procedure cases. Only after the Court's "clear and to the point" decision in *Miranda v. Arizona* (1966) did the lower courts come around to accept the holding of *Escobedo v. Illinois* (1964) (criminal suspects have

---

[14] Justices can take a number of strategic actions, of course, to achieve their goals (Murphy 1964). In some cases, this strategic behavior might mean refusing to hear cases that could generate controversy (Perry 1991). A strategic justice may also need to manipulate legal context to circumvent supervisory constraints. Smith and Tiller (2002) argue that when faced with judicial review, executive agencies make policy through adjudication rather than rule making to make it more difficult for the reviewing court to change the agency policy. Another strategic action might be to decide a case on constitutional, rather than statutory grounds, so as to increase the costs on Congress to respond (Epstein, Segal and Victor 2002). Justices could, likewise, moderate the policies of their opinions (Gely and Spiller 1990), or limit their decisions to the facts of the case at hand, as they did in *Bush v. Gore* (2000). A further option available to them, and the one we study here, is to alter the clarity of their opinions.

a right to counsel during police interrogations) (Romans 1974, 51). By writing a clear opinion, the Court removes ambiguity that opponents can use to evade it.

Other studies agree. In her analysis of plurality opinions, Corley (2009) notes: "ambiguity gives the lower courts increased discretion in analyzing and applying precedent and consequently, 'affords lower courts considerably more leeway to minimize or even disregard entirely the precedential value' of ... opinions" (35, *quoting* Novak 1980, 779). Additionally, in their study of remands, Pacelle and Baum (1992) find lower courts are more likely to side with the Supreme Court's winner when the Court reverses and remands rather than vacates and remands. Vacation and remand orders, they argue, afford lower court judges more wiggle room to justify their previous decisions, which they use to stick with their original ruling. In fact, lower court judges took advantage of this flexibility roughly 50% of the time to maintain their original rulings. On the other hand, where the Court reversed and remanded – and gave the lower courts less flexibility – the lower courts stuck with their original rulings only 10% of the time. Clarity, in other words, led to more compliance.

Clarity helps monitoring and whistle-blowing. For the modern Supreme Court, clearer opinions can expose, and thereby dissuade, noncompliance by making it easier to detect (Staton and Vanberg 2008).[15] When an official receives a clear directive, it is easier for others to determine whether he or she follows it. Staton and Vanberg (2008), for instance, argue that "[t]he more clearly an opinion states the policy implications of the decision, the easier it is to verify whether policy makers have faithfully complied, making it more likely that external actors can monitor and impose costs for noncompliance" (507). Spriggs (1996) argues likewise, stating a comprehensible Supreme Court opinion makes it easier for litigants in cases involving federal agencies to take politically stubborn bureaucrats back to court. McNollgast (1994) argues the Court tries to "isolate" noncompliant lower court judges so "[t]he Court can then focus its attention on the most egregiously nonconforming lower court decisions ... " (1634). According to Songer, Segal, and Cameron (1994), litigants help the Court to audit lower courts (and, presumably, other government officials) by appealing cases and informing the High Court of shirking. When they observe noncompliance, they can help parties litigate

---

[15] As Staton and Vanberg (2008) point out though, a court with *low* levels of legitimacy would be unable to use its legitimacy to leverage officials into compliance.

cases and appeal to the Supreme Court to seek reversal (Black and Owens 2011*b*; Brent 2003).

A number of actors can perform such oversight. Lower court judges can dissent and signal noncompliance to the High Court (Cross and Tiller 1998). The Solicitor General can petition the Court to hear cases that are out of compliance (Black and Owens 2012*b*). Interest groups can file amicus briefs alerting the Court to noncompliance (Black and Owens 2009; Caldeira and Wright 1988). Knowing some actors can and will perform this fire-alarm oversight (McCubbins and Schwartz 1984), officials may not stray from upper Court policies. We have every reason to believe the same dynamic applies to external actors that might wish to use public opinion as a license to shirk Supreme Court policies. If monitoring parties can better recognize when implementing actors deviate from the Court's policies, they can take those actors to federal court to seek redress.

In fact, the Court might use its legitimacy to enhance this risk of exposure and pressure officials to comply with its decisions. Officials should perceive they face a greater risk of incurring costs when they shirk a clear Court decision. The Supreme Court has a foundation of legitimacy, or diffuse support, among citizens (Easton 1965, 1975). As Gibson and Caldeira (2009) explain, the public generally holds a "positivity bias" toward the Court, rooted in perceptions of judicial symbols and impartiality that compel the vast majority of citizens to confer legitimacy on decisions – even those with which they might initially disagree (see also, Gibson, Caldeira, and Baird 1998; Ura 2014). What is more, citizens generally view the Supreme Court as different than an ordinary political institution, commonly conferring legitimacy on decisions based on a perception that they are principled (Gibson and Caldeira 2011). Thus, although elected officials normally possess an acute desire to avoid supporting policies that contradict public opinion, potential (non)compliance with Supreme Court decisions should change this decision making calculus. By shirking a clear opinion, officials risk being caught out of step with a Court that has a considerable foundation of institutional support. Officials, as a result, should perceive that they risk incurring costs, including jeopardizing their own standing among the mass public, if the public and others catch them shirking a Court decision.

To be sure, we do not contend heightened clarity enables justices to induce perfect compliance. External actors might sometimes be willing to accept even extreme costs to pursue their own goals. But we contend that on average, officials will be mindful of the heightened risk involved with shirking a clear Supreme Court opinion, and they will adjust their behavior accordingly. External actors should often find it costly to be caught out of step with the Court's policies. Therefore, justices should have reason to believe writing clearer opinions can help to monitor compliance and therefore meaningfully increase the likelihood of faithful compliance.

Clarity offers better instructions. We also suspect clearer opinions enhance compliance because they simply make it easier for actors to understand what the Court wants. As anyone who has ever put – well, anything – together knows, a clearer set of instructions is a godsend. The effect of Supreme Court opinion clarity is probably similar. In fact, Baum (1976) makes precisely this point. As he puts it, ambiguity "leav[es] loyal judges uncertain as to their superior's intent" (92) which, in turn, can lead them to drift – unwittingly – from the Court's policy goals.

In many respects, this argument follows a team-based approach towards studying the judicial hierarchy. The team-based approach suggests justices and judges both want to observe the "correct" outcome, but make decisions oftentimes with different information available and under different contexts (see, e.g., Caminker 1994*b*). Similarly, Cameron and Kornhauser (2005) discuss how lower courts follow signals sent by the Supreme Court in order to decide cases correctly. Assuming these models apply (or even apply some of the time), it makes sense that increased clarity can enhance the lower court's (and other actors') abilities to decide consistent with the Court's directives. Enhanced clarity may send more precise signals.

2.2.2   Using clarity to manage public support

Justices also write clearer opinions (particularly when ruling against public opinion) to minimize any loss of support they fear they might incur from a wrathful public. Justices should be mindful of public opinion when making decisions (e.g., Casillas, Enns, and Wohlfarth 2011; Enns and Wohlfarth 2013; Epstein and Martin 2010; McGuire and Stimson 2004; Mishler and Sheehan 1993). This is the case because frequent rulings against the public could cause the Court to lose legitimacy. The Court's legitimacy is the foundation of its support. As Justice Frankfurter once claimed: "The Court's authority ... rests on sustained public confidence in its moral sanction" (Caldeira 1986, 1209). A consistent pattern of shirking public opinion could damage the Court's legitimacy. Caldeira (1986) finds, in part, the Court's legitimacy decreases as it strikes more federal laws and sides with criminal defendants. Related work shows courts that systematically ignore *stare decisis* can jeopardize their institutional legitimacy (see, e.g., Zink, Spriggs, and Scott 2009). Bartels and Johnston (2013) suggest ideologues who oppose specific Court decisions are more likely to challenge the Court's legitimacy than those who approve of its decisions (cf., Gibson and Nelson 2015). Collectively, these results suggest citizens respond negatively to Court decisions they dislike.

When ruling against public opinion, justices will enhance the clarity of majority opinions. By writing clearer opinions, justices can attempt to minimize the loss of support they might suffer – or *think* they might suffer – from jilting the public. While we believe justices know they have strong institutional support (and will use that support when they can), they surely must be concerned about managing that goodwill and support. As Gibson, Caldeira, and Spence (2003) state, such goodwill is not limitless. Justices must be concerned about replenishing it after drawing it down. Opinion clarity can help the Court mitigate negative responses to its own legitimacy.

Scholars have argued opinion clarity affects the public, and might affect their views about the Court. As Vickrey, Denton, and Jefferson (2012) put it: "The challenge for the nation's judges ... is to make sure that the public understands what is expressed in a supreme court opinion ... [O]pinions serve as the court's voice because rulings communicate not only to lawyers, but also to the public ..." (74). Opinion clarity is essential. Clarity "is crucial in order to demonstrate fairness, ensure public and media understanding of the role of the court, and encourage acceptance of High Court judgments. Effective communication starts with a well-reasoned and well-written opinion" (78).

Similarly, Benson and Kessler (1987) find plain legal writing is more credible and persuasive than "legalese." The authors conducted an experiment in which they showed respondents legal briefs and petitions for rehearing that employed common language and those that contained legalese. Respondents who read legalese were significantly more likely to think the brief was unpersuasive and the writer was unconvincing. The authors further demonstrate that arguments presented in legalese were 26% less persuasive than the simple text.

We believe justices have a sense of this. Surely, they must know that when they rule against public opinion, they are at risk. Why enhance that risk by writing an unclear opinion the public will find to be less persuasive, less convincing, and less believable? We suspect they will not. We suspect they write clearer opinions in such instances.

Empirical evidence confirms our general belief that justices alter the content of their opinions in anticipation of negative public reactions. For example, Black, Owens, and Brookhart (2014) find the Court is more likely to cite foreign sources of law – to expand the debate and provide additional reasons for their decisions – when they render controversial decisions. Corley, Howard, and Nixon (2005) show the Court is more likely to cite the *Federalist Papers* in controversial opinions. Nelson (n.d.) shows after the influx of television advertising in judicial campaigns, elected judges began to write opinions that were easier to read. The logic is simple. When judges had more to fear from the public, they performed "better." This finding is consistent with our argument: when justices decide cases with outcomes against the public's broad policy preferences – and therefore, have more to fear from public reaction – they write clearer opinions.

Recent comments by judges themselves corroborate our belief. As highlighted earlier, Justice Thomas once remarked: "We're there to write opinions that some busy person or somebody at their kitchen table can read and say, 'I don't agree with a word he said, *but I understand what he said*'" (Friedersdorf 2013; *emphasis supplied*). Similarly, Judge Steve Leben of the Kansas Court of Appeals recommends that judges:

> ...explain things so that a layperson can understand them, whether it's an oral ruling or a written opinion. *A person involved in a court proceeding is more likely to accept a court decision that he or she can understand*, and the failure to explain legal concepts to the layperson leads to an unnecessary lack of understanding of what judges do
>
> (Leben 2011, 54)(Emphasis supplied)

Our argument about the use of opinion clarity is also related to literature on legitimacy and procedural fairness. Scholarship shows procedural fairness can facilitate legitimacy. Even losers in proceedings believe institutions to be legitimate when they receive fair procedural treatment. Casper, Tyler, and Fisher (1988) find procedural and distributive fairness influenced how defendants evaluated their treatment by the judicial system, independent of their sentences. Sunshine and Tyler (2003) find the fairness of police procedures has a strong influence on police legitimacy. Like the positive effect of procedural fairness, opinion clarity can stanch the Court's bleeding when it rules against public opinion. When the Court explains more clearly why it ruled the way it did, the public might feel treated more fairly than if justices wrote an obfuscated opinion. Vickrey, Denton, and Jefferson (2012) make precisely this point, stating: "Litigants, *especially losing litigants*, care less about the length of opinions and more about *clarity* and the scope or soundness of the reasoning" (76)(Emphasis supplied).

To be sure, a fountain of scholarship suggests the Court's legitimacy is unlikely to diminish seriously by a single "bad" decision (e.g., Gibson, Caldeira, and Spence 2003). Yet, even such scholarship recognizes judicial carelessness with public opinion might diminish the Court's legitimacy. Gibson, Caldeira, and Spence (2003) state: "A few rainless months do not seriously deplete a reservoir. A sustained drought, however, can exhaust the supply of water" (365). To prevent erosion of public confidence, justices should want to take steps to justify and mitigate decisions against public opinion.

2.3   Face validity for the theory

By now, it should be clear what our theory is. But does that theory have face validity? We believe so. On top of the literature we cited previously, we looked to the justices' private communications – the memos they exchanged during the opinion-writing process. There, we discovered substantial evidence that justices think about and shape opinion clarity.

The book's introduction showcased one such instance. Other examples abound. Consider the memo in Figure 2.1 from Chief Justice Burger to Justice White in *California Human Resources Dept. v. Java* (1971). Chief Justice Burger makes two explicit references to ways he could improve the clarity of the opinion in line with Justice White's suggestions.

In *Healy v. James* (1972), Chief Burger wrote to his colleagues underscoring the importance of clarity in the final majority opinion. He argued their decision needed to hand down guidelines with a high level of clarity. Specifically, he wrote: "To be sure that the decisional processes in administering such an institution are in fact even-handed and are seen to be even-handed, guidelines should be specific, known to all, applied with uniformity and articulated with some clarity" (Wahlbeck, Spriggs, and Maltzman 2009).

These concerns are not isolated. In *Levitt v. Committee for Public Ed.* (1973), Justice Powell wrote to Chief Justice Burger, stating: "I think the wiser course would be to state – with some clarity – in dictum in the opinion that the permissible forms of aid to state-required testing could be funded under a properly redrawn statute." In another case, *Monell v. Department of Social Services* (1978), Justice Brennan wrote a memo to his colleagues expressing his intent to increase the clarity of the opinion. The last sentence of the memo in Figure 2.2 expresses this sentiment.

Later in *Monell*, Brennan responded to a suggestion made by Justice Potter Stewart to remove a footnote. Brennan refused, stating the

Supreme Court of the United States
Washington, D. C. 20543

CHAMBERS OF
THE CHIEF JUSTICE

April 5, 1971

Re: No. 507 - California Human Resources Dept. v. Java

Dear Byron:

Thank you for your note of April 3.

I have a feeling that what you suggest is already there, but the point is somewhat elusive and it can readily be cleared up.

I think if we add the following to the first sentence at the top of page 12, that should clear it up:

"allowed, as a result of a hearing at which both parties are able to present their respective positions;"

For even more clarity we could add after that sentence

"Since both parties are given notice of the initial interview and have, as we note elsewhere, full opportunity to present claims and challenge opposing positions that initial confrontation is crucial."

However, I will work at this to be sure the point you make is clarified. We are of one mind on the fundamentals.

Regards,

Mr. Justice White

cc: The Conference

Figure 2.1: Supreme Court justices' concern about the clarity of opinion language (Wahlbeck, Spriggs, and Maltzman 2009).

footnote should be retained "given the need for clarity." He then suggested additional sentences aimed at enhancing the opinion's clarity (Wahlbeck, Spriggs, and Maltzman 2009, 18).[16]

---

[16] More examples from other cases exist; see also *Rose v. Mitchell* (1979), where Justice Powell requested a small change in language to Justice Blackmun's opinion in order to increase clarity. Also, see *Gertz v. Robert Welch, Inc.* (1973), where Chief Justice Burger expresses (in a private memo) his preference that Justice Powell should clarify his concept.

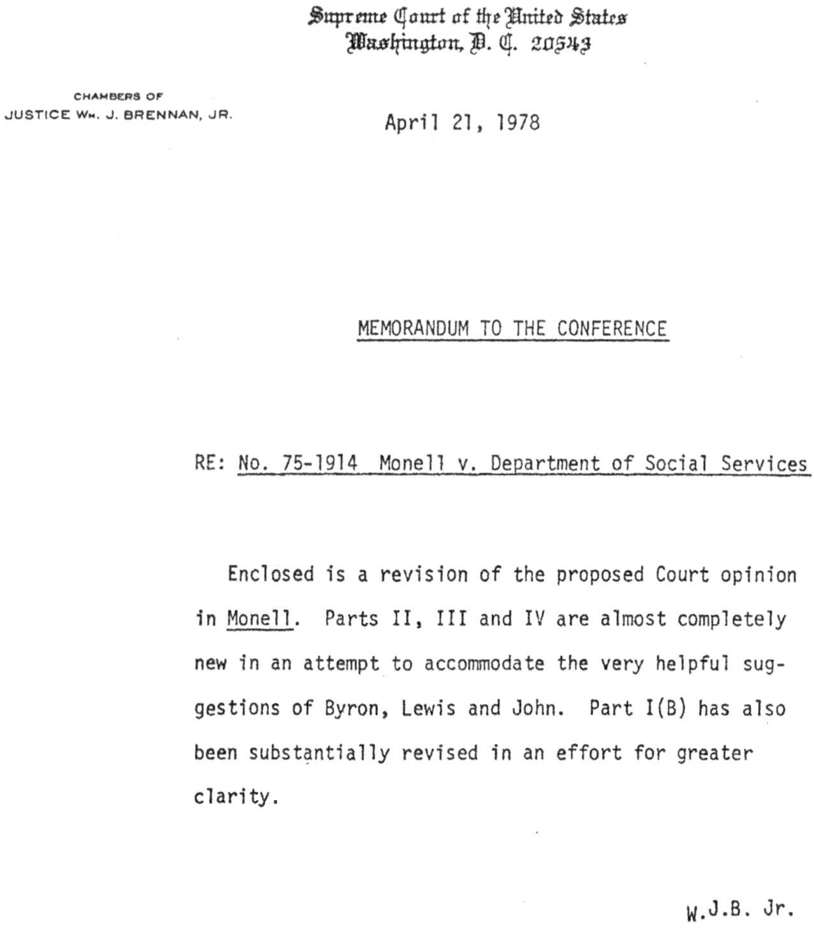

𝔖𝔲𝔭𝔯𝔢𝔪𝔢 𝔔𝔬𝔲𝔯𝔱 𝔬𝔣 𝔱𝔥𝔢 𝔘𝔫𝔦𝔱𝔢𝔡 𝔖𝔱𝔞𝔱𝔢𝔰
𝔚𝔞𝔰𝔥𝔦𝔫𝔤𝔱𝔬𝔫, 𝔇. 𝔔. 20543

CHAMBERS OF
JUSTICE WM. J. BRENNAN, JR.   April 21, 1978

MEMORANDUM TO THE CONFERENCE

RE: No. 75-1914 Monell v. Department of Social Services

Enclosed is a revision of the proposed Court opinion
in Monell. Parts II, III and IV are almost completely
new in an attempt to accommodate the very helpful suggestions of Byron, Lewis and John. Part I(B) has also
been substantially revised in an effort for greater
clarity.

W.J.B. Jr.

Figure 2.2:   Justice Brennan striving for increased clarity of opinion language
(Wahlbeck, Spriggs, and Maltzman 2009).

Another memo shows justices managing opinion clarity. As Figure 2.3
reveals, in *Brockington v. Rhodes*, Justice Harlan sought to make the
Court's holding clear. Indeed, in the last paragraph, Harlan proposes
deleting a footnote to "eliminate a possible source of confusion" with
the goal of not "undermining the holding in the case" (Wahlbeck,
Spriggs, and Maltzman 2009). In short, Justice Harlan directly articu-
lates concern for how the Court's audience will read and interpret the
opinion.

Supreme Court of the United States
Washington, D. C. 20543

CHAMBERS OF
JUSTICE JOHN M. HARLAN

November 4, 1969

Re: No. 31 - Brockington v. Rhodes

Dear Potter:

I agree entirely with the result you reach in this case, and with all of the opinion, except that I have trouble with two minor matters.

First, the considerations recited in the last paragraph on page 3 appear to relate only to the difficulty of obtaining mandamus relief, rather than to the impossibility at this date of ordering Brockington placed on the November 1968 ballot. While those considerations might provide the basis for an adequate-state-ground holding, would it not be better to delete all but the first sentence of that paragraph, in order to make clear our holding on the mootness ground?

Second, footnote 3 appears to suggest that appellant's having voted in the Democratic primary was possibly the ground for the trial court's denial of mandamus. However, I understand the appellees to concede that this would not be a proper ground for denial under state law, and the trial judge did not expressly rely on that ground. I believe that deletion of this footnote might eliminate a possible source of confusion without undermining the holding in the case.

Sincerely,

J. M. H.

Mr. Justice Stewart

CC: The Conference

Figure 2.3:   Justice Harlan's concern with opinion clarity and whether the holding will be undermined (Wahlbeck, Spriggs, and Maltzman 2009).

In *United Airlines, Inc. v. McDonald* (1977), then-Justice Rehnquist sent a memo to Justice Stewart asking for several changes in opinion language in exchange for joining the majority opinion draft:

> I also have some reservation about the seemingly blanket endorsement of the lower court decisions contained in the language on page 9 of the draft opinion. If all of these make clear that the motion to intervene had been filed within the 30 day period for taking an appeal, I have no objection to them; but if any of them do not make that clear, I fear that their apparent endorsement in the text of the opinion may leave room for misunderstanding as to one of the limitations on the rule as I conceive it.
>
> (Wahlbeck, Spriggs, and Maltzman 2009)

In *Upjohn Co. v. United States* (1981), Justice Brennan requested that Justice Rehnquist clarify issues regarding attorney-client privileges. In particular, Brennan was concerned the draft opinion language was vague, despite the opinion's goal to provide the attorney and client the ability to be "able to predict with some degree of certainty whether particular discussions will be protected." Brennan asked Rehnquist to "consider stating the test for application of the privilege more concretely." Figure 2.4 displays Rehnquist's response memo, showing that he would consider the issue and that he agreed with the goal of "predictability."

Nevertheless, despite this face validity for our theory, skeptical readers might reasonably respond that few citizens actually read Supreme Court opinions, or they have an outdated perception of the Court. To this response, we make the following arguments. First, our theory does not hinge on whether the public actually reads opinions; all that matters is justices *believe they might.* A dormant public can be alerted by politicians, thereby inducing widespread public attention. Indeed, politicians regularly make decisions based on the threat their actions *could* receive significant attention. As Key (1961, 266) explains of policymakers:

> Even though few questions attract wide attention, those who decide may consciously adhere to the doctrine that they should proceed as if their every act were certain to be emblazoned on the front pages ... and to command universal attention.

Arnold (1990, 68) makes a similar argument in his study of congressional policymaking:

> Latent or unfocused opinions can quickly be transformed into intense and very real opinions with enormous political repercussions. Inattentiveness and lack of information today should not be confused with indifference tomorrow.

Supreme Court of the United States
Washington, D. C. 20543

CHAMBERS OF
WILLIAM H. REHNQUIST

December 16, 1980

Re: No. 79-886   Upjohn v. United States

Dear Bill:

        Thank you for your suggestion that I state in more
concrete form the attorney-client privilege test and its
metes and bounds. I found that to be one of the
difficulties in writing the opinion in the first place --
everybody wanted to reject the "control group" test, as I
read it, but not too much else was said. At first blush,
your suggested formulation of the test seems to me to
introduce by the back door the very "control group" test
which the opinion as now written turns away at the front
door. But I fully agree with you as to the desirability of
predictability, insofar as possible, in this area, and will
reexamine my opinion to see if I can clarify the statement
of the attorney-client privilege and its applicability to
corporate situations. My present feeling is that I will not
be able to agree with the "one possible formulation" which
you describe in your letter, but will go over the opinion
again to see if the principles by which the privilege is to
be governed can be clarified.

                              Sincerely,

                              Wm

Mr. Justice Brennan

Copies to the Conference

Figure 2.4:   Justice Rehnquist responds to Justice Brennan's request for more clarity
on attorney-client privileges (Wahlbeck, Spriggs, and Maltzman 2009).

Existing literature shows in nonsalient cases, justices are concerned
their decisions could trigger rebuke from an otherwise dormant public
(Casillas, Enns, and Wohlfarth 2011). In other words, even if the public
does not read every decision, justices are likely to worry they might.

    Second, the media often lift passages directly from Court opinions, so
it is likely many members of the public are in fact exposed to and read
portions of Court opinions. An existing study shows the media borrow
non-trivial amounts of the Supreme Court's opinions when reporting on

them (Zilis n.d.). Specifically, the *New York Times* quoted 69% of salient opinions between the 1980 and 2008 terms. This finding suggests the public is directly exposed to at least some opinion language.

Third, even if the public does not read the Court's opinions, legal and political elites do – and the logic of our argument remains the same under this context. After all, elite explanation to the public likely turns on the content of the Court's opinion. By writing a clearer opinion, justices make the "translation" from elite to public smoother. In fact, existing scholarship suggests elites must respond to the way the Court frames arguments in its opinions (Wedeking 2010). A clearer opinion might make it easier for the media to report on the Court's decision – and a clearer opinion might allow the media to portray the Court's decision closer to how the Court would like it portrayed.[17]

Fourth, while one part of our theory focuses on public reaction to the Court's opinion, the other focuses on how external actors can help enhance compliance with the Court's opinion through whistle-blowing. And these actors (e.g., interest groups, lawyers, judges) surely read the Court's opinions. Like Arnold's (1990) conception of the "talented instigators" that stand ready to activate widespread attention to congressional policymaking, legal and political elites are surely prepared to do the same in response to Court opinions.[18]

Finally, we recognize members of the public are more concerned about a case's outcome than its clarity. Our argument is not that opinion clarity can overcome this. Rather, we believe justices should perceive – for all of the reasons described earlier – that enhanced opinion clarity is an especially important attribute of their decision given the potentially negative effects of ruling against the public.[19] Indeed, could anyone credibly claim a poorly written counter-majoritarian opinion would trigger the same public response as a well-crafted counter-majoritarian opinion? We suspect not. In fact, the remarks from the judges quoted

---

[17] This could be important given the variety of media sources (e.g., sensationalist versus sober) citizens use (Johnston and Bartels 2010).

[18] We should also point out that American legal education is based in large part on reading Supreme Court opinions. This method of teaching involves law students (and future judges) reading legal opinions and distilling them, all while subject to the effects of the opinion's clarity.

[19] Justices may generally perceive opinion clarity as a desirable quality that may affect how relevant audiences perceive their opinions (e.g., Baum 2006). The enhanced scrutiny and attention that will accompany a counter-majoritarian decision should magnify this incentive.

earlier – including Justice Thomas's – suggest judges and justices care about clarity.[20] In short, clarity is not a get-out-of-jail-free card for justices. It is, however, a tool they can use to enhance compliance with their decisions and manage public support for the Court.

∗∗∗

The literature provides some guidance as to the conditions under which justices might write clearer opinions. It also lays the foundation for our theory that justices write clearer opinions to enhance compliance and to manage public support for the Court. What is left for us, now, is to examine our theory empirically. To that end, the first order of business is to explain how we measure opinion clarity. We do so in the next chapter.

---

[20] At any rate, if one believes the bottom line is the only thing that matters to the public or elites, then studying opinion content would be superfluous. It would also ignore the hundreds of books and articles, many of them written by judges and justices, that bespeak the importance of clear writing, to say nothing of legal education in this country, which focuses on reading and dissecting legal opinions.

3

Estimating the clarity of Supreme Court opinions

The goal of this book is to determine whether justices alter the clarity of their opinions to enhance compliance with their decisions and to manage public support for the Court. This goal is easier set than met, however. Estimating clarity is a difficult endeavor. Clarity might mean doctrinal clarity, cognitive clarity, rhetorical clarity, or clarity of another sort. If we are to examine the clarity of Supreme Court opinions – and whether justices strategically modify clarity – we must be transparent and forthright about how we measure it. That is, we must be clear about how we estimate clarity.

In this chapter, we describe how we empirically estimate opinion clarity in the chapters that follow. We begin by briefly noting several ways previous scholars have measured clarity. These previous attempts examine important concepts. We, however, opt for an alternative approach that relies on *textual readability*. We focus on the ability of general readers to understand the opinion. Put simply, we examine how easily a member of the public could pick up an opinion, read it, and understand it.[1] An opinion is less readable if it requires extensive education to understand. Conversely, if it requires little education to understand it, an opinion is more readable.

In what follows, we begin by discussing previous efforts to estimate opinion clarity. We then explain how we estimate our measure of clarity. Finally, we offer evidence to validate the measure.

3.1 Previous efforts to measure opinion clarity

For years, scholars have employed various approaches to estimate opinion clarity. Some scholars looked simply at the size of the majority coalition,

---

[1] As we show later, the measure also has other useful features. For example, it taps into the general complexity of opinions. It also correlates with how readers perceive the likelihood others will comply with the Court's decision.

arguing dissents lead to more ambiguous law. Others argue the number of words in a text relate to its clarity, with a greater number of words correlated with increased specificity and, therefore, clarity (see, e.g., Richards, Kritzer, and Smith 2006). In addition to these two approaches, Owens and Wedeking (2011, 1038) identify three other types of clarity: doctrinal, cognitive, and rhetorical. Doctrinal clarity focuses on "how the Court's specific treatment of doctrine [in an issue area] has remained stable or inconsistent ... over time" (Owens and Wedeking 2011, 1038). This approach to measuring clarity is perhaps the oldest and most common, but costliest (because it must use laborious human coding). Cognitive clarity addresses the clarity of the underlying ideas being expressed. Rhetorical clarity, which we examine in this book, refers to the nature of an opinion's written content. We briefly address each of these approaches before turning to our own.

Coalition size as a measure of clarity. One longstanding method of estimating the clarity of a Court decision is to consider the number of justices who dissented in the case, or the number of dissenting opinions (Johnson 1979). Some argue when the number of dissents increases, the clarity of the Court's opinion diminishes. This is the case for at least two reasons. First, dissents signal weakness in the coalition. So, many dissents signal increased weakness. Second, majority opinion writers often need to devote attention in their opinions to the dissenting opinions. As such, the flow of Court opinions can be interrupted, leaving a choppy and potentially inconsistent opinion.

Along these lines, Corley (2009) finds plurality opinions – opinions that do not receive a majority of justices but still receive more votes than any other opinion – are more likely to be treated negatively by lower courts. Examining all circuit court cases decided between 1976 and 2005 that applied Supreme Court decisions, Corley finds the federal circuits were much less likely to comply with plurality opinions than with majority opinions. Plurality decisions, and the numerous separate opinions with which they are associated, create ambiguity. As a consequence, the probability a lower court treated a plurality opinion negatively increased 42% versus a Supreme Court majority opinion.

To be sure, coalition size taps into something related to clarity, but we doubt it reflects the kind of clarity relevant to our examination. Certainly, some unanimous opinions are clear while 5-4 cases are ambiguous. But surely some unanimous opinions are horribly unclear, while some 5-4 opinions are quite clear. Indeed, Staudt, Friedman, and Epstein (2008) argue ideological homogeneity (i.e., minimum winning coalitions) actually is associated with more consequential decisions.[2] In short, while the size of the opinion coalition may be important in some respects, we do not believe it is a good proxy of opinion clarity.

The number of words as a measure of clarity. Other scholars measure clarity (or specificity) by counting the number of words in a text. Their argument is more words represent greater specificity. Consider the work of Randazzo, Waterman, and Fine (2006). The authors find Congress can constrain judges by enacting detailed legislation – they measure detailed legislation as the natural log of the number of words in the statute under review.[3] According to the authors, Congress recognizes it has few practical *post hoc* tools to punish or incentivize federal judicial behavior, but it recognizes it does have the *ex ante* power to define clearly what courts can do and how they can do it. Riding the same wave, Randazzo, Waterman, and Fix (2011) examine state legislation and find, likewise, more detailed legislation limits the discretion of liberal state judges (but strangely, enhances the ideological voting of conservative state judges).[4] Black and Spriggs (2008) examine the length of Supreme Court opinions, claiming length can highlight "an opinion's clarity, scope, and amount of dicta, among other potential qualities" (626). They find salient cases, complex cases, opinions by minimum winning coalitions, and opinions that overrule precedent are longer (and, thus, less clear) than average opinions. And, opinions that observe considerable bargaining behind the scenes are also longer.

Similarly, in a study of the jurisprudential effect of *Chevron U.S.A., Inc. v. Natural Resources Defense Council, Inc.* (1984), Richards, Kritzer, and Smith (2006) look to the number of words in a statute to determine its

---

[2] In fact, it is not even all that clear that dissents signal weakness with a decision (Johnson 1979; *but see* Benesh and Reddick 2002, Murphy 1964).

[3] In a similar fashion, but looking beyond the Court, Huber and Shipan (2002) find that legislatures can use broad or detailed statutory language to expand or limit executive discretion. When a legislature does not trust an agency, it "will not want to give free rein over policy to the agency, but instead will prefer to constrain the agency by filling enacting legislation with specific policy details and instructions" (332). Epstein and O'Halloran (1994) argue that congressional delegation to agencies is a function of preference similarities, with Congress granting agencies more discretion when they are politically aligned, but more clearly delineating the boundaries of agency authority when the two are ideologically distant. Bawn (1997) examines the conditions under which legislators employ specific statutory control provisions to direct future agency implementation.

[4] In a similar analysis, Hinkle et al. (2012) find that lower court judges are more likely to use "hedging" language to make it more difficult for reviewing courts "to falsify their conclusions and overturn their legal analyses" (438).

specificity.[5] *Chevron* examined how courts should defer to agency inter-pretations of law. The Court held that judges must first determine whether Congress spoke to the issue at hand. If it did, then courts and agencies must give effect to Congress's intent. Only if the statute at issue is ambiguous will the courts defer to reasonable agency interpretations. Richards, Kritzer, and Smith (2006) focused on the first part of the test, looking to determine whether – after *Chevron* – justices were more likely to defer to agencies when the statute at issue was longer and, presumably, more detailed. Their findings suggested *Chevron* made justices more likely to defer to agencies when facing ambiguous statutes.

While the word count approach toward measuring clarity is interesting (and is systematic and reliable), it is blunt and fails to take advantage of readily available information. Simply because an opinion is long does not necessarily mean it is unclear – or at least any less clear than a short opinion. Again, a short opinion could be horribly written and unclear while a long opinion, despite its length, might be easy to understand.

Doctrinal clarity: using human coders to measure clarity. The oldest method of measuring opinion clarity is to employ human coders to read Court opinions and rate their clarity. Perhaps the best example of this approach comes from Spriggs (1996). As we explained last chapter, Spriggs examines the conditions under which federal administrative agencies faithfully implement Supreme Court decisions. Spriggs analyzes agency responses to Supreme Court opinions that reverse earlier agency decisions. One of his main covariates is how specific (i.e., clear) the Court's opinion was in terms of what it wanted the agency to do on remand. To measure the specificity of the Court's opinions, Spriggs read and analyzed more than 200 Court opinions and rated, on a scale of 1–4, the clarity of each opinion. Johnson (1986) undertakes a similar analysis. Seeking to determine whether the clarity of a Supreme Court opinion effects lower court compliance with it, he analyzed lower court treatment of fourteen Supreme Court decisions. He and his coders determined the clarity of each opinion "based on whether the reader could easily determine relevant facts, issues, holdings, and reasoning" (328) (see also Gruhl 1980). Human coders made subjective determinations about the clarity of the text.

While this approach is intuitive and somewhat flexible, its costs and risks are legion. First, employing human coders is time consuming and

---

[5] *Chevron U.S.A., Inc. v. Natural Resources Defense Council, Inc.*, 467 U.S. 837 (1984).

expensive. The researcher must spend significant amounts of time reading each opinion – or training and overseeing others as they read them. With any sample of significant size, the time needed to read a full sample of opinions is prohibitive. Second, multiple coders – or even the same coder over lengthy periods of time – may not agree on how to code cases. One coder may have different views than another coder. Similarly, a coder may measure cases differently over time as she becomes more familiar with the material. So, even with the same human coder, a learning effect can threaten the coding scheme's validity. Third, and particularly true when coding legal or political material, a person's own ideological or jurisprudential views can cloud how he or she codes an opinion (Harvey and Woodruff 2013). It may be hard to separate one's own biases from the measurement score. In short, human coding schemes have several potential pitfalls to both validity and reliability. And, though these problems can be overcome with substantial effort, the approach remains costly and does not guarantee a measure will have more validity or less error.

Cognitive complexity as a measure of clarity. With the advancement of computational linguistics and sentiment analysis, social scientists have increasingly been able to address age-old questions with more objective (and cheaply obtained) data. We can now measure difficult psychological concepts that, in many cases, surpass the benefits provided by human coders.[6] In particular, scholars have found it easier to employ measures of "cognitive complexity" as a proxy for clarity.

Cognitive complexity (or what others sometimes call "integrative complexity") captures the levels of "conceptual organization of decision-relevant information" (Gruenfeld 1995, 5) and refers to an individual's ability to "differentiate" and "integrate" information. Differentiation represents the degree to which an individual can see multiple perspectives or dimensions in an issue. It examines whether an individual perceives and explains events in black and white or shades of gray. Integration represents the degree to which a person recognizes relationships and connections among these perspectives or dimensions and integrates them into their decision or judgment.

These two concepts are theorized to comprise a one-dimensional construct on which individuals (or, more specifically, the words they

---

[6] For an excellent summary of the benefits of computer text analysis, as well as a review of the common assumptions and relative costs across different methods of one form of text analysis – text categorization, which has many parallels to measuring text clarity – see Table 1 of Quinn et al. (2010).

use) can be scaled (i.e., individuals can be given a cognitive complexity score for words they speak or write). Less complex language relies on "one-dimensional, evaluative rules in interpreting events" in which actors make decisions "on the basis of only a few salient items of information" (Gruenfeld 1995, 5). With more complex language, on the other hand, individuals tend to "interpret events in multidimensional terms and to integrate a variety of evidence in arriving at decisions" (Tetlock, Bernzweig, and Gallant 1985, 1228). In short, cognitive complexity is theorized to capture a person's cognitive worldview.

A number of studies have used measures of cognitive complexity to examine Supreme Court justices and their opinions. For example, Tetlock, Bernzweig, and Gallant (1985) examine how liberal, moderate, and conservative justices interpret policy issues. They find justices with liberal and moderate voting records present more integratively complex styles of thought in their opinions than justices with conservative voting records. On the other hand, Gruenfeld (1995) finds ideology and cognitive complexity are not correlated; rather, majority opinions display higher levels of cognitive complexity than dissents. As such, it was not that conservatives were less complex than liberals in Tetlock, Bernzweig, and Gallant (1985), but, rather it was that conservatives in their study simply happened to be in the dissent more than in the majority. Later work by Gruenfeld and Preston (2000) argues justices upholding precedent interpret the law with more complexity than justices overturning precedent.[7] Using this cognitive complexity measurement strategy, Owens and Wedeking (2011) find, in part, Justices Scalia and Breyer write the clearest majority opinions (and Ginsburg writes the least clear), criminal procedure opinions tend to be the clearest, and dissents are clearer than majority opinions on average.[8]

It is unlikely, however, that cognitive complexity is the best measure of clarity for our purposes. After all, some may perceive less cognitive

---

[7] Scholars have employed similar measures elsewhere. Tetlock (1981b) and Tetlock (1984) examine legislators, while others analyze presidents and revolutionary leaders (Suedfeld and Rank 1976; Tetlock 1981a). Pennebaker and Lay (2002) analyzed whether Rudy Giuliani's governing style and personality changed over the course of his tenure as mayor of New York by examining the words he used throughout his press conferences. Pennebaker, Slachter, and Chung (n.d.) examined the words of John Kerry, John Edwards, and Al Gore.

[8] In related work, Owens and Wedeking (2012) measure the cognitive complexity of Supreme Court nominees to determine whether one aspect of their cognitive style – their degree of cognitive (in)consistency – correlates with ideological drift later in their career. It does. Justices with more cognitive consistency (or rigidity) in their pre-nomination utterances are less likely to drift ideologically once on the Court.

complexity as simple thought. Others, however, may perceive it as an "ability to penetrate to the essence of key issues" (Tetlock, Bernzweig, and Gallant 1985, 1238). Similarly, some may see larger levels of cognitive complexity as advanced thought that captures multiple perspectives, while others see it as "muddled, confused, and vacillating thought" (Tetlock, Bernzweig, and Gallant 1985, 1238). Simply put, while measures of cognitive complexity certainly have value in a number of contexts, we opted for a different estimate of clarity, what Owens and Wedeking (2011) call "rhetorical clarity." More specifically, we examine the textual readability of Supreme Court opinions.

3.2   Our approach: textual readability

We measure opinion clarity by analyzing the textual readability of Supreme Court opinions. Generally speaking, textual readability is the ease with which a layperson can read and understand the language of the Court's opinions. Readability scores offer "quantitative, objective estimates of the difficulty of reading selected prose" (Coleman 2001, 489). These measures originally were developed by reading specialists who sought to define the appropriate reading level for school textbooks. Today, scholars and practitioners use them in various contexts to measure the degree of difficulty inherent in reading a text (DuBay 2004). In fact, insurance companies and government agencies are often required by law to employ these measures to enhance the general readability of the documents they generate (Grossman, Piantadosi, and Covahey 1994).[9] As we apply the scores (and explain more fully later on), they measure the difficulty a general reader is likely to encounter when reading a court opinion.

Estimating clarity by measuring the textual readability of opinions has advantages. First, the measures are efficient. We can quickly generate readability scores through computational means – a virtue that allows us to code significant numbers of cases for analysis. In fact, we can examine every Supreme Court opinion during our sample period. Our computers neither want (nor need) to be paid, nor do they complain about working

---

[9] Even policymakers use similar theoretical approaches. Some states that use retention elections to retain state court judges have created judicial performance evaluations to help voters determine whether to retain those judges. According to the American Bar Association, one criterion of this evaluation is how clear and logical the judge writes his or her opinions. As the ABA states: "All judges must be able to communicate effectively. Effective communication skills include the ability to speak and write so that what is expressed is understood" (www.americanbar.org).

too much. (We also take substantial comfort in knowing that August 29, 1997 has long since come and gone with little evidence our computers are fully self-aware.)

Second, because our measure is computer-generated, it is empirically reliable. Unlike human coders, who may get tired or learn over time, our automated measure will produce the same result every time. It treats the first text the same as the very last text. Researchers could take the Supreme Court opinions we have and generate the exact same measures.

Third, and most importantly, opinion readability substantially taps into the broader concept of opinion clarity. The measure is valid. As we discuss later, we spend considerable time examining the validity of our readability measure, and find it to be significantly related to our concept of interest.

Research supports our measurement approach. As highlighted in Chapter 2, Benson and Kessler (1987) show plain legal writing is more credible and persuasive than legalese. In their experiment, subjects were randomly assigned to read short texts (framed as either a brief excerpt or a petition for rehearing) that were written either in plain language or legalese. Although this research was conducted more than twenty years ago, we were able to access the texts used in their experiments and calculate clarity scores with the same approach we utilize in this book. The brief sample excerpt written in plain language was more than nine times clearer than the same excerpt written in legalese. Similarly, the clarity scores for the petition for rehearing put the plain language text in roughly the top 5% for clarity compared with the *bottom* 5% for the legalese text. We highlight these differences in clarity because the authors find a number of important results in their experiments. Respondents were significantly more likely to think legalese was unpersuasive, unconvincing, unbelievable, and incomprehensible. More generally, Benson and Kessler find the unclear text is 20% less persuasive than the clear text for a brief and 32% less for the rehearing petition. In short, rhetorical clarity matters. Indeed, Vickrey, Denton, and Jefferson (2012, 74) write:

> The challenge for the nation's judges …is to make sure that the public understands what is expressed in a Supreme Court opinion … [O]pinions serve as the court's voice because rulings communicate not only to lawyers, but also to the public.…

Our approach also finds support in an entirely different area of research: marketing. Chebat et al. (2003) experimentally examine the effect of advertising content while manipulating several variables:

readability, argument strength, and personal interest/involvement. Readability interacts with argument strength. Readability increases the depth of information processing, but does so in a significantly stronger way when a subject is exposed to strong (+32%) vs. weak (+11%) arguments. We would argue, of course, that judicial opinions typically make strong arguments. Readability also increases the depth of information processing when a subject is not very involved – in fact, it does so more when the subject is not involved than when the subject is very involved. This is noteworthy because people usually are not very involved when they read Supreme Court opinions (or media accounts of them) since the opinions seldom directly impact them. Readability also, for strong arguments, significantly improves how subjects' attitudes toward a product change as well as their behavioral intent to buy it. Interestingly, for weak arguments, increased readability has the opposite effect. As Chebat et al. (2003, 616) say:

> Low readability cancels the effects of argument strength, whereas strong arguments enhanced attitudes under high readability for all measures except attitude toward execution cues. Under high readability participants were able to assess the arguments and to transfer their evaluation of the arguments on the attitudes. Low readability canceled this transfer because of the reduced comprehension of the arguments. The findings support the proposition that low readability inhibits the ability to process the information.

In recent years, a host of scholars have begun to use readability measures to estimate the clarity of Supreme Court opinions and government documents. For example, Owens, Wedeking, and Wohlfarth (2013) examine whether the separation of powers influences the clarity of Supreme Court opinions. They find when the Court becomes increasingly distant ideologically from Congress, justices write less readable opinions. They do so, the authors argue, to increase the costs on Congress to read and react to the Court's opinions. Coleman (2001) uses readability measures to compare the writings of Justice Cardozo and Lord Denning with their contemporaries, finding "strong empirical support for the widely-held claim that Cardozo and Denning's judicial opinions are written in a style that is comparatively plain and clear" (491). Goelzhauser and Cann (2014) employ readability measures to determine the clarity of State Supreme Court decisions, and whether elected judges write clearer opinions across multiple issues than non-elected judges (they do not). On the other hand, Nelson (n.d.) uses readability measures to discover that elected judges write more readable opinions in search and seizure cases than non-elected judges, but they write less readable opinions when they live in electorally competitive states.

Law and Zaring (2010) use a readability index to measure the complexity of federal statutes. They find the Supreme Court is more likely to refer to legislative history when it interprets complex statutes. Coleman and Phung (2010) examine the readability of more than 9,000 party briefs spanning more than three decades of Supreme Court decisions and find a "gradual historical trend towards plainer legal writing" (103). Black and Owens (2012b), likewise, measure the readability of party briefs to determine whether the Office of the Solicitor General's advantage in the Court is a function of its brief-writing prowess. It is not.

There are, however, a surprisingly large number of readability indexes from which to choose; scholarship has not settled on the dominance of one. Some are more popular than others. For example, owing to its inclusion in Microsoft Word, two of the most well-known measures are the Flesch-Kinkaid Reading Ease and Grade Level scores. Yet there are many more. And while all of these measures purport to tap into the same general construct – the readability of a text – they each have slight differences that, if ignored, might cast doubt on the measure. Stated less charitably, "cherry-picking" one readability measure might lead to erroneous inferences about (non)significant outcomes in the data. It is possible we might find a statistically significant finding for the relationship between readability and another concept if we measured readability using one index, but a non-significant finding if we employed another. Indeed, if at least twenty measures of readability exist (and they do), we would expect by chance alone to recover a significant relationship even if one did not exist.

So, rather than pick one or two readability measures, we take advantage of computational power and use as many of them as possible. We began by collecting every Supreme Court majority opinion from 1946–2012. We then used the R package koRpus to deploy 19 separate readability formulas for each of these opinions. These 19 distinct formulas yield a total of 28 measures (i.e., some formulas produce more than one readability score).[10] Figure 3.1 identifies the general types of inputs that go into the calculation of the scores.

In the figure, the words, sentences, characters, and syllables columns indicate that a formula calculates the total number of these items (e.g., total number of characters). The final three columns are for indicator

[10] Formulas for all of the measures used can be found on pages 78–84 of the documentation for koRpus (version 0.05-5, dated 2/20/15).

	Words	Sentences	Characters	Syllables	3+ Syllable Words	<2-3 Syllable Words	<6-7 Character Words
Anderson's Readability Index (RIX)		X					X
Automated Readability Index (ARI)	X	X	X				
Coleman–Liau	X	X				X	
Danielson–Bryan		X	X				
Dickes–Steiwer Handformel	X	X	X				
Fang's Easy Listening Formula		X				X	
Farr–Jenkins–Paterson	X	X				X	
Flesch	X	X		X			
Flesch–Kincaid	X	X		X			
FORCAST	X					X	
Fucks' Stilcharakteristik	X	X	X				
Gunning Frequency of Gobbledygook (FOG)	X	X			X		
Kuntzsch's Text–Redundanz–Index						X	
Linsear–Write	X				X	X	
LIX Score	X	X					X
Neue Wiener Sachtextformeln (nWS)	X					X	X
Simple Measure of Gobbledygook (SMOG)		X			X		
Strain Index		X		X			
Wheeler–Smith	X	X				X	

Figure 3.1: Readability formula inputs

variables that count the frequency of, for example, words with at least three syllables. Taking these variables as input, the readability formulas perform a variety of arithmetic functions to produce a single score for a given text. As an example, the Flesch-Kincaid Grade Level is computed as follows:

$$0.39 \times \frac{\text{Total Words}}{\text{Total Sentences}} + 11.8 \times \frac{\text{Total Syllables}}{\text{Total Words}} - 15.59$$

We then subjected these distinct measures to a Principal Component Analysis, which returned a single principal component with an eigenvalue greater than one that explained 77% of the variance in the data. By combining the various measures of readability, we capture much of what is important conceptually for readability that is common to all of the different measures. For example, while one measure focuses on word and sentence length to capture the difficulty associated with reading a text, another might focus on the number of syllables or novel words as they relate to readability. The strength of our approach is it captures what is common among them without being skewed by various idiosyncrasies of each individual formula.

We scale our measure such that larger scores reflect *more readable* text while smaller scores reflect *less readable* text. Our readability measure has a mean of 0, a median of 0.04, and a standard deviation of 4.65. It ranges from −44.0 to 24.5. The 10th and 90th percentile values for our measure are −5.6 and 5.7, respectively. The 25th and 75th percentile values are −2.9 and 2.9. In short, with the exception of a handful of very unreadable opinions, the distribution is a symmetric, bell-shaped distribution. Indeed, even up through the 1st and 99th percentile the values (−11.4 and 10.8) are basically mirrors of each other.

We pause to point out one item. The readability measures look at things like the number of words per sentence, and other features contained within sentences. The readability measures often use periods to determine the stopping point of sentences. Because many legal citations include periods (e.g., the citation to volume 100, page 1 of the U.S. Reports is 100 U.S. 1), there is a concern the software might falsely impose sentence stops and, thereby, result in a higher count for the number of sentences for a given number of words (among other things). This might wrongly determine texts with greater numbers of citations are more readable. We wanted to be sure our readability measure did not simply pick up the amount of legal authority contained in an opinion, which is, of course, distinct from readability. Legal authority thus would be a confounder. So, we treated this issue like any other possible confounder: we measure it and control for it. Thus, all our models in the remaining chapters control for what we call *False Full Stops*.[11]

To add context to the measure, consider this example from what is arguably the Court's most well-known opinion – *Brown v. Board of Education* (1954)(*Brown I*). *Brown I* has a readability score of −2.23. This puts it roughly one-half of a standard deviation below the mean in terms of reading difficulty. This shows that, overall, *Brown I* was not all that much more difficult to read than an "average" opinion. Consider this excerpted passage from the landmark opinion:

> Today, education is perhaps the most important function of state and local governments. Compulsory school attendance laws and the great expenditures for education both demonstrate our recognition of the importance of education to our democratic society. It is required in the performance

---

[11] We should note, also, that we examined the most common false full stops from the data, which resulted in reclassifying about 30% of the 2.1 million full stops that our koRpus identified. We then regressed our scores on the number of false full stops to see how much of the variation in our scores was driven by them. Happily, the R-squared for this regression was just 0.09, which indicates that virtually all of the variation is being driven by other factors.

of our most basic public responsibilities, even service in the armed forces. It is the very foundation of good citizenship. Today it is a principal instrument in awakening the child to cultural values, in preparing him for later professional training, and in helping him to adjust normally to his environment. In these days, it is doubtful that any child may reasonably be expected to succeed in life if he is denied the opportunity of an education. Such an opportunity, where the state has undertaken to provide it, is a right which must be made available to all on equal terms (347 U.S. 483, 493).

The public could readily grasp *Brown I*. What was not so clear, however, was how the Court was going to apply a remedy in the case. In fact, *Brown I* stated that the formulations of the decrees presented problems of considerable complexity. As such, it ordered reargument on the issue.

In *Brown v. Board of Education* (1955)(*Brown II*), the Court was less clear. The opinion has a readability score of −11.62, suggesting it is much less readable than the "average" opinion. In fact, it is about two standard deviations less readable than *Brown I*. *Brown II* is in the lowest 1 percent of all opinions, making it among the most difficult to read. *Brown I*, by contrast, clocks in at around the 30th percentile of readability.

For some more detailed examples, consider *Glona v. American Guarantee Co.* (1968). Its majority opinion has a readability score of 15.86 and is, therefore, one of the easiest to read opinions in our sample (it is in the 99th percentile of readability). Following is a short excerpt of the majority opinion, which addressed whether a parent to a child born out of wedlock could obtain relief in the case of a child's wrongful death:

> Louisiana follows a curious course in its sanctions against illegitimacy. A common-law wife is allowed to sue under the Louisiana wrongful death statute. When a married woman gives birth to an illegitimate child, he is, with a few exceptions, conclusively presumed to be legitimate. Louisiana makes no distinction between legitimate children and illegitimate children where incest is concerned. A mother may inherit from an illegitimate child whom she has acknowledged and vice versa. If the illegitimate son had a horse that was killed by the defendant and then died himself, his mother would have a right to sue for the loss of that property.

In contrast, consider *First National Bank of Arizona v. Cities Service Co.* (1968), a hard to read opinion. The opinion has a score of −17.69, which places it alongside *Brown II* as one of the most demanding opinions. Following is a sample of the opinion, which addressed whether an award of summary judgment in the lower court in favor of respondent Cities Service accorded with one of the Court's earlier precedents:

In reply to Cities' motion, petitioner's counsel reiterated his contention that the course of dealings between Waldron and his associates, on the one hand, and various of Cities' executive personnel, especially its president, W. Alton Jones, on the other, raised an inference of conspiracy because the most probable conclusion to be drawn from Cities' decision to pass up the assertedly extremely beneficials deal proposed by petitioner, notwithstanding its need for additional supplies of imported oil, was that in some manner Cities either had been 'reached' or had used its negotiations with Waldron as a means of forcing its way into the alleged Middle East oil cartel. Petitioner also suggested that Cities might well have made some sort of informal agreement with the other defendants concerning the Consortium that was not revealed by the documents and that Cities might have expected, at the time such an agreement was made, a more profitable share therein than it was eventually offered.

The sentence length alone makes this excerpt difficult to follow. Unfortunately, the opinion in the case is filled with many paragraphs like this. A few other examples of generally familiar cases include *Stenberg v. Carhart* (2000), with a readability score of 4.57, which is about one standard deviation above the mean; *Planned Parenthood v. Casey* (1992), which has a score of −0.335,; and *Milliken v. Bradley* (1974), which is about one standard deviation below the mean with a score of −4.44.

3.2.1 Validating our readability measure

Do these computer-based measures actually capture the clarity of a given text? To answer this question, we turned to human raters and had them assess the validity of our computer-based measures. We also use human raters to code whether the readability measure corresponds with a human rater's prediction of compliance.

More specifically, 72 undergraduate students rated eight excerpts from Supreme Court majority opinions. We varied the excerpts on three dimensions. First, we selected cases we expected to be either "interesting" or "boring" based on the issue areas. We classified First Amendment cases as interesting and economics or federal taxation cases as boring.[12] Second, we varied the case's overall salience as measured by whether the opinion received front page coverage by the *New York Times* the day after it was decided (Epstein and Segal 2000). Third, and of primary importance for our analysis, we varied the readability of the excerpt itself, selecting excerpts with either low or high readability. We employed 16 different

---

[12] We identified issues using the Supreme Court Database's *issueArea* variable.

levels of readability (from 16 different excerpts) in the examples. These 16 different values ranged from 9 to 15 on the easy-to-read end and from −24 to −15 on the hard-to-read end of our measure. Thus, we have a total of eight different excerpt types:

1. Interesting, Salient, Low Readability
2. Interesting, Salient, High Readability
3. Interesting, Not Salient, Low Readability
4. Interesting, Not Salient, High Readability
5. Boring, Salient, Low Readability
6. Boring, Salient, High Readability
7. Boring, Not Salient, Low Readability
8. Boring, Not Salient, High Readability

As another check on the qualitative differences of similar cases, we identified two opinion excerpts for each type, giving us a total of 16 different excerpts. Our coders rated one excerpt from each type, being randomly given a specific excerpt within each type. To help contextualize the excerpts, we created short introductory texts for each excerpt, which appeared before the excerpt itself. Here, we provide an example of the contextual introduction and excerpt from *Santa Fe v. Doe* (2000) (the case name was not given to raters), which we used as an excerpt for the interesting, salient, and low readability condition.

> [our excerpt]
> In the case below, the Court was ruling on whether school districts can have student-led prayer at football games (or other athletic events). The school district argued it could because it was private speech. In this segment, the Court is deciding whether the school district's policy is a state-sponsored religious practice.
>
> [opinion excerpt]
> Most striking to us is the evolution of the current policy from the long-sanctioned office of "Student Chaplain" to the candidly titled "Prayer at Football Games" regulation. This history indicates that the District intended to preserve the practice of prayer before football games. The conclusion that the District viewed the October policy simply as a continuation of the previous policies is dramatically illustrated by the fact that the school did not conduct a new election, pursuant to the current policy, to replace the results of the previous election, which occurred under the former policy. Given these observations, and in light of the school's history of regular delivery of a student-led prayer at athletic events, it is reasonable to infer that the specific purpose of the policy was to preserve a popular "state-sponsored religious practice." Lee, 505 U.S. at 596. School

sponsorship of a religious message is impermissible because it sends the ancillary message to members of the audience who are nonadherants "that they are outsiders, not full members of the political community, and an accompanying message to adherants that they are insiders, favored members of the political community." *Lynch v. Donnelly*, 465 U.S. at 688 (1984) (O'CONNOR, J., concurring). The delivery of such a message over the school's public address system, by a speaker representing the student body, under the supervision of school faculty, and pursuant to a school policy that explicitly and implicitly encourages public prayer is not properly characterized as "private" speech.

After reading the background text and the opinion excerpt, we asked the raters three objective comprehension questions about the excerpt. For the excerpt from *Santa Fe v. Doe*, for example, we asked raters the following question: "In the reasoning, what was a reason given as to why the Court did not characterize the student prayer as private speech?" Raters were able to pick from four multiple choice options: (A) Because the purpose of the policy was to preserve a state-sponsored religious practice; (B) Because the prayer sends an ancillary message to members if they are insider or outsiders; (C) Because the delivery of the message was done over the school's public address system; and (D) Because the delivery of the message was done by randomly selecting a student. Choice (C) is the correct response.[13]

We also asked raters seven subjective questions about the excerpt. We asked them how likely they believed people would be to comply with the decision (seven-point scale), how clear they believed the text was (five-point scale), how well written the excerpt was (seven-point scale), how interesting they thought the excerpt was (five-point scale), the ease or difficulty of understanding the excerpt (four-point scale), whether they knew all the words in the excerpt (four-point scale), and how important they believed the topic in the excerpt was (three-point scale).

The results suggest our raters did, in fact, perceive all the intended differences among our excerpt types. When asked to assess their interest in the opinion text on a five-point scale ($5 =$ very interesting, $1 =$ very boring), they rated First Amendment cases as 3.5 (average) and tax/ economics cases as 2.9 – a difference that is statistically significant ($p < 0.001$, $t = -5.92$, two-tailed test). Raters also perceived excerpts

---

[13] The two other objective questions for this excerpt were: (1) Did the Court conclude that the purpose of the District's policy was to preserve a popular state-sponsored religious practice? and (2) Did the school district intend, according to the opinion, to preserve the policy of having prayer before football games?

coming from salient opinions differently than those from non-salient ones. When asked to rate importance on a three-point scale, raters gave salient texts an average score of 2.4 compared to an average score of 2.2 to non-salient texts. This difference is also statistically significant ($p < 0.001$, $t = -3.87$, two-tailed test).

Our primary interest, however, is whether raters could detect differences between low readability and high readability excerpts. They could, and they did. Although our interest and importance concepts were directly linked to a single question asked of the rater, we have multiple indicators for each rater of both a subjective (e.g., how clear do you believe the text was) and objective (e.g. whether they correctly answered content questions) nature. We followed Jones et al. (2005), who argue that readability is comprised of: (a) comprehension, (b) time to complete and answer questions about the reading, and (c) how an individual subjectively perceives the text. We estimated an exploratory factor analysis model with six variables. This included the four subjective ratings (i.e., clarity, quality of the writing, ease of understanding, and difficulty with words), an objective measure of the number of correct responses to our comprehension questions, and the (logged) number of minutes it took a rater to read the text and answer the questions. The Cronbach's alpha for these six items is 0.77. The factor analysis model returned a single factor with an eigenvalue greater than one. We used these loadings to calculate *Comprehension*, which is a factor score from our model.

For our validation test, *Comprehension* serves as our dependent variable. Our main independent variable is *Opinion Readability*, which is a readability score for each of our 16 opinion excerpts. As noted, large values indicate high readability (i.e., easier texts) and small values indicate low readability (i.e., harder text).

We also include a series of controls. We include separate dummy variables for whether an opinion excerpt came from a *First Amendment Opinion* (1 = yes, 0 = no) and for whether it came from a *Salient Opinion* (1 = yes, 0 = no). To identify raters who might not have been taking their task as seriously as others, we imbedded two "filter" questions into the excerpt rating process. We code *Incorrect Filter Response* as 1 if a rater incorrectly answered either of those two questions and 0 if the rater answered them both correctly.[14] Finally, as our excerpts come from legal opinions, they can contain a large number of citations. These citations

---

[14] Because our results are unchanged if, instead, we omit these not especially attentive individuals, we retain these observations for our analysis.

have a large amount of punctuation within them, which in turn can affect how an excerpt is scored in terms of our *Opinion Readability* measure. To control for this potential confound, we counted the percentage of the excerpt that was periods, commas, quotations, and colons (obtained through the program Linguistic Inquiry and Word Count [LIWC]).

Because our dependent variable, *Comprehension* is continuous, we estimate an ordinary least squares model with robust standard errors clustered on rater. The results appear in Table 3.1. The left column in Table 3.1 provides parameter estimates for our model. As expected, we find a positive and statistically significant relationship between our *Opinion Readability* measure and a rater's overall level of comprehension of the excerpt. In other words, excerpts that our automated readability statistics identified as being easier and more readable yielded higher comprehension levels than excerpts that were more difficult. These findings provide systematic support for our computer-generated readability measure.

In terms of the substantive magnitude of the effect, although the coefficient on the *Opinion Readability* is just 0.03, it is important to remember the underlying measure ranges for these 16 opinion segments between roughly -23 and $+16$. Holding all other variables at their median values, we estimate a comprehension score of just 0.03 when a text is at the sample minimum level of readability. This is just about at the median level of comprehension in our sample. When, however, the excerpt is at the sample maximum level of readability, we predict a comprehension score of 1.22. This corresponds to approximately the 87th percentile of comprehension in our sample. What is more, that absolute change – about 1.19 – is equivalent to about 1.25 standard deviations within our *Comprehension* measure, which is a sizable substantive increase in comprehension. In summary, this provides systematic and important evidence that our automated content analysis of Supreme Court majority opinion readability is directly related to how human raters assess the readability of those same texts.

What is more, the right column of Table 3.1 provides a direct link between the readability of an opinion excerpt and a rater's assessment of the likelihood that officials will comply with the opinion. To obtain the results in the right column of Table 3.1, we estimated a second linear regression model where the dependent variable is each rater's response to our compliance question (higher values indicate more likely to observe compliance). We employed the same independent variables. We expect the relationship between *Opinion Readability* and predicted compliance

Table 3.1: *The impact of opinion readability on comprehension and compliance attitudes*

	Dependent Variable	
	Comprehension	*Compliance*
Opinion Readability	0.030**	0.064**
	(0.009)	(0.016)
First Amendment Opinion	0.616**	0.362**
	(0.087)	(0.156)
Salient Opinion	0.519**	0.539**
	(0.083)	(0.153)
Incorrect Filter Response	−0.092	0.148
	(0.136)	(0.408)
Periods in Segment	−0.067**	−0.102**
	(0.021)	(0.031)
Commas in Segment	−0.055**	−0.084**
	(0.015)	(0.026)
Quotations in Segment	−0.020	−0.123**
	(0.020)	(0.042)
Colons in Segment	−1.167**	−0.119
	(0.315)	(0.550)
Constant	0.895**	6.716**
	(0.243)	(0.395)
N	559	568
R^2	0.22	0.05

Note: Column entries are ordinary least squares coefficients; robust standard errors clustered on the 72 unique raters appear in parentheses below each coefficient. * $p < 0.05$ (one-tailed test). The *Comprehension* variable is a factor score generated from an exploratory factor analysis of several variables (see text above for details) and ranges between −2.3 and 1.5. The *Compliance* variable ranges between 1 (not at all likely to comply) and 7 (very likely to comply). Treating this variable as ordinal and estimating an ordered logistic regression model does not alter any of the substantive results.

to be positive – that is, raters should predict that officials will be more likely to comply with easy-to-read opinions than difficult-to-read ones. This is precisely what we find. When an opinion excerpt is of minimum readability, we observe a compliance likelihood score of 4.2. When the text comes from an opinion of the highest readability, by contrast, the estimated likelihood of compliance jumps by 60% to a value of 6.7. As the scale has a maximum value of 7, this is an especially impressive substantive effect.[15] Put simply, readability indeed appears related to the likelihood of observing compliance – and this supports our theory that justices use clarity to enhance compliance with their decisions and manage public reaction to those decisions.

***

We discussed existing approaches scholars have employed to measure opinion clarity. We then discussed our approach. We focus on the textual readability of opinions. Importantly, we find our measure is reliable *and* valid. Readability is strongly attached to comprehension. As such, we can now proceed to our empirical analyses. Do justices alter the clarity of their opinions to address specific audiences and enhance compliance with those opinions? It is to this question we now turn.

---

[15] We obtain substantively identical results by estimating an ordered logistic regression model. The probability of observing the highest compliance rating for excerpts of maximum and minimum difficult are 0.08 and 0.65, respectively.

4

Supreme Court opinions and federal circuit courts

Supreme Court justices have two primary goals while managing the federal judicial hierarchy. The first is a legal goal. Justices seek to ensure lower courts apply federal law uniformly (Lindquist and Klein 2006; Perry 1991). The second is a policy goal. Justices want to ensure lower court judges faithfully apply the policies the High Court creates (Murphy 1964). The problem, however, is lower court judges sometimes have their own goals that may not coincide with the Supreme Court's – or with the goals of judges in other circuits. As we stated in the book's introduction, Ninth Circuit Court of Appeals Judge Stephen Reinhardt once claimed to "follow the law the way it used to be, before the Supreme Court began rolling back a lot of people's rights" (Baum 2006). Defiance, indeed. At the same time, it is not uncommon for lower court judges to split on how to interpret federal law. For example, on July 22, 2014, the Circuit Court of Appeals for the District of Columbia decided *Halbig v. Burwell* (2014), holding the Affordable Care Act unambiguously restricted IRS subsidies to insurance purchased only on exchanges "established by the State." That same day, however, the Fourth Circuit Court of Appeals decided the language of the Act was broad enough to allow the IRS to subsidize insurance purchased on exchanges created by the federal government. The conflict between these circuits was huge, with the D.C. Circuit's interpretation threatening effectively to wipe out the controversial law.

In this chapter, we consider how the preferences of lower court judges influence Supreme Court justices' goals and opinions; that is, whether lower court judges influence the clarity of Supreme Court opinions. We begin with a discussion about justices' legal motivations and how clarity can help them achieve those goals. Next, we discuss how clarity can help justices achieve their ideological goals. After discussing these two goals, and how they relate to justices' opinions, we examine how ideological conflict among lower courts leads justices to write clearer opinions, and how ideological distance between the two levels of courts influences Supreme Court opinion clarity.

4.1 A theory of opinion clarity and federal circuit courts

For those readers just joining us, our broad theory (as laid out in Chapter 2) is that justices alter the clarity of their opinions to enhance the likelihood of compliance with their decisions and to manage public support for the Court.[1] There are three reasons why opinion clarity can help the Court enhance compliance. First, opinion clarity can remove discretion from actors opposed to the Court's decision. When the Court renders a clear decision, a lower court judge's ability to evade decreases (see, e.g., Romans 1974). A clear command from the Supreme Court tells lower courts what to do and how to do it. An ambiguous opinion, however, does not impose a clear command and leaves them free to shirk and claim innocence.

Second, opinion clarity can help whistle-blowers monitor and report on the behavior of judges who defy the Court (Cross and Tiller 1998). Dissenting judges, the Solicitor General, and amicus groups are likely to have an easier time monitoring whether actors comply with their decisions when the decisions themselves are clear. And when they observe noncompliance, they can help bring cases to the Supreme Court to seek reversal. So justices can use opinion clarity as a built-in alarm system.

Third, clear opinions can serve as instructions that help guide actors who are inclined to follow the Court's decisions but might be less able to do so. We suspect there may be institutional actors who want to comply with High Court decisions but lack the resources to interpret some opinions. Without clear guidelines, these actors may not be able to determine what the Court really wants, and so they may miss the mark. Justices may need to anticipate this and provide more helpful instructions to actors that require them.

4.2 Lower court audiences and legal motivations

One of the Supreme Court's most important duties is to ensure lower courts uniformly interpret federal law. Since the Court's beginning, justices declared the importance of unity in federal law (Hellman 1995). Justice Story once emphasized "the importance, and even necessity, of uniformity of decisions throughout the whole United States upon all subjects within the purview of the Constitution ... The public mischiefs that would attend [disunity] would be truly deplorable ..."[2] Modern scholars

---

[1] The goal of managing public support for the Court is not operative in this context.
[2] See *Martin v. Hunter's Lessee* 14 U.S. 304, 347–348 (1816); Hellman (1995).

have pointed to the practical realities of uniformity as well. As Korobkin (2000) argues, uniformity in law can establish predictability and reduce the amount of needless litigation (56). Uniformity among the circuits in terms of legal interpretation makes it easier for parties in a dispute to know how the courts will decide cases. Disuniformity, on the other hand, leads to indeterminacy and inefficient outcomes, such as a greater likelihood of litigation (Korobkin 2000, 56). With heightened uncertainty as to the application of legal rules in a case, parties to litigation may wrongly believe a judge or jury will rule in their favor, and therefore litigate when they should not (Priest and Klein 1984).

Indeed, the uniformity of legal interpretations is strongly connected to the rule of law (Owens and Wedeking 2011). In *The Morality of Law*, Fuller (1964) argues the rule of law constitutes an "internal" morality of law. His discussion of the hypothetical King Rex, who failed to live up to the rule of law, focuses on eight attributes that make law possible. Taken together, these attributes focus on individuals' ability to know what the law is and to be able to comply reasonably with it.[3] They point toward the importance of legal uniformity – and underscore the Supreme Court's special role in ensuring it.

The Court can help ensure legal uniformity among lower courts in at least two stages of its decision making process: the agenda stage and the merits stage. When the Court sets its agenda, it can grant review to cases where the lower courts disagree over the proper interpretation of federal law. At the merits stage, the Court can write clear opinions to head off conflict before it occurs.

4.2.1   Ensuring legal uniformity through agenda-setting

Perhaps nowhere is the Court's goal of legal uniformity more frequently observed than in its agenda-setting behavior. The Supreme Court's own rules highlight the importance of uniformity. Rule 10 states the Court is more likely to grant review to cases when a circuit court renders a decision in conflict with the decision of another circuit court, or makes a decision that conflicts with a state supreme court decision. Perry's (1991) interviews with justices and their clerks suggest legal conflict (i.e., the absence of uniformity) strongly influences whether the Court reviews a

---

[3] Fuller, of course, is not the only legal scholar to consider the value of clarity. For other important works, see Dworkin (1986), Dworkin (1985), Dworkin (1978), Hart (1963), and Hart (1961).

case. When multiple lower courts disagree on the proper interpretation of federal law, the Court will wade into the conflict to declare the correct interpretation. One justice said emphatically: "...there are certain cases that I would vote for, for example, if there was a clear split in circuits, I would vote for cert. without even looking at the merits." (Perry 1991, 269). Justice Ginsburg likewise stated the Court must "keep federal law fairly uniform ... [and] resolve splits among federal or state tribunals over the meaning of" federal law (Ginsburg 1994, 884).

The Court's own opinions highlight the importance of resolving conflict and ensuring uniformity. Consider *Thompson v. Keohane* (1995). When discussing its decision to grant review to the case, the Court stated: "Federal Courts of Appeals disagree on the issue *Thompson* asks us to resolve ...Because uniformity among federal courts is important on questions of this order, we granted certiorari to end the division of authority."[4] In their treatise on Supreme Court practice, Stern et al. (2002) spend pages explaining the importance of legal conflict to the Court's agenda decisions.

Empirical evidence shows justices grant review to clear up legal conflict and establish uniform federal law. Black and Owens (2009) observe that when justices' policy goals and the legal goal of circuit uniformity collide, legal considerations sometimes win out. When looking at whether a justice casts a policy-based deny vote (i.e., voting to deny review because the merits outcome is likely to be worse ideologically for her than the status quo), they find the probability of a policy-based deny vote decreases from 0.89 in the absence of legal conflict to 0.61 in the presence of strong legal conflict. Black and Owens (2011a, 2012b) find similar results when examining the Solicitor General's (SG) influence on agenda-setting. Conflict among the lower courts constrains a justice's willingness to agree with an SG recommendation. When the SG makes a recommendation that contravenes the legal factors in the case (e.g., to deny review when there is strong conflict among the circuits), justices are roughly 45% less likely to follow that recommendation, regardless of their ideological congruence with the SG.

4.2.2   *Ensuring legal uniformity by writing clear opinions*

Another way justices can ensure lower court uniformity – the one we focus on in this chapter – is to help prevent conflict before it occurs by writing

---

[4] See *Thompson v. Keohane*, 516 U.S. 99, 106 (1995); *cited in* Stern et al. (2002).

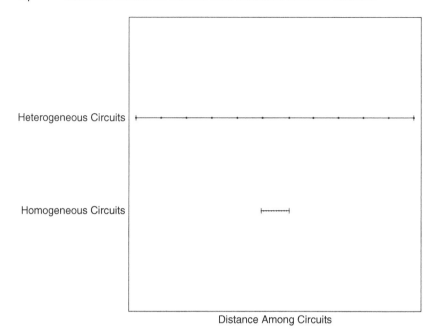

Figure 4.1:   Ideological dispersion in the federal circuit courts.

clear opinions. We believe justices write clearer opinions when the federal circuits are divided ideologically from one another. When some circuits are extremely liberal and others are extremely conservative, they are more likely to conflict with each other than if all the circuits are homogenous. Consider Figure 4.1. The line on the bottom represents a group of circuit courts that are fairly homogenous. The most liberal circuit is not especially distant on this scale from the most conservative circuit. In this scenario, justices are not likely to worry about legal conflict among the circuits, since those judges all see the law similarly. On the other hand, the top line reflects a world in which the circuits are much more heterogeneous. Here, the most liberal circuit is, relatively speaking, much more distant from the most conservative circuit. It is in these situations the Court can expect to observe heightened legal conflict among the circuits.

By writing clear opinions, justices might be able to help lower courts coordinate on the correct legal interpretation – and, most importantly, fend off future conflict. Thus, we expect Supreme Court justices will write clearer opinions as the federal circuit courts become increasingly distant from each other ideologically.

4.3   Lower court audiences and ideological motivations

Justices also seek to effectuate policy goals. They want to ensure that those who apply their policies do so faithfully. Scholars have, of course, recognized justices try to constrain lower court judges and lead them to behave in an ideologically friendly way. Once again, however, most of this research has focused on how justices set their agenda and audit lower courts to ensure compliance. As we argue, justices also may consider the ideological propensities of lower court judges – and how those predispositions match their own ideological goals – when they write opinions.

4.3.1   Ensuring policy compliance through agenda-setting

If there is one fixed star in the constellation of studies on Supreme Court auditing, it is that justices will grant review to overturn ideologically disagreeable lower court decisions. Cameron, Segal, and Songer (2000) develop a signaling model to generate predictions about how the Court will allocate its limited docket space. The authors examine how the Court uses signals and indices to determine which cases to review. When a lower court renders a decision that accords with Supreme Court ideology in a case, the Court need not rely on indices to determine whether to review – the signal tracks with the Court's goals. On the other hand, when the lower court renders a decision that the Supreme Court dislikes (i.e., it sends a signal of which the Court is skeptical), justices rely on unmanipulable indices to verify the veracity of the lower court's signal.

Similarly, Lindquist, Haire, and Songer (2007) examine the conditions under which the Court audits lower court decisions. The authors find the Supreme Court reviews circuit court decisions when the median judge on the circuit becomes more ideologically distant from the median justice, and when the circuit itself observes more dissents, more reversals of district courts, and a higher rate of reversal by the Supreme Court. These findings, the authors state, suggest the Court "expend[s] its institutional resources strategically to enhance the effects of its auditing activity" (Lindquist, Haire, and Songer 2007, 620).

In a recent article, Black and Owens (2011b) find justices audit lower court decisions most offensive to them. Justices are more likely to review ideologically distant decisions rendered by ideological foes than ideologically close decisions rendered by ideological allies. They find a conservative justice will vote with a 0.21 probability to review a liberal lower court decision by a majority panel of liberal judges. That same conservative justice is least likely (pr $=$ 0.06) to review a conservative panel's conservative decision. In other words, when voting to grant review to cases, justices often focus on the ideologies of the lower court judges who decided the case, in addition to the ideological direction of the lower court decision.[5]

4.3.2   Ensuring policy compliance through opinion clarity

Justices also use opinion clarity to manage lower court behavior. As we stated earlier, clarity can remove discretion from actors opposed to the Court's decision. It can help whistle-blowers monitor and report on the behavior of judges who defy the Court (Cross and Tiller 1998). And, it can serve as better instructions to help guide actors who are inclined to follow the Court's decisions but might be less able to do so.

Opinion clarity removes lower court discretion, furthers the auditing of those courts, and helps courts who want to follow the High Court. As a consequence, opinion clarity can enhance lower court compliance. And because justices should have the most concern over noncompliance when facing ideologically unfriendly lower courts, we expect the Supreme Court will write clearer opinions as the ideological distance between it and the federal circuit courts increases.

***

In summary, we theorize justices seek to ensure legal uniformity among the lower courts, and to ensure lower court judges apply Supreme Court policies faithfully. Justices seek legal uniformity because it enhances the Court's power (and, indirectly, their own). They also seek legal uniformity because legal norms strongly compel it – and violating such norms could reduce the Court's legitimacy. At the same time, justices must concern themselves with the policy behavior of their lower court agents. They therefore have an interest in ensuring lower court judges apply the policies the Supreme Court sets. Opinion clarity helps justices secure both goals.

---

[5] The authors also discovered justices give their ideological allies the benefit of the doubt when they render counter-ideological decisions. So, for example, a conservative justice has a 0.12 probability of voting to review a liberal decision by a conservative panel of judges, but a 0.21 probability of voting to review a liberal decision by a liberal panel of judges. Conversely, a liberal justices has a 0.13 probability of voting to review a conservative decision by a liberal panel of judges but a 0.23 probability of voting to review a conservative decision by a conservative panel of judges.

4.4 Data and measures

To examine whether justices alter the clarity of their opinions because of lower court dynamics, we analyze the Court's majority opinions in all signed, orally argued decisions during the 1953–2007 terms. We begin our analysis in 1953, as that represents what many people believe to be the beginning of the modern Court. We conclude our analysis in 2007 because that was the most recent year of data available in the Judicial Common Space (JCS) (Epstein et al. 2007) when we conducted this analysis. We analyze whether justices craft more readable opinions to decrease conflict and to enhance faithful policy compliance with their decisions. Our dependent variable is *Opinion Readability*, which we explained in Chapter 3. This measure reflects the general readability of each Supreme Court opinion using a principal component analysis of 28 different readability measures. The scale of the measure, recall, is such that larger scores represent greater readability while smaller scores represent less readability.

Uncertainty in the federal circuits. Our first covariate of interest, *Intercircuit Uncertainty*, reflects how ideologically scattered the circuit courts are each year. When the ideological locations of the circuits become increasingly scattered, justices should expect a greater likelihood those courts will conflict over the interpretation of federal law. Anticipating this, justices will write clearer opinions. To measure circuit court judges' ideologies, we turn to the JCS (Epstein et al. 2007). The JCS places Supreme Court justices (as measured by Martin and Quinn (2002)) on the same ideological scale as federal circuit court judges, with scores ranging from negative (liberal) to positive (conservative). The JCS uses the coding method suggested by Giles, Hettinger, and Peppers (2001), who argued when the norm of senatorial courtesy applies to a judge's appointment, that judge's ideal point estimate mirrors the home state senators' preferences. The estimate for such a judge is thus her home state senators' Poole and Rosenthal first-dimension Common Space scores.[6] If there are two home state senators from the president's party, the point estimate is the mean of the two; if only one senator hails from the president's party, the point estimate is that senator's score. When senatorial courtesy does not apply to the judge's appointment, the judge's ideal point estimate is the president's first dimension Common Space score.

As Table 4.1 illustrates, we located each judge's JCS score in each circuit during each year. Then we determined the JCS score of the median judge in each circuit in each year. Then, using the twelve values we generated

---

[6] www.voteview.com/dwnomjoint.asp

Table 4.1: *Judicial Common Space (JCS) scores for select individual judges and court medians in 2006*

Term	Circuit	Judge Name	Judge JCS	Circuit Median	Average of Medians	Interdecile Score
2006	CA1	Crosby	0.002	0.120	0.260	0.557
2006	CA1	Rodgers	0.120	0.120	0.260	0.557
2006	CA1	Nelson	1.087	0.120	0.260	0.557
2006	CA2	Adams	−1.233	−0.266	0.260	0.557
2006	CA2	House	−0.266	−0.266	0.260	0.557
2006	CA2	Barrington	1.210	−0.266	0.260	0.557
2006	CA3	Harris	−1.260	−0.147	0.260	0.557
2006	CA3	Dorsey	−0.147	−0.147	0.260	0.557
2006	CA3	Boykin	0.110	−0.147	0.260	0.557
2006	CA4	Lang	−1.070	0.288	0.260	0.557
2006	CA4	Peppers	0.288	0.288	0.260	0.557
2006	CA4	Sherrod	0.780	0.288	0.260	0.557
2006	CA5	Kuhn	−1.300	0.346	0.260	0.557
2006	CA5	Neal	0.346	0.346	0.260	0.557
2006	CA5	Flynn	1.010	0.346	0.260	0.557
2006	CA6	Jones	0.095	0.226	0.260	0.557
2006	CA6	Masthay	0.226	0.226	0.260	0.557
2006	CA6	Perry	0.053	0.226	0.260	0.557
2006	CA7	Shields	−0.037	0.305	0.260	0.557
2006	CA7	Hayward	0.305	0.305	0.260	0.557
2006	CA7	Bulaga	1.075	0.305	0.260	0.557
2006	CA8	Bush	0.024	0.276	0.260	0.557
2006	CA8	Lacey	0.276	0.276	0.260	0.557
2006	CA8	Matthews	0.520	0.276	0.260	0.557
2006	CA9	Tolzien	−1.600	−0.209	0.260	0.557
2006	CA9	Clinton	−0.209	−0.209	0.260	0.557
2006	CA9	Quarless	0.081	−0.209	0.260	0.557
2006	CA10	Dorsey	0.130	0.228	0.260	0.557
2006	CA10	Hill	0.228	0.228	0.260	0.557
2006	CA10	Hyde	0.330	0.228	0.260	0.557
2006	CA11	Hornung	0.005	0.348	0.260	0.557
2006	CA11	Bennett	0.348	0.348	0.260	0.557
2006	CA11	White	0.920	0.348	0.260	0.557
2006	CADC	Hutson	0.014	0.516	0.260	0.557
2006	CADC	Ringo	0.516	0.516	0.260	0.557
2006	CADC	Nitschke	0.660	0.516	0.260	0.557

Note: JCS scores for judges and medians in the Supreme Court's 2006 term. For illustrative purposes, we use artificial names and scores of judges and fewer than the total number of judges in each circuit.

(one circuit median score for each of the twelve circuits), we computed the distance between the 10th and 90th percentiles (i.e., the interdecile score). So, for example, in Table 4.1, *Circuit Median* shows the median JCS score of the judges within each circuit. The 10th percentile among the twelve is −0.209. The 90th percentile is 0.346. The Interdecile Score among these twelve medians is 0.557 (the absolute vale of the difference between −0.209 and 0.348).

We use the interdecile score because we believe it captures an important distance between the circuits in this context. If we instead estimated *Intercircuit Uncertainty* by measuring the full ideological range across the circuits – and, for instance, there was one circuit significantly more liberal (conservative) than all others – we might overestimate the amount of real dispersion among the circuits. On the other hand, if we looked at the standard deviation of JCS scores across the circuits, we might not capture enough of the relevant dispersion. In short, we want a dispersion measure that is not pulled too much by outliers, but also looks across the spectrum of the circuits. This is why we settled on the interdecile range.[7]

Figure 4.2 illustrates the degree of *Intercircuit Uncertainty* during the 1953 to 2007 Supreme Court terms. As the data illustrate, there has been substantial variance in the heterogeneity of circuit medians over time. The federal circuits displayed a consistently moderate level of dispersion during the Warren Court era, and then grew more homogenous over Warren Burger's tenure as Chief Justice. Yet, around the time William Rehnquist took over as Chief in 1986, the circuits began to polarize, as conservatives increased their numbers on circuits long held by liberals.

Ideological distance between the Supreme Court and the circuits. Our second covariate of interest captures the ideological differences between the Supreme Court and the circuits – or how ideologically dissimilar the two levels of courts were. To measure *Ideological Distance*, we employ an institutional-based approach that measures the ideological distance between the *average of the circuit court medians* and the *Supreme Court median* each term. To do so, we again obtain the JCS score of every circuit's median judge during each term. Then, for each term, we calculate the mean of those median JCS scores, as we showed in Table 4.1. Next, we obtain the JCS score of the median justice on the Supreme Court each term (Epstein et al. 2007). Finally, we calculate the absolute value of the

---

[7] The results still show justices write clearer opinions to ensure uniformity even if we estimate *Intercircuit Uncertainty* using the full range or standard deviation of circuit court medians each year.

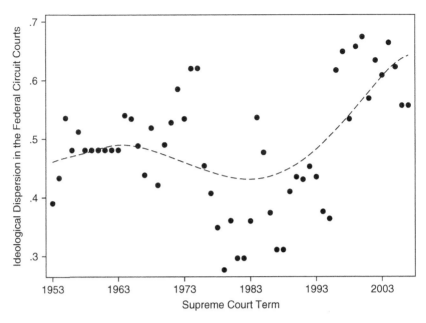

Figure 4.2:   Ideological dispersion in the U.S. Courts of Appeals, 1953–2007.
Estimates reflect, for each term, the interdecile ideological distance (90th vs. 10th
percentile) among circuit medians in the U.S. Courts of Appeals using the Judicial
Common Space scores. The dashed line displays a lowess smoother of the over-time
trend.

distance between the average circuit median and the median justice on the
Supreme Court. So, for example, in Table 4.1, the average of the median
circuit judges in the Supreme Court's 2006 term was 0.260. The Supreme
Court median in 2006 was −0.00216. The absolute value of the difference
between these two estimates is 0.262. This measure reflects the average
institutional distance between the Supreme Court and the circuit courts.[8]
Figure 4.3 illustrates the extent of ideological divergence over time.

A cursory look at the figure shows a multitude of values taken by this
measure. Although the smoother suggests not much movement until the
early 2000s, the raw data tell a different story. Descriptively, the measure

---

[8] Alternatively, one might construct this ideological distance indicator using the median
justice within each Supreme Court majority coalition (instead of the Court's median
justice). The subsequent effect for ideological distance is not robust to this alternative
measurement strategy, but the impact of *Intercircuit Uncertainty* is robust and substantively
consistent using both measurement approaches.

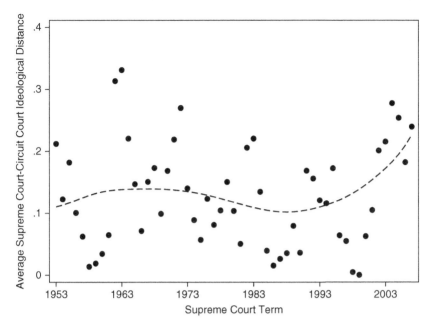

Figure 4.3: Ideological distance between the Supreme Court and the U.S. Courts of Appeals, 1953–2007. Estimates reflect, for each term, the ideological distance between the average of the circuit court medians and the Supreme Court median using the Judicial Common Space scores. The dashed line displays a lowess smoother of the over-time trend.

ranges from 0 (i.e., the Supreme Court and the average circuit are identical ideologically) to 0.33, which suggests there is significant distance between the circuits and the Supreme Court. The mean and median are both 0.12. The standard deviation for the variable is 0.08.

Because the variable is measured on the JCS scale, it allows us to apply some substantively meaningful labels to these values. For example, the average distance between the Supreme Court and the circuit courts is approximately the same as the ideological distance between Justice Souter and Justice Stevens during the Court's 2007 term, with Stevens being a bit more liberal than Souter. During the 2007 term, Stevens voted liberally 76% of the time compared with Souter's 71% (according to the *direction* variable in the justice-centered version of the Supreme Court Database).

As for the sample maximum (0.33), this is approximately equivalent to the JCS score difference between Justice Kennedy and Chief Justice Roberts, also in the Court's 2007 term. In terms of raw voting behavior,

Kennedy voted liberally 50% of the time that term compared to Roberts' 40% of the time. Although these differences might not seem overwhelming at first, it is important to emphasize they are capturing the *average* distance between the Supreme Court and the circuit courts.

Control variables. In addition to *Circuit Uncertainty* and the High Court's *Ideological Distance* from the circuits, there are a host of other factors that may also affect the clarity of Supreme Court opinions. We control for them. We first control for whether the Court alters one of its precedents. Justices likely believe lower court judges might be less compliant with a decision that breaks with precedent. As we explained in Chapter 2, Benesh and Reddick (2002) argue among all Supreme Court cases, those that alter precedent should be the most vulnerable to noncompliance since lower courts "have the opportunity to make a good case against compliance, given that the High Court is not even holding its decision in high regard" (535). Benesh and Reddick find that among all High Court opinions, circuits take the longest to comply with those that reverse precedent. Justices, as a result, might enhance the clarity of opinions when formally altering a prior precedent. (Of course, they may also write more clearly to explain why they overruled precedent.) We code *Precedent Alteration* as 1 if, according to the Supreme Court Database, the Court majority formally altered an existing precedent; 0 otherwise.[9]

We next control for whether the Court's opinion struck down either a federal law or state action as unconstitutional. When the Court takes the major step of nullifying an act of the elected branches, it likely should be clear as to why, perhaps as a way to instruct and constrain subsequent implementation. We code *Federal Judicial Review* as 1 if, according to the Supreme Court Database, the Court struck down an act of Congress; 0 otherwise.[10] And, we measure *State Judicial Review* using a dichotomous indicator to reflect when the justices constitutionally nullified a state's law, regulation, or constitutional provision, as identified by the Supreme Court Database.[11]

---

[9] We utilize the *precedentAlteration* variable in the Supreme Court Database to identify decisions that formally altered prior precedent.

[10] Technically, the Court engages in judicial review any time it reviews the constitutionality of a law – even when it upholds that law. For ease of presentation, we refer to the Court's invalidation of laws as using judicial review.

[11] We utilize the *declarationUncon* variable in the Supreme Court Database. Specifically, *Federal Judicial Review* and *State Judicial Review* take on a value of 1 when *declarationUncon* equals 2 and 3, respectively.

We next control for the ideological heterogeneity of the Supreme Court majority coalition in each case. Since justices might expect a fractious or ideologically unconnected coalition may send weaker signals to lower courts, they may write clearer opinions to anchor those decisions. To measure *Coalition Heterogeneity*, we obtain all the justices' JCS scores per term and then calculate, for the majority coalition justices, the standard deviation of their JCS scores. We also include *Majority Votes*, which examines the size of the majority coalition as a way to account for the degree of internal (dis)agreement on the Court. One might expect a smaller majority – and thus, greater internal disagreement within a Court decision – will lead to a less clear opinion.[12]

Next, we account for the potential that more complex cases might lead to less clear opinions. Scholars have found greater amicus curiae participation corresponds with greater case complexity (Collins 2008). We measure *Case Complexity* by counting the number of amicus curiae briefs filed in each case. We obtain amicus participation from the 1953 to 2001 Supreme Court terms from Collins (2008), and collect amicus data from 2002 to 2007 using Lexis. We also code for whether there was dissent in the lower court that heard the case. When a lower court judge dissents in a case, it often signifies the case is complicated or otherwise ideologically charged. We suspect justices might write less clear opinions in such cases. So, we include a binary indicator called *Lower Court Dissent* which measures whether a judge in the court that decided the case dissented.[13]

We also control for the separation of powers dynamic and its potential influence on opinion clarity. Greater ideological divergence between the Court and Congress might lead justices to obfuscate opinions (Owens, Wedeking, and Wohlfarth 2013). We measure *SOP Constraint* as the absolute value of the distance between the Court's median justice and the closest chamber median. That is, when the median justice falls between the House and Senate chamber medians, *SOP Constraint* equals 0. When the median is more liberal or conservative than both the House and

---

[12] We use the *majVotes* variable from the Supreme Court Database to code *Majority Votes*, which is the size of the majority coalition.

[13] We use the *lcDisagreement* variable in the Supreme Court Database to identify whether one or more of the members of the court whose decision the Supreme Court reviewed dissented. While we would prefer a better measure of lower court dissents, for a project of this size, there are no other alternatives, aside from reading every single Supreme Court opinion in our sample ($n = 5774$), and all the lower court opinions in those cases.

Senate medians, *SOP Constraint* equals the absolute value of the distance between that justice and the closest pivot.[14]

We account for variance in opinion clarity that might be due to shifts over time, different legal contexts and issue areas, or the idiosyncrasies of majority opinion authors (see, e.g., Owens and Wedeking 2011). Accordingly, we include a predictor reflecting the *Court Term* associated with each majority opinion, fixed effects to control for the primary *Issue Area* of each case, and fixed effects accounting for the identity of the *Majority Opinion Author* within each case.[15] Finally, as we note earlier in the book, we also control for potential false full stops that might otherwise drive our measure of opinion clarity.

4.5   Methods and results

Our model analyzes how the Court alters the readability of its opinions as a function of lower court preferences. Because the dependent variable (readability) is a continuous indicator, we estimate OLS regression models. In all models, we estimate robust standard errors to account for the possibility of correlated errors, though the results are consistent if we alternatively fit the models with classical standard errors. Model 1 regresses opinion readability on our two primary covariates (i.e., *Intercircuit Uncertainty* and *Ideological Distance*). Model 2 includes these variables, the full set of control predictors, and fixed effects for both issue area and majority opinion author (parameter estimates not shown to conserve space, trees, and attention spans).

Table 4.2 shows that the empirical results from both models support our hypotheses. Justices write clearer opinions when the circuits are more ideologically dispersed, as well as when the circuits become more distant ideologically from the High Court. What is more, these results are substantively consistent even after we control for variance in opinion readability driven by the complexity inherent across different issue areas, the idiosyncrasies of different justices' opinion writing, and other relevant factors.

---

[14] All subsequent empirical results are consistent, including the impacts of *Intercircuit Uncertainty*, *Ideological Distance*, and *SOP Constraint*, when using the median of the Court's majority coalition in each case to construct the *SOP Constraint* control predictor.

[15] We followed the broad "IssueArea" and "majOpinWriter" in the Supreme Court Database to specify these fixed effects.

Table 4.2: *The impact of circuit court context on Supreme Court opinion clarity*

	(1)	(2)
Intercircuit Uncertainty	5.055**	2.380**
	(0.509)	(0.483)
Ideological Distance	3.242**	1.796**
	(0.701)	(0.633)
Precedent Alteration		0.220
		(0.289)
Coalition Heterogeneity		−0.611
		(0.672)
Lower Court Dissent		−0.200**
		(0.112)
Case Complexity		−0.060**
		(0.014)
Majority Votes		0.273**
		(0.038)
Federal Judicial Review		−1.126**
		(0.387)
State Judicial Review		0.347*
		(0.229)
SOP Constraint		−3.417**
		(0.544)
Court Term		0.032**
		(0.008)
False Full Stops		0.022**
		(0.001)
Constant	−3.050**	−67.044**
	(0.248)	(15.289)
Majority Opinion Author Controls	No	Yes
Issue Area Controls	No	Yes
N	5774	5774
R^2	0.02	0.26
BIC	32907.52	31679.69

Note: Table entries are OLS coefficients with robust standard errors in parentheses. $^*\,p < 0.10$ and $^{**}\,p < 0.05$ (one-tailed). The dependent variable represents the composite readability score of each Supreme Court majority opinion (per curiam opinions excluded), 1953-2007, with larger values reflecting greater clarity.

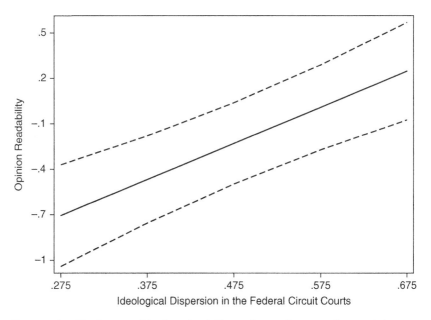

Figure 4.4:   The impact of the *Intercircuit Uncertainty* on Supreme Court opinion clarity, 1953–2007. Estimates reflect the predicted degree of opinion readability (with 95% confidence intervals) generated from Model 2 in Table 4.2.

Figures 4.4 and 4.5 highlight these legal and policy effects, respectively, using the regression results from Model 2 in Table 4.2. First, the data suggest justices write an opinion that is nearly one unit clearer on the readability scale when moving across the observed range of *Intercircuit Uncertainty*. Figure 4.4 illustrates that when the circuit medians become more ideologically dispersed and justices have greater reason to expect them to apply federal law differently, justices will write opinions that are meaningfully clearer. (What is more, we show in Chapter 8 the magnitude of this shift in readability in fact increases the probability circuit courts positively interpret their precedent!)

We also find justices write clearer opinions when the circuits become increasingly distant ideologically from the Supreme Court – and, thus, justices should have concerns over the faithful application of their policy decisions. As Figure 4.5 illustrates, the Court will write an opinion as much as approximately 0.65 units clearer on the readability scale as the ideological distance between the median justice and the average of the circuit medians each year shifts across its observed range.

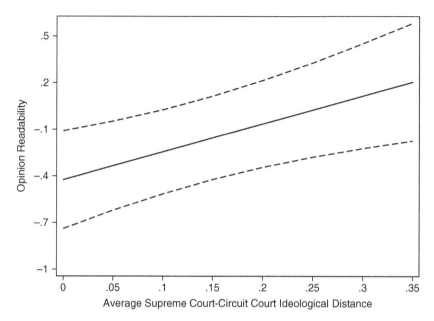

Figure 4.5:   The impact of *Ideological Distance* between the Supreme Court and federal circuit courts on Supreme Court opinion clarity, 1953–2007. Estimates reflect the predicted degree of opinion readability (with 95% confidence intervals) generated from Model 2 in Table 4.2.

Of course, it is worth noting the *Ideological Distance* measure simply calculates the distance between the Supreme Court and the *average* ideological complexion of all circuit medians each year. In some years, individual circuit courts display a much greater degree of ideological distance from the High Court. For instance, during the 2004 Court term, the median judge serving on the legally important and prestigious D.C. Circuit Court of Appeals had a JCS ideal point of 0.502, which amounts to a distance from the Supreme Court median of 0.583 units. If we measured the predicted impact of *Ideological Distance* using the median judge of the D.C. Circuit in 2004, the empirical results would generate an expected opinion that is more than one unit clearer than the effect of the minimum average circuit distance during the sample period, and approximately 0.8 units clearer when considering the most proximate circuit (i.e., Third Circuit) during the 2004 term. Thus, the magnitude of the predicted impact of *Ideological Distance* on opinion clarity can be even greater if isolating an individual circuit court. In short, then, the results suggest justices meaningfully alter the readability of majority opinion language based on their desire to reduce intercircuit legal conflict and to ensure circuit courts faithfully apply their policies.

Our control variables also exhibit statistically significant effects on majority opinion readability. As expected, opinions become less readable in complex cases (as measured by the degree of amicus participation). They are also less readable in cases where a lower court judge dissented below. And, as the justices display greater consensus in support of a decision (as evident through the majority coalition size), the majority opinion tends to exhibit clearer language. The data also suggest justices write less clear opinions when they strike down acts of Congress as unconstitutional and when the Court faces greater SOP constraints (i.e., greater ideological distance between the Court and nearest congressional pivot when the Court is spatially constrained). It may be justices obfuscate opinion language to shield their decisions when the Court is more vulnerable to congressional rebuke (see, e.g., Owens, Wedeking, and Wohlfarth 2013). Additionally, the data suggest justices have somewhat enhanced the average degree of opinion clarity in more recent Supreme Court terms. Lastly, the results show justices tend to write clearer opinions in criminal procedure cases (i.e., the baseline category) compared to most of the broad issue areas on the Court's docket. Majority opinions generally display the least clear opinion language when justices issue decisions primarily involving First Amendment, privacy, and union issues.

4.6   Discussion

We examined how Supreme Court justices write clearer opinions to manage the judicial hierarchy. The empirical results support our hypotheses. First, we discovered justices write clearer opinions when the lower courts are ideologically dispersed and thus are likely to generate legal conflicts. By writing clearer opinions, justices might stave off conflict. This finding is important as it provides an alternative perspective on circuit conflicts, legal ambiguity, and the Court's efforts to address them. It shows justices do not simply react to circuit conflicts by granting review to cases. Rather, they seek to get out ahead of those conflicts and stop them before they begin. Just as importantly, it shows a legal motivation among justices at the merits stage, something scholars have been at pains to find. Second, the data show justices write clearer opinions when they have reason to believe lower federal court judges will oppose – and fail to comply fully with – their policy decisions. Justices write clearer opinions to minimize the discretion afforded to those judges and to make the detection of non-compliance easier. Thus, not only do justices use opinion language for legal reasons (preventing conflict), they also use it (if less often) for policy-based reasons (to enhance compliance).

Managing the federal judicial hierarchy is a tricky business for the Supreme Court. They have few tools available to audit and punish lower court judges. Certainly, in the classic principal-agent sense, they are remarkably weak principals. Yet, they are not powerless. Justices can take advantage of their positions and craft opinions that impose costs on lower courts should they evade the High Court. If our data have anything to say on the matter, it is that justices strategically craft clearer opinions so as to enhance compliance with their decisions. When they expect problems, they write clearer opinions.

Nevertheless, while these results are consistent with our theory, questions remain. The relationship between the Supreme Court and lower court judges may be unlike other relationships. Justices might expect lower court judges to be compliant, given their subordinate status in the judicial hierarchy. Other actors, like federal agencies and the states, might not be so "eager" to comply. Do justices also use opinion clarity to enhance compliance when dealing with those actors? And how might the Court use clarity when ruling against the public?

5

Supreme Court opinions and federal agency implementors

Judge Guido Calabresi – a senior judge on the U.S. Court of Appeals for the Second Circuit – claimed we live in "the age of statutes" (Calabresi 1985). Calabresi was right, but only partially. Today, we not only live in an age of statutes, we also live in an age of regulations. From major issues like health care regulations and regulations governing the air we breathe and the water we drink, to minor issues like sporting events[1] and school lunches, nearly every facet of modern life involves federal regulation. Regulation is ubiquitous and sometimes controversial.

It should come as no surprise, then, that parties often challenge agency action (and inaction) in courts of law. De Tocqueville once stated: "There is hardly a political question in the United States which does not sooner or later turn into a judicial one" (de Tocqueville 2010). One could say the same for regulatory questions turning into judicial questions. And while the lower federal courts bear the brunt of most of these cases, the Supreme Court weighs in on important administrative law questions. Indeed, some of the Court's most important decisions have enmeshed federal agencies. *Chevron U.S.A. v. Natural Resources Defense Counsel* (1984), *INS v. Chadha* (1983), and *Massachussetts v. EPA* (2007) are among the most significant High Court decisions in recent years – and all involved agency action. In fact, since 1946, more than 22% (n = 1,641) of all Supreme Court decisions involved disputes that originated in federal administrative agencies.[2]

The concern for justices, however, is that when they speak, agencies do not always listen (Spriggs 1996). For some agencies, compliance with High

---

[1] See, e.g., www.packers.com/tickets/pay-online-sweepstakes-rules.html).

[2] To generate this number, we looked to the Supreme Court Database *adminAction* variable. We excluded instances where the administrative agency was established under an interstate compact (*adminAction* = 65) and those that involved a state agency (*adminAction* = 117) as well as those cases where there was no administrative action preceding the case (*adminAction* = 124). Data include orally argued signed and per curiam opinions and judgments of the Court during the 1946–2012 Court terms. Data exclude original jurisdiction cases.

Court decisions is a lesser priority than others. What is more, those that do listen may not be able to comply fully. Some agencies are more competent and professional than others, with large staffs, large budgets, professionalized legal advisors, and specific jurisdictional goals. Others are less competent, with small staffs, minuscule budgets, poor appellate legal advisors, and unclear goals. Additionally, some agencies are more independent from political actors than others and, thus, may have different incentives to follow or evade the Court. These resource-based and political factors, we believe, influence the Court's expectations of compliance and, therefore, how clearly the Court writes its opinions. In other words, we believe agency characteristics influence how clearly justices write their opinions because those same characteristics can influence whether they comply with Court decisions.

In this chapter, we examine whether the clarity of Supreme Court opinions is a function of federal agency characteristics. We examine whether Supreme Court justices try to use opinion clarity to influence federal agencies to comply with their decisions. As we argue throughout this book, we believe justices modify the clarity of their opinions based on their audiences and how they expect their audiences will react to their decisions. What that means is when the Court decides cases involving less competent agencies, it will write clearer opinions. And, when the Court decides cases involving competent agencies, justices do not need to shoulder the costs to write such clear opinions.

We begin this chapter by revisiting our main theory. We then explore how often federal agencies appear before the Supreme Court. The data show agencies participate regularly before the Court and are, therefore, important audiences. We then explain why we believe agency professionalism will influence opinion clarity, as well as how ruling against less professionalized agencies might lead justices to write clearer opinions. Next, we discuss our data and measures, and then move on to our methods and results. We conclude with a discussion of what our findings mean for our broader theory and where they fit within the entirety of our book.

5.1 A theory of opinion clarity and federal agencies

As we stated in Chapters 1 and 2, the Supreme Court faces numerous audience-based obstacles when it makes decisions. The Supreme Court's audiences have the capacity to block or escape the Court's policies. Court decisions do not always end controversies: they often transform them.

Rarely does the Court have the last say or take the last action in a case. So justices must devise ways of accomplishing their goals, knowing others may want to stop them. That is, justices pursue their goals in an inter-dependent environment in which their decisions are a function not only of their preferences, but also the preferences of those with whom they interact. And so we theorize that justices write clearer opinions to enhance compliance with its decisions and to manage the Court's public support. Clear opinions can help justices enhance compliance for three primary reasons.

First, opinion clarity can remove discretion from actors opposed to the Court's decision. When the Court renders a clear decision, an actor's ability to evade decreases. Removing ambiguity allows actors less wiggle room to feign ignorance. A clear opinion tells them what to do, how to do it, and when to do it. Clarity, that is, puts actors on notice of exactly what to do.

Second, opinion clarity can help whistle-blowers monitor and report on the behavior of actors who defy the Court. Clarity can enhance com-pliance by making it easier for people to monitor how actors respond to High Court decisions. If the Court issues a clear opinion, interest groups, members of Congress, the executive branch, the public, and others all have an easier time determining whether actors comply with the Court's decision. Conversely, if an opinion is vague and unclear, people will find it harder to detect noncompliance.

Third, clear opinions can serve as instructions that help guide actors who are inclined to comply with the Court's decisions but might be less able to do so. We suspect there may be instances in which clarity can enhance compliance simply because it lowers the cost for those who want to comply with a Court decision but who might not otherwise be able to determine how to do so. A lower court judge or implementor might want to comply with a High Court ruling but find it so confusing that they are not sure whether they actually are complying. A clear opinion can help those actors comply.[3]

Put plainly, we believe justices recognize the interdependence they face. They recognize their need to enhance the likelihood of compliance among their audiences. And they can influence, or at least believe they can influ-ence, such compliance by crafting clearer opinions.

---

[3] Our theory also relates to how the Court manages public support for its decisions but this goal is not operative in this context here.

5.2   The Supreme Court and federal agencies

Federal agencies appear frequently before the Supreme Court and are engaged in substantial policymaking across the country. As we stated earlier, more than 22% of all Supreme Court decisions between the 1946 and 2012 Court terms involved disputes that originated with some federal agency action. As Figure 5.1 shows, the high-water mark in terms of total cases coming from a federal agency occurred in the 1946 term, when the Court decided 43 such cases. The Court has decided a substantial number of federal regulatory cases since then. For example, in its 1982 and 1983 terms, the Court decided 32 and 38 cases coming from federal agencies. And though the number of such cases has decreased – along with the overall decrease in the number of cases on the Court's docket overall (Owens and Simon 2012) – the *proportion* of federal agency cases decided by the Court remains respectable. Recent Court terms have seen a sizable proportion of cases coming from agencies on the docket. In the

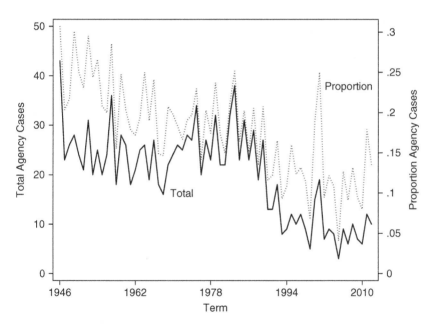

Figure 5.1:   Frequency of U.S. Supreme Court cases originating in federal agencies, 1946–2012. The solid line represents the total number of agency cases with its vertical axis on the left; the dotted line represents the proportion of Supreme Court cases, with its vertical axis on the right, that originated with agency action.

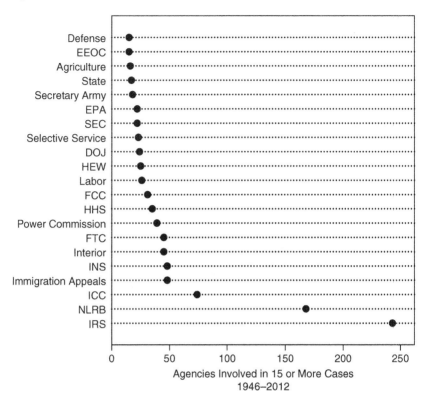

Agencies Involved in 15 or More Cases
1946–2012

Figure 5.2: Most frequent federal agencies appearing before the U.S. Supreme Court, 1946–2012.

1983 and 2001 terms, at least 25% of the Court's docket involved cases that originated in federal agencies.

If we, instead, look at cases in which agencies appeared as *parties* to Supreme Court cases, the results are similar and highlight the important status of federal agencies as litigants. A federal agency appeared as a party in just less than 20% (n = 1,347) of the Court's cases between the 1946 and 2012 terms.[4] As Figure 5.2 shows, some agencies litigated often, while

---

[4] These numbers also come from the Supreme Court Database and include instances when an agency of the federal government (or the US or Attorney General) was the petitioner or respondent in the case, and federal administrative action preceded the litigation. We again excluded instances where the administrative agency was established under an interstate compact (adminAction = 65) and those that involved a state agency (adminAction = 117) as well as those cases where there was no administrative action preceding the case

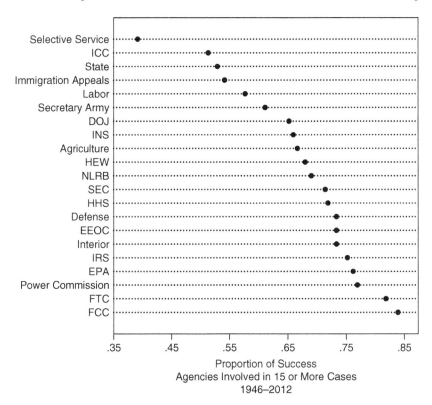

Figure 5.3:   Federal agency success rate before the U.S. Supreme Court, 1946–2011.

others did so rarely. For example, the IRS appeared more often before the Court than any other agency, showing up in 242 cases as a party. The National Labor Relations Board was the second-most frequent agency party, with 168 total appearances. The now defunct Interstate Commerce Commission came in third, appearing roughly 75 times.

Not surprisingly, the rates of success for these agencies differed substantially. As Figure 5.3 shows, the Federal Communications Commission won 84% (26) of the 31 cases in which it was involved. The Federal Trade Commission also fared well, winning 82% (36) of the 44 cases in which it appeared. The Federal Power Commission won 77% (30) of its 39 cases,

(adminAction = 124). Cases decided during the 1946–2012 Court terms. Data include orally argued signed and per curiam opinions and judgments of the Court. Data exclude original jurisdiction cases.

while the EPA won 76% (16) of its 21 cases. The Internal Revenue Service won 75% (182) of the 242 cases in which it appeared.

At first glance, it appears that some of the most successful agencies are those that are professionalized and independent, as opposed to less professional and political. For example, the top three most successful agencies (the FPC, FTC, and FCC) all are independent agencies with expert boards and partisan balance. Surely their independence and overall quality and professionalism must factor at least somehow into their success – and the Court's treatment of them. Indeed, from the Court's perspective, factors like agency competence, political status, and other agency characteristics are likely to influence how justices behave. As we explain next, we believe an agency's past performance influences how clearly justices write their opinions.

5.3   How past performance and agency characteristics influence Supreme Court opinion clarity

We have reason to believe policymakers take notice of and modify their behavior when dealing with agencies that have performed ably (and poorly) in the past. For example, Gilmour and Lewis (2006) show the Office of Management and Budget devotes budgetary resources to agencies based on their past performance assessments. Using the grades agencies earned from the Program Assessment Rating Tool (PART) adopted in the early 2000s to measure agency performance and efficiency (see more later in the chapter), Gilmour and Lewis (2006) find that better performing agencies receive budget increases. Similarly, Blanchard (2008) finds evidence that Congress and the president take agency performance into consideration when making budgeting decisions, with the president proposing larger budget increases for higher performing agencies, and Congress concurring.[5] Norcross and Adamson (n.d.), likewise, suggest "there is a tendency for Congress to award more budget increases to effective and moderately effective programs, and fewer increases to ineffective" programs (27). In short, political actors take agency performance into consideration when making decisions. We suspect justices do too.

We expect the Court will write clearer opinions when it decides cases involving agencies that have a poor record of overall executive

---

[5] Stalebrink and Frisco (2011) find that members of Congress with business experience were more likely to support performance-based measures of agencies.

performance. This is the case, again, for three reasons. First, enhancing the clarity of the Court's opinion can minimize the discretion of those errant agencies. By writing clear instructions, the Court takes away opportunities for agencies to run afoul. Second, by writing clearer opinions, justices may better craft its directives to politically constrain these agencies, as clearer language is likely to illuminate subsequent shirking to external actors (Staton and Vanberg 2008). On the other hand, agencies that have performed well in the past have a stronger record of smooth functioning, and the Court may be more likely to trust them. Thus, justices will not need to invest as much time or as many resources into writing clearer opinions. Third, agencies with poor performance records have shown they are simply not good at operating effectively. They may not have the resources or institutional capacity to comply with complex orders. Justices should have some expectation that such agencies are less able to follow the Court's policy directives simply due to their own resource limitations or relatively diminished competency. Enhancing the clarity of their opinions should better enable agents to follow.

Agencies require information, expertise, and other formal resources (e.g., budgets and staff). Agencies require clear guidelines to adjust their policies to conform effectively to judicial directives (Baum 1976; Canon 1991; Milner 1971; Shapiro 1968). One critical resource is information. As Spriggs explains, agencies require the "information necessary to formulate expectations about the actions of those with whom they interact" (Spriggs 1996, 1126). Accordingly, agencies require sufficient expertise and competence to comply with judicial orders. Agencies also depend on more formal resources like their budgets and, more specifically, legal staffs. For instance, agencies must use a staff of attorneys to read and analyze the Court's decisions. Then, those attorneys must work with relevant policy analysts to revise the agency's policy in a way that satisfies the Court's legal policy. In many instances, complying with Court opinions can be a tricky thing. And, there is considerable variance in the competence, expertise, and formal resources of agencies.

Empirical studies show the Court's opinions can influence how agencies behave. Perhaps the most impressive work to date on agency responses to High Court opinions comes from Spriggs (1996). Spriggs examines whether agencies follow the Supreme Court's directions when it reverses them. More specifically, he analyzes whether the agency complies fully by engaging in major policy change or evinces less than full compliance. Spriggs finds the language of the Court's opinions can influence compliance. The specificity of the Court's opinions leads to enhanced compliance. Whereas agencies make major policy changes in response to *unclear* opinions a mere 3.4% of the time, they make major policy changes in response to *clear* opinions 95.5% of the time.[6] This means that opinion language, as we have suggested throughout this book, can influence compliance. It also means justices have incentives to write opinions in an effort to enhance compliance. They should have greater incentives to write clearly when they are most concerned about noncompliance. Those concerns, we believe, can be triggered by poor past performance.[7]

We expect the Supreme Court will write clearer opinions in cases that involve poorly performing agencies, and this effect should be more pronounced when directing an agency to change its policy.

5.4   Data and measures

To examine how agency characteristics such as past performance influence the clarity of Supreme Court opinions, we employ the same dependent variable outlined in Chapter 3, and used throughout this book: the readability of the Court's opinions. The measure reflects the general readability of each Supreme Court opinion using a principal component analysis of 28 different readability measures. The scale of the measure, again, is such that larger scores represent greater readability while smaller scores represent less readability.

We examined every Supreme Court opinion between the 2001 and 2007 terms in which administrative action occurred prior to the onset of the Court's decision. We examined these years because they correspond with the federal government's PART scores – the data we use to measure agency performance, as well as the terms for which Judicial Common Space (JCS) data were available when we conducted this analysis.[8] We include cases decided in 2001, the year before the PART measures came out, because agency action then likely turns up in the scores the following years.

---

[6] In a similar study, Spriggs (1996) finds some evidence that the specificity of the policy change leads to greater agency compliance.

[7] To be clear, we do not examine past agency compliance with High Court decisions but, rather, the overall performance of the agency in the execution of its regulatory duties. While it would be interesting to determine whether justices alter their opinions based on past noncompliance, that undertaking would be considerable and is not within the reach of this study.

[8] We used the Supreme Court Database's *adminAction* variable to identify whether any federal agency action occurred prior to litigation.

Agency performance measures. Measuring the performance of federal agencies is notoriously difficult. As a consequence, few studies have examined agency performance systematically. Thankfully, PART, adopted by the Office of Management and Budget (OMB) in 2002, serves as a measure we can employ. As Lewis (2008) explains: "the PART system was developed through the Federal Advisory Commission Act process in cooperation with the President's Management Council, the National Academy of Public Administration, and other interested parties" (174). In 2002, OMB first began to use the PART procedure to generate objective measures of how well agencies executed their programs (Stalebrink and Frisco 2011).[9] The goal was to identify agencies that did not execute their programs well and to make budget decisions "based on results" (Gilmour and Lewis 2006, 170).

To these ends, OMB gave each agency-program an overall grade that derived from four component grades. That is, in a series of interviews with different agencies over time, OMB examiners asked agencies four categories of questions:

- The purpose and design of specific programs (i.e., whether the program design and purpose was clear and defensible);
- The strategic planning that went to the long-term planning of the agency vis-à-vis the program (i.e., whether the agency set long-term goals);
- Program management (i.e., how well the programs were administered and overseen);
- The results of the program (i.e., rate the overall performance of goals met) (Lewis 2008, 174).

Interviewers asked their respondents a series of yes or no questions on each of these four dimensions. For example, if a respondent answered "yes" to 5 out of 10 questions in a category, the score for that category would be 50 out of 100 (Gilmour and Lewis 2006, 170). OMB then gave each agency-program a score on each of these four dimensions. Then, it generated a weighted score (ranging from 0–100) for each program based on the four scores. Based on this final weighted score, programs received one of four possible ratings from OMB: ineffective (final scores from 0–49), adequate (final scores of 50–69), moderately effective (final scores of 70–84), or effective (final scores of 85–100).

---

[9] While OMB *executed* the procedure, it did not actually *create* it.

The PART system has a number of advantages. For starters, it is transparent and objective. As Lewis (2008) states: "[t]he PART system defines good performance in a defensible, transparent, and largely policy-neutral way. It attempts to take into account variations in management environment ..." (173). What this means for us, then, is we do not need to create and take a stand on a new measure, or otherwise reinvent the wheel. Indeed, numerous scholars have already employed the PART scores as measure of agency performance. In addition, the PART system covers a substantial number of agencies over its time period because all federal managers were required to participate (see, e.g., Gilmour and Lewis 2006, and cites contained therein). This provides variation across agencies.

To be sure, the PART scores have limitations. Some argue they are ideologically biased, though there is dispute about that (see, e.g., Lewis 2008, 175). Some argue they are biased against traditionally "liberal" agencies, while others argue they are biased in favor of agencies that are better able to quantify their behavior. Without wading into that argument, we merely note we refit all our models while controlling for whether Lewis (2008) identifies the agency as traditionally liberal or conservative. Our results remain the same.

A second limitation is the PART scores apply to the execution of specific *programs* as opposed to the overall quality of the agency. While this is not something we would have done if we had our way, we tried to account for it. When the Court identified which agency program was involved in a case, we turned to the most recent PART score for that program. In other words, when the Supreme Court opinion identified which agency program was involved in the litigation, we measured *PART Score* by using the most recent PART score for that program. When, however, the opinion did not identify a specific agency program at issue in a case, we measured *PART Score* by calculating the average PART score for all programs executed by that agency up to the year of the case.

One other issue with the PART scores is worth discussing briefly. One might wonder whether these scores actually capture *the justices'* beliefs about agencies, or whether they simply reflect OMB's beliefs. In other words, how well-known are these scores, and by default, the overall performance of the agencies? While we cannot determine what justices think about every agency, we are comfortable asserting these scores are likely to reflect *general* beliefs about the competency of most agencies. While justices are not likely to know the State Department and Federal Trade Commission received "effective" ratings while the Departments of Education received many "ineffective" ratings, they are likely to observe differences among actors and programs within those entities. But the reader should keep this in mind.[10]

Ruling against the US. We next account for whether the Supreme Court's decision supported the federal government's position on the merits of the case. If the decision was pro-US, we coded the variable as 0. If the decision did not favor the United States, we coded the variable as 1.[11]

Interactive term. We then interacted our agency PART scores with whether the Court ruled against the United States. Our argument, again, is that justices will take an agency's past behavior and capabilities into consideration and will write clearer opinions when the Court rules against poorer performing agencies.

Agency characteristics. We also account for a host of agency characteristics that could influence the Court's opinions. We start with whether the agency is independent. Independent agencies may be less susceptible to political constraints, and may be more professional than political agencies. If this is the case, we would expect the Court to be less likely to invest scarce time and resources into writing a clear opinion when dealing with independent agencies versus non-independent agencies. To code whether an agency was *Independent*, we first looked to Black et al. (2007) and their definitions of independent agencies. We then followed up and checked each agency's website to verify whether it was independent or not.

We next looked at whether each agency was headed by a commission that required partisan balance. Under federal law, certain agencies must be politically balanced. Commonly, the law declares there may not be, for example, more than three members of the same political party on a five-person commission. The reason for limiting the agency's composition is to reduce the influence of partisanship while enhancing expertise and neutrality. As such, we might expect the Court writes clearer opinions when an agency is free to be stocked with partisans. To determine whether the agency must observe *Party Balance*, we referred to Lewis (2008).

We also examined whether the agency heads served for *Fixed Terms.* We expect the Court will write clearer opinions in cases dealing with agencies

---

[10] It is possible that our approach is biased against our results. If justices are not particularly adept at noticing the differences among agencies, our results actually undersell the relationship between agency performance and opinion clarity.

[11] We made this determination by looking at the *petitioner, respondent,* and *partyWinning* variables in the Supreme Court Database. If the United States or one of its agencies was listed as the petitioner (respondent) and the Database listed the respondent (petitioner) as the winning party, we code *Against US* as 1; 0 otherwise.

whose heads do not have fixed terms versus those that serve at the pleasure of the president. To determine whether the agency heads enjoyed *Fixed Terms*, we again turned to Lewis (2008).

Controls. We also control for a handful of features likely to influence how the Court writes its opinions. We believe the ideological spread of the majority coalition may matter, with more diverse coalitions being less likely to write readable opinions. *Majority Coalition Spread* is the standard deviation among the Martin Quinn (2002) scores of justices in the majority. Next, we control for *Lower Court Dissent.* When there is dissent in the lower court that decided the case, it signals salience, complexity, or both. As such, we might expect a less readable opinion. If there was a dissent in the lower court, we code the variable as 1; 0 otherwise.

Next, we accounted for the number of justices who voted in the majority. We might expect that in minimum winning coalitions, justices can write clearly and succinctly while larger coalitions involve more bargaining and lose clarity. We code *Majority Votes* as the number of justices in the majority coalition. We also controlled for whether the Court exercised *Federal Judicial Review* and struck down a federal statute as unconstitutional, expecting when it does so, it might craft a clearer opinion.

We also control for the separation of powers dynamic and its potential influence on opinion clarity, as greater ideological divergence between the Court and Congress might lead justices to obfuscate opinions (Owens, Wedeking, and Wohlfarth 2013). We measure *SOP Constraint* as the absolute value of the distance between the Court's median justice and the closest chamber median. When the median justice falls between the House and Senate chamber medians, *SOP Constraint* equals 0. When the median is more liberal or conservative than both the House and Senate medians, *SOP Constraint* equals the absolute value of the distance between that justice and the closest pivot.

We account for the general complexity of each case with the expectation that a more complex decision will lead to an opinion with less clarity. *Case Complexity* reflects the total number of amicus curiae briefs filed in the case.[12] We account for variance in opinion clarity that might be due to shifts over time and different issue areas. Accordingly, we include a predictor reflecting the *Court Term* associated with each majority opinion

---

[12] We obtain amicus participation from 1960–2001 from Collins (2008), and collected amicus data during the 2002–2007 Court terms from Lexis.

as well as fixed effects for the primary *Issue Area* of each case.[13] Finally, as we note earlier in the book, we also control for potential false full stops that might otherwise drive our measure of opinion clarity.[14]

5.5 Methods and results

To determine whether Supreme Court justices write clearer opinions based on agency capabilities, we estimate the readability of the Court's majority opinions using OLS regression. We estimate robust standard errors clustered on each federal agency to account for the possibility of correlated errors among different agencies. As Table 5.1 shows, the data confirm our expectations. Justices craft the language of majority opinions based, in part, on agency characteristics. In particular, justices write opinions with a view toward an agency's performance record as they issue a ruling contrary to that agency's position. What is more, this effect is evident in both a baseline model and when accounting for other factors possibly related to opinion clarity.

Figure 5.4 displays the magnitude of the substantive effects, which we derive from Model 1 (though figures based on Models 2 and 3 look substantively the same). Along the x-axis we plot agency professionalism, which ranges from low to high. The solid line in the figure reflects cases in which the Court ruled against an agency, while the dashed line reflects those in which it ruled in favor of the agency. As the figure shows, when the Court rules against a federal agency, a decrease in agency professionalism (as manifested through its PART score) prompts justices to write clearer opinions. When the Court hands a loss to a highly professional agency, we estimate that its opinion has a readability score of around 1.4, which is the 62nd percentile across all opinions in our data. When that

---

[13] We determined whether there was a dissenting vote below by looking to the *lcDisagreement* variable in the Supreme Court Database. We determined the number of justices in the majority by looking to the Supreme Court Database *majVotes* variable. To measure whether the Court exercised judicial review, we looked to the *declarationUncon* variable in the Supreme Court Database. We determined the issue of the case by looking at the *issueArea* variable in the Supreme Court Database.

[14] There is one aspect of the model that is somewhat different from models we present in the other chapters of this book. In particular, we do not control for the alteration of precedent. This is because among the 92 cases we examine, there is a not a single case in which the Court altered its own precedent. Without any variation in the variable, we cannot estimate its impact on opinion clarity.

Table 5.1: *The impact of administrative agency characteristics on Supreme Court opinion clarity*

	(1)	(2)	(3)
Rule Against U.S.	9.182**	10.462**	5.279*
	(3.247)	(4.228)	(3.320)
PART Score	0.069**	0.062*	0.088**
	(0.030)	(0.044)	(0.040)
Rule Against U.S. x PART Score	−0.122**	−0.138**	−0.067
	(0.050)	(0.062)	(0.051)
Independent Agency		−1.520*	−1.664**
		(1.014)	(0.756)
Party Balance		−1.929	0.068
		(1.909)	(1.333)
Fixed Terms		2.230*	1.877**
		(1.485)	(1.026)
Coalition Heterogeneity		0.178	0.950
		(0.926)	(0.844)
Lower Court Dissent		−0.209	−0.385
		(0.880)	(0.775)
Majority Votes		0.674**	0.623**
		(0.276)	(0.329)
Case Complexity		−0.050	−0.100*
		(0.052)	(0.070)
Court Term		0.301**	0.311**
		(0.133)	(0.156)
Federal Judicial Review		−3.624**	−4.334**
		(2.117)	(2.187)
SOP Constraint		−3.449	−1.632
		(4.265)	(5.718)
False Full Stops		0.022**	0.021**
		(0.007)	(0.007)
Constant	−3.038*	−612.314**	−632.533**
	(1.935)	(265.718)	(311.693)
Majority Opinion Writer Controls	No	No	Yes
Issue Area Controls	No	Yes	Yes
N	92	92	92
R-Squared	0.07	0.39	0.64
BIC	516.87	559.57	561.37

Note: Table entries are OLS coefficients with robust standard errors clustered on each originating agency/bureau shown parentheses. $*$ $p < 0.10$ and $**$ $p < 0.05$ (one-tailed). The dependent variable represents the composite readability score of each Supreme Court majority opinion, 2001–2007, with larger values reflecting greater clarity.

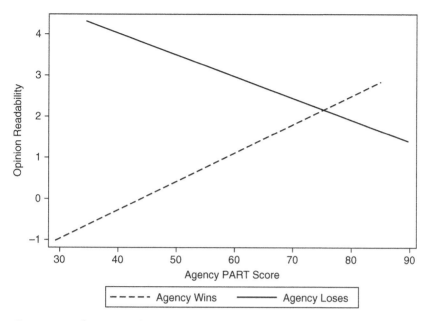

Figure 5.4: The impact of agency professionalism on Supreme Court opinion clarity. Negative scores for readability represent less readable opinions while positive scores represent greater readability. Note that the uneven lengths of the two lines is intentional and reflects the in-sample ranges over which we observe agency professionalism for each type of case.

opinion is targeted towards a highly *un*professional agency, however, the Court writes in a way that is significantly clearer. Such an opinion has an estimated readability score of 4.2, which puts it in the 83rd percentile of all Supreme Court majority opinions. In short, the characteristics of federal agencies can have a substantively meaningful effect on the way justices craft majority opinions. Justices alter the clarity of their opinions to direct subsequent agency implementation.

Several control predictors also influence opinion readability. Looking to the empirical results in Models 2 and 3, opinions written in cases involving independent agencies tend to be less readable than cases involving executive-controlled agencies. Perhaps this is because independent agencies may be more objective and therefore need less clarity to enhance their compliance. We also observe that the Court writes increasingly readable opinions when the size of the majority coalition in the case increases. That is, at least in this subset of cases, smaller coalition size can produce less readable opinions, perhaps due to the internal bargaining that is necessary to sustain a majority coalition during the Court's opinion-writing process. The data also suggest the average opinion has become more readable over time, as evident in the impact of the control predictor accounting for the term of the Court's decision. Opinions that strike down federal legislation are more difficult to read than those that do not. Lastly, there are several significant effects among the issue area controls (that are not displayed in Table 5.1). Compared to the baseline category of criminal procedure cases, justices tend to write decreasingly readable opinions in cases primarily involving issues of privacy and increasingly readable opinions in due process cases.

5.6   Discussion

Scholars of policy implementation and administrative decision making have long documented the institutional incentive of bureaucrats to craft policy consistent with their own programmatic goals and preferences (e.g., Niskanen 1971; Wildavsky 1992; Wilson 1989). What we show here is that opinion clarity is a function of agency characteristics. Specifically, when the Court decides cases involving less competent agencies, it writes clearer opinions, and when the Court decides cases involving competent agencies, justices do not increase the clarity of their opinions.

When we consider this chapter's theory and evidence as part of the book's larger theoretical and empirical argument, we see that federal agencies comprise another crucial audience justices consider when deciding cases. Agencies make some of the most important decisions on issues in terms of the impact the issues have on our daily lives. And as we pointed out at the beginning of this chapter, virtually all facets of our daily lives are regulated by federal law. Agency competence factors in to their decisions. When they worry about future compliance, justices adjust the clarity of their opinions.

Combined with support from the previous chapter, we now observe that lower courts and federal agencies can influence how justices write their opinions. We next consider whether other actors – outside the federal government – influence the Court's opinions. More specifically, we turn to the states as another audience of the Court.

6

Supreme Court opinions and the states

In *Alexander v. Choate* (1985), the Supreme Court decided whether the changes Tennessee made to its Medicaid procedures violated the Federal Rehabilitation Act of 1973. Faced with a budget shortfall, Tennessee decided to reduce (from 20 to 14) the number of inpatient hospital days it would cover for Medicaid recipients. In response, a class of Medicaid recipients challenged the reduction, claiming it discriminated against the handicapped in violation of the Rehabilitation Act. Their argument was that since handicapped people used Medicaid services more than non-handicapped people, the reduction would disproportionately harm them. And this, they said, ran afoul of the law. The Supreme Court disagreed.

In a unanimous decision by Justice Thurgood Marshall, the Court held states could change their inpatient coverage using such neutral methods. Because the state made its Medicaid benefits equally accessible to handicapped as well as non-handicapped citizens, there was no legal violation. Moreover, there was nothing in the law or legislative history to suggest that, because the handicapped might be affected more than others, Tennessee ran afoul of the Act. The law did not, according to the Court, address neutral motivations that had a disparate impact. As the Court stated:

> The reduction in inpatient coverage will leave both handicapped and non-handicapped Medicaid users with identical and effective hospital services fully available for their use, with both classes of users subject to the same durational limitation ... Medicaid programs do not guarantee that each recipient will receive that level of health care precisely tailored to his or her particular needs. Instead, the benefit provided through Medicaid is a particular package of health care services, such as 14 days of inpatient coverage.

While the majority opinion in the case is of roughly average clarity, earlier drafts were not so clear. And some justices believed that lack of clarity might lead to poor compliance among states. For example, in response to an earlier opinion draft in the case, Justice Powell told Marshall: "there is a substantial amount of dicta that is unnecessary to a decision of this case, and that may cause trouble for us ... " Justice O'Connor put the matter more strongly: "I am concerned that because of its length and complexity it may not furnish the helpful guidance that [state] agencies affected by section 504 [of the Rehabilitation Act] need for their day to day operation." Then-Justice Rehnquist also voiced concerns over the clarity of the opinion. Only after Marshall's fifth draft of the opinion were his colleagues satisfied (Wahlbeck, Spriggs, and Maltzman 2009).

Of course, *Alexander v. Choate* was not the only case in which justices expressed concern over how the clarity of an opinion would lead states to respond. In *Wardius v. Oregon* (1973), Justice Powell complained the Court's draft opinion failed to guide states effectively. As he put it: "Unless we [decide an unaddressed issue in the draft opinion], we are not affording state legislatures the most helpful type of guidance." He followed up with a memo two weeks later, again stating the draft opinion "really will hang up state legislatures." In his mind, states would have trouble understanding and complying with the Court's unclear opinion (Wahlbeck, Spriggs, and Maltzman 2009). And, of course, the Court's treatment of the *Swann* opinion, as discussed in the book's introduction, showed that justices anticipate noncompliance by state actors.

These cases, and others we could mention, suggest that, in order to enhance compliance with their decisions, justices predict how states will respond. They are concerned about how willing and able states are to follow their opinions. But states are not all the same. Some states have the capacity – and political will – to follow Court decisions faithfully, while others do not. Some states have highly professionalized legislatures with large salaries and staff while others are part-time citizen legislatures with few resources. These features are likely to influence their compliance. Similarly, some governors enjoy extensive powers while others suffer from institutional weakness. Whether these legislative and gubernatorial characteristics influence how the Court writes its opinions is the focus of this chapter.

We examine whether state legislative professionalism and gubernatorial power influence the clarity of Supreme Court opinions. We seek to determine whether the Court writes clearer opinions when it decides cases dealing with less professionalized legislatures and governors. We expect the Court will write clearer opinions when deciding cases with citizen legislatures and institutionally weak governors. Consistent with this book's central theory, they will do so to enhance compliance with High Court decisions.

We examine just a little more than 1,000 Supreme Court opinions from 1960–2005 from cases in which a state government was a party. Our results suggest justices do, in fact, modify the clarity of their opinions as a function of state characteristics, with legislative professionalism – or the lack thereof – playing a large role. The Court writes clearer opinions when it decides cases dealing with citizen state legislatures than when it decides cases with professionalized state legislatures. In cases that involve state legislatures that lack resources and quality information, the Court produces clearer opinions. What is more, this effect is exacerbated when the citizen legislature is unified in terms of party control of the state government. We find no support, however, for the effect of gubernatorial institutional powers.

In what follows, we begin by revisiting the book's overall theory. We then discuss the role of legislative and gubernatorial professionalism, highlighting existing works that show their effects on policy and electoral outcomes. We then discuss how decreasing levels of professionalism might lead the Court to write clearer opinions. Next, we discuss our data and measures and present our results. We conclude with a discussion about the interaction between the Court and the states and opinion clarity as a tool in the hands of forward-looking justices.

6.1   A theory of opinion clarity and states

The Supreme Court faces audience-based obstacles when it makes decisions. The Supreme Court's audiences have the capacity to block or escape Court policies. So justices must devise ways of accomplishing their goals, knowing that others may want to stop them. In other words, justices pursue their goals in an interdependent environment in which their decisions are a function of their preferences and the preferences of those with whom they must interact. They must devise ways to achieve their goals while maintaining the Court's status. We focus on how justices enhance the clarity of the Court's opinions to do so.

As we have stated repeatedly, justices write clearer opinions to enhance compliance with their decisions (and to manage the Court's public support). Since this chapter is primarily concerned with how the Court might enhance compliance among states, we focus on the compliance portion of the theory. More specifically, clear opinions can help justices enhance compliance for three primary reasons.

First, opinion clarity can remove discretion from actors opposed to the Court's decision. Clearer opinions can remove discretion from those opposed to the Court's decisions. When the Court renders a clear decision, a lower court judge's ability to evade decreases. This was a key finding of Romans (1974) in his study on compliance with the Supreme Court's criminal procedure cases, as stated earlier. Only after the Court's "clear and to the point" decision in *Miranda v. Arizona* (1966) did the lower courts come around to accept the holding of *Escobedo v. Illinois* (1964) (criminal suspects have a right to counsel during police interrogations) (Romans 1974, 51). Clarity removes ambiguity that opponents can use to evade.

More broadly, looking at congressional control of bureaucracies, Huber and Shipan (2002) find that legislatures can use broad or detailed statutory language to expand or limit executive discretion. When Congress and executive agents disagree ideologically, Congress will increase the amount of policy detail in legislation. As Huber, Shipan, and Pfahler (2001) put it, when the legislature does not trust an agency it "will not want to give free rein over policy to the agency, but instead will prefer to constrain the agency by filling enacting legislation with specific policy details and instructions" (332). Randazzo, Waterman, and Fine (2006) similarly find that Congress can pass detailed legislation to constrain lower court judges. "Members of Congress," they argue, "can constrain judicial decision making over the long term by enacting detailed legislation" (1015).[1] Likewise, Randazzo, Waterman, and Fix (2011) find that detailed state statutes limit the discretion afforded to state court judges.

Second, opinion clarity can help whistle-blowers monitor and report on the behavior of states who defy the Court. Clarity can enhance compliance by making it easier for people to monitor how actors respond to High Court decisions. If the Court issues a clear opinion, interest groups, members of Congress, the executive branch, the public, and others all have an easier time determining whether actors comply with the Court's decision. Conversely, if an opinion is vague and unclear, people will find it harder to detect noncompliance. According to Songer, Segal, and Cameron (1994), litigants help the Court audit lower courts by appealing their cases and informing the High Court of shirking. The Supreme Court, in turn, grants review, reverses the lower courts, and impose its policies. The same dynamic likely applies with the Court and obstructionist states. If parties challenging a state recognize that it has deviated from the Court's policy, they can take the state to federal court to seek redress. And a clearer

---

[1] The authors made no theoretical claim about whether members intentionally passed detailed legislation in an effort to constrain lower courts, however.

opinion can enhance their ability to do so by making noncompliance easier to detect (Staton and Vanberg 2008). Indeed, Spriggs (1996) suggests that a comprehensible Supreme Court opinion makes it easier for litigants in cases involving federal agencies to take politically stubborn bureaucrats back to court. "[T]he Court," he says, "can reduce agency discretion [and, thus, noncompliance] by writing very explicit formal rules" (1127). A clear Court opinion can have the same effect on states (Brent 2003; Cross and Tiller 1998). Indeed, as applied to legislative professionalism, Berkman (2001) finds that increased legislative professionalization leads to more interest group involvement. In other words, if more professionalized legislatures induce more interest group auditing, the Court may want to make more of an effort to deputize interest groups in cases dealing with less professionalized states.

Third, clear opinions can serve as instructions that help guide states who are inclined to comply with the Court's decisions but might be less able to do so. We suspect there may be instances in which clarity can enhance compliance simply because it lowers the cost for those who want to comply with a Court decision but who might not otherwise be able to determine how to do so. A lower court judge or implementor might want to comply with a High Court ruling but find it so confusing that they are not sure whether they actually are complying. A clear opinion can simply help states execute what might otherwise be a complicated Court ruling. Some of the issues the Court addresses are complicated and may surpass the capabilities of even the most professionalized states. The Court's practice of calling for the views of the Solicitor General in complex cases (Black and Owens 2012a) suggests that some cases are considerably harder than others. States may simply need better guidance to implement the Court's decisions faithfully, and a clear opinion can offer such guidance.

Put plainly, we believe justices recognize the interdependence they face. They recognize their need to enhance the likelihood of compliance among their audiences. And they can influence, or at least believe they can influence, such compliance by crafting clearer opinions. In this chapter, we examine how they use opinion clarity when deciding cases that involve states.

6.2   Legislative and gubernatorial professionalism

A state's legislative and gubernatorial professionalism will influence the clarity of the Supreme Court's opinions. The professionalism of a state government signifies its capacity, and perhaps its willingness, to comply.

For instance, scholars often rely on measures of legislative professionalism to capture the capability and institutionalization of a state legislature. Legislatures that pay their members well, have many tangible resources, enjoy large staffs, and convene often are considered to be professionalized. Conversely, legislatures that pay their members little, have few tangible resources, have small staffs, and meet infrequently are widely considered the least professionalized (Ellickson and Whistler 2001) and are often called "citizen legislatures." Average citizens often hold these offices for a short duration, while keeping their normal, full-time jobs.[2]

Prevailing research suggests professionalism affects policy outcomes. For example, Shipan and Volden (2006) find professionalized state legislators learn from, and adopt, policies that localities in their states employ. They are able and willing to do so because they have frequent contact with their constituents, greater resources, and ambition for higher office (which leads them to focus more on public opinion). Citizen legislators, on the other hand, did not show such learning behavior in their study. Other scholars argue increased legislative professionalism leads to a more experienced collection of legislators who are of higher quality (see, e.g., Squire 2007). For example, Squire (1998) finds more professionalized legislatures are able to pass a higher percentage of their bills than less professionalized legislatures. Maestas (2000) shows professionalized state legislatures make policy that is more congruent with statewide public opinion. Professionalized legislators engage in more contact with their constituents than do citizen legislators (Squire 1993). And, Berkman (2001) finds increasingly professionalized legislatures are less reliant than citizen legislatures on interest groups for information.

Research also shows increased legislative professionalization helps legislators retain their seats. Professionalized legislators generally have more resources to travel to their districts and campaign (Carey, Niemi, and Powell 2000a; Holbrook and Tidmarch 1991). Perhaps not surprisingly, then, professionalism is also related to member stability (King, Zeckhauser, and Kim 2004; Moncrief, Niemi, and Powell 2004; Squire 1988). For example, Berry, Berkman, and Schneiderman (2000) find increased legislative professionalism keeps incumbents insulated from external political forces. That is, as the level of professionalism in a state legislature increases, the effects of external political and economic shocks on members' chances for reelection decrease. Along the same lines, Hogan

---

[2] Scholars have also pointed to a third group of legislatures – hybrid legislatures – that fall between citizen and professionalized legislatures (Moncrief et al. 1992).

(n.d.) finds professionalized legislators devote less time to legislative work than to constituent-related services (see also Ellickson and Whistler 2001).

Given these findings, we suspect citizen legislatures and less professionalized governors are likely to be more problematic from the Supreme Court's perspective than professional legislatures. This is the case for three reasons, all of which we discuss more fully in the subsections that follow. First, the prevailing literature suggests less professionalized legislatures contain fewer "quality" members than professional legislatures. It also suggests citizen legislatures are more reliant on interest groups for information. Second, citizen legislatures may be more likely to pass anti-Court legislation than professionalized legislatures. Third, because they are smaller, citizen legislatures are likely to employ fewer "whistle-blowers" who will stand up to, or point out, a state's obstruction.

6.2.1   Professionalism, legislator quality, and informational deficiencies

According to the literature, citizen legislatures contain fewer "quality" members than professionalized legislatures.[3] Whereas professionalized legislatures "attract better-qualified legislators, in terms of academic credentials, [and] occupational status" (Squire 2007, 215), citizen legislatures are likely to consist of individuals who are not skilled professionals or policy experts. Citizen legislators have little institutional memory about the legislative branch and a dearth of resources to enact policy.

Additionally, citizen legislatures lack the information more professionalized legislatures enjoy and, therefore, are more reliant on interest groups. Professional legislators have staff to collect information and analyze it. They also have the resources to find and hire good experts. Professional legislatures often have institutions like legislative reference bureaus and legislative fiscal bureaus to help them collect and analyze data and draft legislation. Consequently, Berkman (2001) finds professional legislatures rely less on interest groups for information than do citizen legislatures (see also Thompson 1986). And, since interest groups have their own goals in mind when they provide information, it is quite possible the information on which citizen legislators rely is of poorer quality.

As a result of poorer quality members and inferior information, scholars have argued citizen legislatures are less effective than professional

---

[3] We take no position on whether one style of legislature is normatively superior to another.

legislatures. Consider, for example, the study of state management performance by King, Zeckhauser, and Kim (2004). The authors examine the conditions under which state governments receive high or low management performance ratings. Their results show a strong correlation between effective managerial performance and legislative professionalism. Less professional legislatures lack sufficient policy expertise, support staff to process legislation, and competitive wages to attract quality members. Thus, "professional legislatures," they find, "appear to be a hallmark of successful state governments" (21). Ka and Teske (2002) find that professionalized legislatures are more likely to engage in complex deregulatory legislation than citizen legislatures. Shipan and Volden (2006), similarly, argue professionalized legislatures are more likely to pass legislation that is "substantively effective" (827) because they have "higher capabilities" (840).

6.2.2   Professionalism and obstructionist legislation

Citizen legislatures also may be more likely to pass obstructionist legislation than professionalized legislatures. Hogan (n.d.) finds professionalized legislators devote less time to legislative work and more time to constituent related services. He finds the "average effort devoted to legislative activities is higher than constituency activities in citizen and hybrid chambers while constituency efforts are higher than legislature activities in professional chambers" (14). Ellickson and Whistler (2001) likewise find ambitious representatives – those of the type seen in professionalized legislatures – "are more likely to engage in show horse behaviors ... rather than spending their time and energy on work horse activities ... " (562). And, Woods and Baranowski (2006) find increased legislative professionalism often leads to less democratic control over state agencies. As they see it, the professionalized state legislature has more career-oriented members who care less about controlling state agencies than they do with reelection. In other words, just when members have the most ability to control agencies, they are least likely to do so (but see, Clynch and Lauth 1991; Huber, Shipan, and Pfahler 2001).

Because citizen legislatures tend to focus more on legislation than professionalized legislatures (and, as we discussed earlier, tend to pass lower quality legislation) they are more likely to pass obstructionist legislation. Indeed, some evidence suggests citizen legislatures are, in fact, more likely than professional legislatures to pass anti-Court legislation. Ross (2002) analyzed state legislation passed in response to the Warren

Court's controversial decisions in the early 1960s. After the Court's decision in *Baker v. Carr* (1962), which came on the heels of a number of other rulings against the states, officials from various states came together and proposed a set of three constitutional amendments aimed at undoing the Court's decisions and empowering the states. Specifically, officials proposed three constitutional amendments that would: (a) allow the states to amend the Constitution without Congress's participation, (b) strip the Supreme Court of jurisdiction in apportionment cases, and (c) create a Court of the Union composed of the Chief Justices of all 50 states that would review decisions by the U.S. Supreme Court (Ross 2002, 484). Eighteen state legislatures approved the amendment that would have allowed states to amend the Constitution without congressional involvement (Shanahan 1963). The state legislatures that approved this amendment were, on average, less professional than states that did not. In fact, a difference of means test shows the mean legislative professionalism score of the adopters was significantly ($t > 0.038$) smaller than the mean professionalism score of the non-adopters.

6.2.3 Professionalism and whistle-blowers

Citizen legislatures are likely to have fewer whistle-blowers to point out their state's (intentional or unintentional) noncompliance with the Court's decisions. One of the main attributes of a professionalized legislature is increased support staff (Berry, Berkman, and Schneiderman 2000). Professionalized legislatures have larger professional staffs who can assist members and provide them with information. Staff help move along legislation, provide fiscal summaries of bills, and provide constituent services. Such staff, we believe, also generate a larger audience that views the actions of the legislature and can, when necessary, blow the whistle on bad behavior.

Consider existing scholarship on political corruption. While no studies of which we are aware directly examine the role of legislative professionalism on corruption, a number of studies suggest more professionalized legislatures might generate less corruption. For example, Alt and Lassen (2003) find that where public sector wages are high (i.e., one component of professionalism), public officials engage in less corruption. Gentzkow, Glaeser, and Goldin (2006) show where third parties exist – such as the media, competing partisans, or even professionals – reporting on corruption increases. Other studies are equally suggestive. Riccucci (1995) discusses how professionals in the SEC blew the whistle on the Savings and Loan scandal that involved a number of members of Congress, including Speaker Wright and powerful senators. Mosher (1982) notes that professionals have a continuing drive to advance their profession and strengthen its public image. And, Moe (1987) believes professionals within the National Labor Relations Board will protect the agency from political attacks.

The more professionalized a legislature becomes – and the more professionals surrounding it – the more potential whistle-blowers there are, and thus, the higher the probability someone will publicly point out a state's obstruction. Because increasingly professionalized state legislatures have more staff, there are more sets of eyes on the policies the legislature makes, and whether those policies comply with Court policy. On the other hand, with fewer staff, it is very likely a citizen legislature has fewer sets of eyes on it. So, professionalized states may have more whistle-blowers to expose noncompliance, while citizen legislatures have less.

Our discussion (and extant literature) has focused predominantly on legislative professionalism to lay the foundation for our claim that justices write clearer opinions when dealing with citizen legislatures. Yet, the institutional power of state governors may reflect similarly on the professionalism of state government and influence the clarity of Court opinions accordingly. Around the same time many states ramped up the powers of their legislatures, many states also sought to strengthen and professionalize gubernatorial powers (Fisher and Nice 2005). States sought "to place governors in a strong position to direct, control, plan, organize, evaluate, and coordinate the activities of the executive branch – to fulfill the role of manager in the classical sense" (Beyle 1983, 82).[4] Thus, to the extent that justices look to a state's gubernatorial professionalism when forming expectations about compliance concerns within a state, those institutional powers (or limitations) might also influence how they craft opinions.

In sum, the literature suggests that when compared to professionalized legislatures (and governors), citizen legislatures tend to be of lesser quality, are more likely to pass obstructionist legislation, and have fewer whistle-blowers. What can the Court do to manage these institutional

---

[4] Much of this executive growth came in response to external institutions such as the number of media outlets in the state, the size of the state bureaucracy, and the number of separately elected officials in the executive branch. Whatever the cause, however, the unmistakable fact is that governors in many (though certainly not all) states are more professionalized and powerful than in years past.

obstacles? How can it overcome the limitations of some states and enhance compliance with its decisions? As we argue throughout this book, the Court can write clearer opinions.

Before we proceed, we pause to address one item. One may wonder whether the justices are aware of legislative and gubernatorial professionalism. We believe the Court is aware of legislative and gubernatorial professionalism through various interactions with the states over time. As we discussed earlier, the states appear as litigants before the Court in roughly 25% of all cases over time. When one includes the number of cases in which various states participate as amici, that familiarity with the states increases dramatically. The Court obtains significant information through these contacts. Similarly, justices regularly travel to various states to give speeches, teach classes, and oversee judicial conferences. As they make these visits, it is likely apparent to them which states have invested resources into their legislatures and executive branch, and which states have not. Finally, we suspect the Court is also aware of state professionalism through the media. In other words, we do not think knowledge of a state legislative or gubernatorial professionalism is hidden or overly complex. Justices are likely quite aware of a state's general degree of professionalism.

6.3   Data and measures

Our goal is to determine whether justices modify the clarity of their opinions because of the institutional characteristics of the states that appear before them. To pursue this goal, we examined every orally argued, signed opinion, or judgment of the Court from its 1960 through 2005 terms in which a state was a party.[5] We include only these years in our sample because those are the years for which we can obtain data on state legislative professionalism. Our dependent variable is the clarity of each Court opinion which, again, measures the readability of the opinion. The measure reflects the general readability of each Supreme Court opinion using a principal component analysis of 28 different readability measures. The scale of the measure, again, is such that larger scores represent greater readability while smaller scores represent less readability.

---

[5] We utilize the *petitionerState* and *respondentState* variables in the Supreme Court Database to identify cases with state governments as litigants. Because we control for opinion author fixed effects, we do not include per curiam opinions in our model. However, our results remain the same if we include per curiam opinions and omit these fixed effects.

Our main covariates of interest measure the professionalism of each state legislature as well as the power of the Governor in each state that appeared before the Court. To measure *Legislative Professionalism*, we turn to the "most commonly used measure of professionalism in the literature" (Malholtra 2008, 9) and the "most appropriate" approach for making overtime comparisons among state legislatures (King 2000, 329) – the Squire Index (Squire 2007).[6] Squire compares the characteristics of state legislatures with those of the U.S. Congress, which is the most professionalized legislature in the world. Squire's professionalism measure compares a state's legislator compensation, session length, and legislative staffing levels to those of Congress. The ultimate score each legislature receives is "the average of legislator compensation, days in legislative session, and legislative resources (all expressed as proportions of corresponding traits of Congress)" (Malhotra 2008, 20). Larger values represent more professionalized state legislatures.

While there is certainly debate over whether scholars adequately can measure legislative professionalism (Rosenthal 1996),[7] most scholars agree existing legislative professionalism scores can measure a legislature's ability to "command the full attention of its members, provide them with adequate resources to do their jobs in a manner comparable to that of other full-time political actors, and set up organizations and procedures that facilitate lawmaking" (Mooney 1995, 48–49). Indeed, scholars who study state governments frequently employ such measures of legislative professionalism (see, e.g., Berkman 2001; Berry, Berkman, and Schneiderman 2000; Ellickson and Whistler 2001; Maestas 2000; Moncrief, Niemi, and Powell 2004; Shipan and Volden 2006; Squire 1988, 1998, 2007).

Figure 6.1 shows the mean legislative professionalism scores for the states between 1960 and 2005. And though what we show here is merely the mean professionalism scores across 45 years, the scores have strong face validity. California, Michigan, New York, and Massachusetts are among the most professionalized states over our sample period. Today, for example, California has 80 members in the state assembly (none

---

[6] More specifically, we obtained the Squire data from the State Politics and the Judiciary dataset compiled by Stefanie Lindquist, which is available online at: http://academic .udayton.edu/sppq-TPR/DATASETS/statedata.xls.

[7] There is also a normative debate about what kind of legislature is "best" (Carey, Niemi and Powell 2000*b*; Carey 1998). We take no position, as there are normative virtues to both types of legislatures.

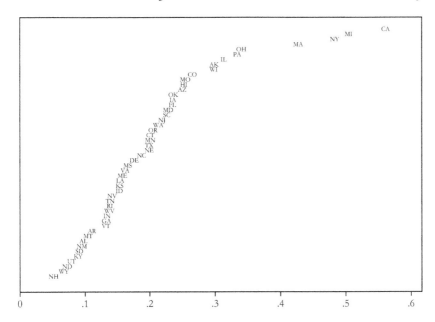

Figure 6.1:   Mean legislative professionalism scores, 1960–2005.

of whom earn less than $90,000 annually), and 40 state senators who meet year round.[8] On the other hand, New Hampshire, Wyoming, and North Dakota are the least professionalized state legislatures. Indeed, New Hampshire is an interesting example, with a part-time House of Representatives containing 400 members, each of whom receives $200 per biennium.[9]

To measure *Gubernatorial Institutional Powers*, we turn to Thad Beyle's gubernatorial powers and resources index (Beyle 1990).[10] These scores are "widely used and often cited" (Dilger, Krause, and Moffett 1995, 554). The Governor's Institutional Powers (GIP) score is a prominent indicator that quantifies (on a scale of 1–5) various concepts attached to heightened gubernatorial power. Beyle measures four dynamics he believes are relevant to a Governor's institutional powers. First, he measures the Governor's Tenure Potential. Governors that serve four-year terms with no constraint on their abilities to seek reelection receive a

---

[8] http://assembly.ca.gov/sites/assembly.ca.gov/files/Assembly%20Members %20Salaries_070513.pdf.
[9] www.gencourt.state.nh.us/house/abouthouse/housefacts.htm.
[10] www.unc.edu/~beyle/I-InstitutionalScore-501.doc.

value of 5. On the other hand, governors that serve two-year terms with limitations on reelection receive a value of 1. As he sees it, governors who have the power to remain in office longer have a broader perspective than shorter term governors, whose political shadows are not nearly so long. Second, Beyle looks to a Governor's Appointment Powers. If a governor alone can appoint people to major functions and offices, he or she receives a value of 5. On the other hand, a governor that lacks such power (because, e.g., those offices are selected by experts or independent commissions) receives a value of 1. Third, Beyle looks to the Governor's Budgetary Powers. Governors who have extensive power to prepare their states' budgets receive a value of 5, while those who must share such responsibility with others who are independent of them receive a value of 1. Finally, Beyle analyzes the Governor's Veto Power. Those who enjoy line item veto powers and a high threshold for legislative override receive a value of 5, while those who have minimal veto powers receive a value of 1.[11] The final Gubernatorial Institutional Power score, then, is the mean of these four scores.[12]

As Figure 6.2 shows, these scores, like the legislative professionalism scores, possess substantial face validity. Texas, South Carolina, and North Carolina have the least powerful governors over our sample period. Indeed, North Carolina's governor heads an executive branch alongside nine popularly elected cabinet-level officials (Bowman, Woods, and Stark 2010, 308). Conversely, New York and New Jersey had the most institutionally powerful governors during this time period. In New Jersey, for instance, the governor is the only statewide elected official (Bowman, Woods, and Stark 2010, 308).

Control variables. Of course, we do not expect legislative profession-alism and gubernatorial powers are the only features that influence the clarity of the Court's opinions. We control for several other factors. We begin by controlling for whether the same party controlled the legislative and executive branches of the state. If the State Politics and the Judiciary dataset codes the state as being uniformly controlled by the same party, we code *Uniform Political Control* as 1; 0 otherwise. Next, we account for whether the Court's decision struck down a state statute. We code

---

[11] In some (but not all) years, Beyle also examined the Governor's Party Control, the Governor's Organizational Powers, Legislative Budget-Changing Authority, and whether there were Separately Elected Executive Branch Officials.

[12] We retrieve the same results if we re-estimate the subsequent statistical models using the individual components of the GIP scores rather than their averages.

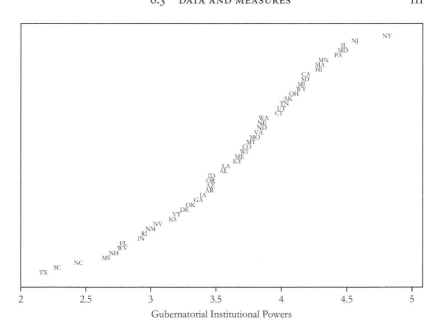

Figure 6.2: Mean gubernatorial powers and resources scores, 1960–2005.

State Judicial Review as 1 if, according to the Supreme Court Database, the Court struck down a state statute or municipal law; 0 otherwise. We likewise account for *Federal Judicial Review*, coding whether (=1) or not (=0) the Court struck down a federal statute.[13]

We next control for whether the state won or lost its case. To measure *State Lost*, we turned to the Supreme Court Database. If the database recorded the state as petitioner (respondent) and listed a favorable outcome for the respondent (petitioner), we coded *State Lost* as 1. If the database recorded the state as petitioner (respondent) and listed a favorable outcome for the petitioner (respondent), we coded *State Lost* as 0.[14] We also control for the ideological position of the state in the case. *State Ideological Distance* represents the absolute value of the distance between the median member of the congressional delegation for each

[13] We utilize the *declarationUncon* variable in the Supreme Court Database. Specifically, *Federal Judicial Review* and *State Judicial Review* take on a value of 1 when *declarationUncon* equals 2 and 3, respectively.

[14] We use the *partyWinning* variable in the Supreme Court Database to identify which party received a favorable disposition within each case.

state and the median justice in the Supreme Court's majority coalition.[15] We use the Judicial Common Space (JCS) scores for this measure, so as to ensure that the relevant legislative and judicial ideological scores were generated on a common scale (Epstein et al. 2007).

We next account for *Majority Votes*, which is the number of justices signing on to the Court's majority opinion.[16] It could be the case that unanimous opinions deal with easy cases and, thus, the opinion might be clearer. We next control for the general complexity of each case – *Case Complexity* – using an indicator of the total number of amicus curiae briefs filed in each case (Collins 2008). We obtain amicus participation from 1960–2001 from Collins (2008), and collected amicus data during the 2002–2007 Court terms from Lexis. We also account for the heterogeneity of the Supreme Court majority crafting each opinion, as a more diverse coalition might produce a less clear opinion. To measure *Ideological Heterogeneity*, we compute the standard deviation of the JCS scores of the justices in each majority coalition. To measure *Majority Votes*, we counted the number of justices in the majority coalition. We further control for whether the Court overruled an existing precedent. If the Supreme Court Database codes the decision as overruling precedent, *Precedent Alteration* equals 1; 0 otherwise.[17]

Next, we control for the separation of powers dynamic and the potential that greater ideological divergence between the Court and Congress might lead justices to obfuscate opinions (Owens, Wedeking, and Wohlfarth 2013). We measure *SOP Constraint* as the absolute value of the distance between the Court's median justice and the closest chamber median. That is, when the median justice falls between the House and Senate chamber medians, *SOP Constraint* equals 0. When the median is more liberal or conservative than both the House and Senate medians, *SOP Constraint* equals the absolute value of the distance between that justice and the closest pivot.[18]

We account for variance in opinion clarity that might be driven by a shift over time, differences across legal issue areas, and the idiosyncrasies

---

[15] The empirical results are robust if using the median justice on the Court to construct the *State Ideological Distance* measure.

[16] We determined the number of justices in the majority by looking to the Supreme Court Database *majVotes* variable.

[17] We use the *precedentAlteration* variable in the Supreme Court Database to identify decisions that formally altered prior precedent.

[18] All subsequent empirical results are consistent when using the median of the Court's majority coalition in each case to construct the *SOP Constraint* control predictor.

of Supreme Court justices' writing styles (see, e.g., Owens and Wedeking 2011). Accordingly, we include a predictor reflecting the *Court Term* associated with each majority opinion, fixed effects to control for the primary *Issue Area* of each case, and fixed effects accounting for the identity of the *Majority Opinion Author* within each case.[19] Finally, as we note earlier in the book, we also control for potential false full stops that might otherwise drive our measure of opinion clarity.

6.4 Methods and results

Because our dependent variable – opinion readability – is a continuous measure, we employ an ordinary least squares regression model with robust standard errors clustered on each state.[20] Recall that positive values of readability represent greater readability while negative values represent less readability. Table 6.1 reports the estimates of our regression model.

The data support our expectation that justices alter the readability of their opinions as a result of states' legislative professionalism. The coefficient on *Legislative Professionalism*, in both a baseline specification (Model 1) and when including all control variables (Model 2), is positive and statistically significant. Larger values of legislative professionalism correlated with smaller values of readability. That is, lower levels of legislative professionalism correlate with clearer Supreme Court opinions. Figure 6.3 illustrates the magnitude of this effect using the empirical results from Model 2. The y-axis shows the readability of a Court opinion while the x-axis signifies the level of state legislative professionalism (moving from citizen legislatures on the left to professionalized legislatures on the right). The solid line represents the predicted level of readability while the dashed lines represent the 95% confidence intervals. As the figure shows, there is approximately a one-unit decrease in opinion readability as a state legislature moves from the least professionalized to most professionalized. This corresponds to moving from the 48th to 60th percentile of all Supreme Court majority opinions. Stated more intuitively, the Court writes opinions that are as much as one-unit clearer, on average, when dealing with citizen legislatures compared to more professional legislatures.

---

[19] We use the *issueArea* and *majOpinWriter* variables in the Supreme Court Database to specify these fixed effects.

[20] The subsequent empirical results are robust if estimating classical standard errors instead of clustered robust standard errors.

Table 6.1: *The impact of state legislative professionalism on Supreme Court opinion clarity*

	(1)	(2)
Legislative Professionalism	−3.125**	−1.770**
	(1.008)	(0.705)
Gubernatorial Institutional Powers	−0.272*	−0.010
	(0.178)	(0.169)
Uniform Political Control		0.290
		(0.260)
State Lost		0.402
		(0.312)
State Ideological Distance		0.239*
		(0.161)
Precedent Alteration		−0.471
		(0.516)
Coalition Heterogeneity		0.152
		(0.206)
Lower Court Dissent		−0.298
		(0.247)
Case Complexity		−0.040**
		(0.021)
Majority Votes		0.349**
		(0.074)
Federal Judicial Review		−4.005**
		(0.973)
State Judicial Review		−0.518*
		(0.342)
SOP Constraint		−0.819
		(1.089)
Court Term		0.027*
		(0.020)
False Full Stops		0.032**
		(0.002)
Constant	1.520**	−57.046*
	(0.610)	(39.847)
Majority Opinion Writer Controls	No	Yes
Issue Area Controls	No	Yes
N	1136	1136
R^2	0.02	0.37
BIC	6627.60	6451.45

Note: Table estimates are OLS coefficients with robust standard errors (clustered on each state) in parentheses. * $p < 0.10$ and ** $p < 0.05$ (one-tailed).

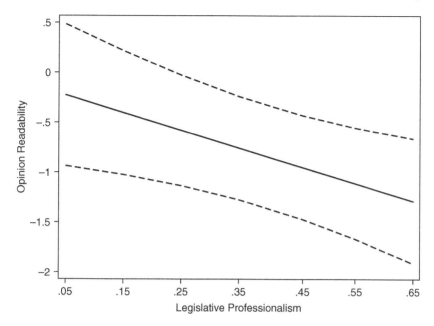

Figure 6.3: The impact of state legislative professionalism on Supreme Court opinion clarity. Larger readability scores amount to increasingly readable opinions.

We decided to probe this relationship further. What happens when the state legislature and governor are controlled by the same party? That is, justices might expect such a unified state could pass responsive legislation with little difficulty. Justices, as a result, might view opinion clarity as an especially effective tool to induce greater compliance among states with unified political control. Table 6.2 reports the statistical results after adding an interactive term between *Legislative Professionalism* and *Uniform Political Control*. The data support our expectations. The Court becomes more likely to write clearer opinions when dealing with unified states that have citizen legislatures, and we see no significant effect of legislative professionalism among states with divided control of government.

Figure 6.4 displays magnitude of the multiplicative effect of legislative professionalism and unified political control on opinion readability. It displays the predicted level of opinion readability across the range of legislative professionalism, with a solid line to represent states with unified political control and a dotted line to signify divided control. Once again, we see that lower values of professionalism correlate with

Table 6.2: *The impact of state legislative professionalism on Supreme Court opinion clarity, conditional on state political control*

	(1)	(2)
Legislative Professionalism	−1.950*	−0.020
	(1.379)	(0.794)
Uniform Political Control	1.165**	1.308**
	(0.630)	(0.424)
Uniform Control × Professionalism	−3.017*	−3.457**
	(1.887)	(1.014)
Gubernatorial Institutional Powers		0.022
		(0.162)
State Lost		0.393
		(0.310)
State Ideological Distance		0.248*
		(0.159)
Precedent Alteration		−0.442
		(0.515)
Coalition Heterogeneity		0.168
		(0.207)
Lower Court Dissent		−0.286
		(0.247)
Case Complexity		−0.041**
		(0.023)
Majority Votes		0.347**
		(0.074)
Federal Judicial Review		−3.891**
		(1.005)
State Judicial Review		−0.528*
		(0.341)
SOP Constraint		−0.717
		(1.124)
Court Term		0.025*
		(0.019)
False Full Stops		0.033**
		(0.002)
Constant	−0.104	−53.651*
	(0.519)	(36.998)
Majority Opinion Writer Controls	No	Yes
Issue Area Controls	No	Yes
N	1136	1136
R^2	0.02	0.37
BIC	6633.53	6446.50

Note: Table estimates are OLS coefficients with robust standard errors (clustered on each state) in parentheses. * $p < 0.10$ and ** $p < 0.05$ (one-tailed). The dependent variable represents the composite readability score of each Supreme Court majority opinion, 1960–2005, with larger values reflecting greater clarity.

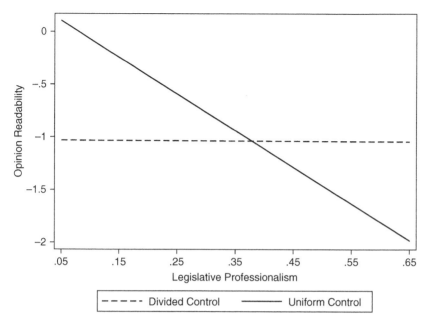

Figure 6.4:   The impact of state legislative professionalism on Supreme Court opinion clarity, conditional on state political control. Predicted values generated using the mgen command as implemented in Stata 14 by Long and Freese (2014).

increasingly readable opinions, but this effect is only prevalent among states with unified political control. Among these states with unified control, there is approximately a two-unit increase in opinion readability as a state legislature moves from the least professionalized to most professionalized.[21] Thus, the magnitude of legislative professionalism's impact on opinion readability is twice the size among states with unified control compared to the average impact when pooling all states.

While we find strong results for legislative professionalism, we find little support for the role of governors. The data fail to show the Court modifies its opinions as a function of gubernatorial power.[22] There is no change in

---

[21] As displayed in the marginal effect figure, this interactive effect is statistically significant below the mean level of state legislative professionalism. See Figures 6.5 and 6.6 in the chapter appendix.

[22] We also considered whether the Court might behave differently towards governors who had ever been a lawyer prior to becoming governor. Of the 281 unique governors in our data, 52% had such experience. This resulted in 58% of our state-year observations

the readability of the Court's opinions relative to gubernatorial power. The Court seems little phased by the power of governors.

These gubernatorial findings, while contrary to our initial expectations, seem to accord with literature that casts doubt on the importance of the governor's institutional powers. For example, Dilger, Krause, and Moffett (1995) find governors are more effective when they have institutional powers, but most effective when they work with professionalized state legislatures (see also Ferguson 2003; Ferguson and Barth 2002). Similarly, in their analysis of state management, King, Zeckhauser, and Kim (2004) find legislative professionalism predicts state performance, but that a strong governor does not. So, it could be that state legislatures matter much more in the actual implementation of the Court's decisions and, knowing this, the Court pays more attention to them than to the states' governors. It is also possible (and perhaps more probable) the institutional powers of the governor are less important than other aspects, such as the governor's popularity and his party's control of the state legislature (which is something confirmed earlier).

As far as our controls are concerned, the data suggest justices write clearer opinions in cases with larger majority coalitions, when the state loses on the merits, and when the ideological distance between the Court and state increases. These latter two results are interesting, as these are also instances in which the Court might expect resistance from states. Conversely, justices tend to write less readable opinions when they strike state or federal legislation and among more complex cases. Among the issue area controls, criminal procedure opinions are the most readable, with all other issue areas (except for federalism cases) significantly less clear.

6.5   Discussion

Scholars have paid considerable attention to the Court's interactions with Congress and the president. A number of high-quality studies have informed our understanding about how the separation of powers influences (or, in some cases, fails to influence) the Court. Yet, there has

being coded as "yes" for a lawyer experience variable. For both this initial and the interactive model we report there was no statistically significant relationship between lawyer experience and opinion clarity.

been little attention devoted to how the states as institutional units can influence the Court.[23] To be sure, scholars have examined the conditions under which states band together in cases before the Court (Provost 2006, 2003) as well as how states have complied or refused to comply with salient Court cases (Canon and Johnson 1999; Peltason 1971). But little is known about whether the institutional dynamics of the states themselves has any effect on Court decisions.

Our goal here was to fill that hole in the literature by examining whether state legislative professionalism and formal institutional gubernatorial powers influence the clarity of the Court's opinions. We found, consistent with our theory, that justices write clearer opinions when deciding cases that affect citizen legislatures. What is more, this effect seems to be exacerbated by unified political control of the state. These findings are intriguing, as they suggest justices are more strategic than even many skeptical scholars have envisioned. It also suggests scholars should focus much more attention on the role of states before the Court. Indeed, states participate in roughly one quarter of the Court's cases, and if the Court modifies its opinions in these cases because of states characteristics, we have much to learn about doctrinal evolution and federalism.

One point worth exploring in the future is whether these results also appear in state supreme courts. Do state supreme court justices also modify the clarity of their opinions for similar reasons? Current research (Nelson n.d.) suggests the results may depend on the state's judicial retention method. For example, judges retained through reelection might have a stronger incentive than non-elected judges to use opinion clarity to reach the public (i.e., voters). Still, the problem of noncompliance exists for all courts, elected or not. And so the use of opinion clarity might remain notwithstanding the judicial retention method. Indeed, that Supreme Court justices – the most insulated of all judges – use opinion clarity suggests that other judges, less insulated, may also use it.

The results are beginning to add up. We have discovered the Court writes clearer opinions when it faces an ideologically scattered judicial hierarchy and when those lower court judges are ideologically opposed

---

[23] Although, some literature examines how states that create (and employ) a formal solicitor general office to handle their appellate litigation can maximize their success before the U.S. Supreme Court (e.g., Owens and Wohlfarth 2014).

to the High Court. We have discovered the Court writes clearer opinions when it decides cases dealing with poor performing federal agencies. And we have now discovered the Court writes clearer opinions when it decides cases dealing with less professionalized states. It enhances the clarity of its opinions, we argue, to enhance the likelihood of compliance with its decisions.

But what about cases in which the Court is less concerned about compliance than it is with public support and its institutional legitimacy? That is, what about those cases in which the Court rules against public opinion? Can this "secondary audience" also lead justices to change the clarity of their opinions? We turn now to those questions.

6.6   Appendix to Chapter 6

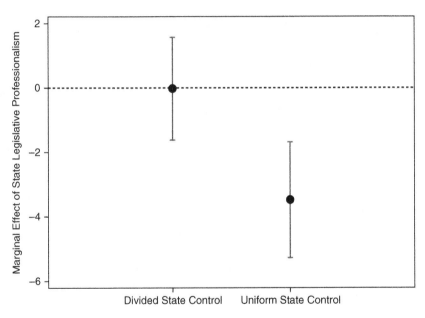

Figure 6.5:   The marginal effect of state legislative professionalism on opinion readability, conditional on state political control. The vertical whiskers represent 95% confidence intervals. This figure indicates that a one-unit increase in legislative professionalism has a null impact when the state is under divided control but a negative impact (i.e., makes an opinion less readable) when the state is under uniform control.

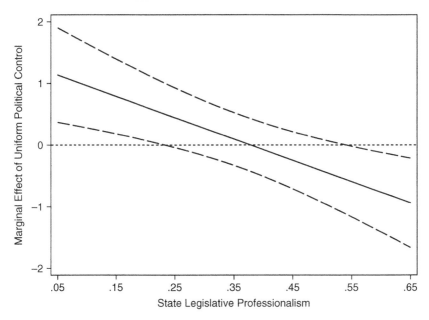

Figure 6.6:   The marginal effect of switching from divided to unified state political control on opinion readability, conditional on state legislative professionalism. The dashed lines represent 95% confidence intervals. This figure indicates that uniform political control leads to more readable opinions when a state's level of legislative professionalism is about 0.25 or less (approximately 53% of the observations in our data). Unified control has no impact for values of 0.25 through around 0.55 (about 40% of the observations in our data); for values above 0.55, unified political control results in less readable opinions (roughly 7% of the observations in our data).

Supreme Court opinions and the secondary population

In *Mapp v. Ohio* (1961), the Supreme Court created the exclusionary rule, which held that courts could not admit evidence obtained illegally against a defendant. Chief Justice Earl Warren assigned the Court's majority opinion to Justice Tom Clark, a former Attorney General of the United States, a man responsible for the prosecution of thousands of criminals. In *Korematsu v. United States* (1944), during the height of World War II, the Court upheld the removal of Americans of Japanese descent to camps away from the West Coast. Chief Justice Stone assigned the Court's opinion to Justice Black, a staunch civil libertarian. These justices seemed unlikely to receive such opinions. But they did receive them. Surely other justices were as qualified. Why did these justices write the opinions? One scholar believes it is because the Chief and other justices were well aware of the need to manage public criticism of the Court's decisions (O'Brien 2008, 273).

The public can be a source of power for the Court, but also a constraint. Public support for the Court enhances its legitimacy. This legitimacy, in turn, gives justices power to rule. Yet frequent rulings against the public could cause it to lose legitimacy. In prior chapters, we demonstrated how Supreme Court justices alter the clarity of their majority opinions with an eye toward multiple audiences in the Court's political and legal environment, including federal circuit courts, federal bureaucratic agencies, and state legislatures. We now extend our focus to a fourth audience – the general public. We examine whether public opinion influences the clarity of Supreme Court majority opinions.

We begin by returning to our central theory – that justices use opinion clarity to enhance compliance with their decisions and, more importantly for this chapter, to manage public support for the Court. We discuss the role of public opinion as a constraint on the Court, highlighting how public opinion influences external actors and, thus indirectly, the Court. We also discuss how frequent rulings against the public could cause the Court to lose institutional support. Next, we discuss why ruling contrary to prevailing popular sentiment might lead justices to write increasingly readable opinions. We then discuss our data and measures, present our results, and conclude with a discussion about the broader importance of public opinion as a constraint on the Supreme Court.

7.1   A theory of opinion clarity and the mass public

The Court's legitimacy serves as the foundation of its support. As Justice Frankfurter once claimed: "The Court's authority ... rests on sustained public confidence in its moral sanction" (Caldeira 1986, 1209). A consistent pattern of shirking public opinion could damage the Court's legitimacy. Frequent rulings against the public could cause it to lose legitimacy (Casillas, Enns, and Wohlfarth 2011). Bartels and Johnston (2013), for example, suggest that ideologues who oppose specific Court decisions are more likely to challenge the Court's legitimacy than those who approve of its decisions (cf., Gibson and Nelson 2015). Other studies provide similar results. Caldeira (1986) finds, in part, that the Court's legitimacy decreases as it strikes more federal laws and sides with criminal defendants. Related work shows courts that systematically ignore *stare decisis* jeopardize their institutional legitimacy (see, e.g., Bailey and Maltzman 2011; Zink, Spriggs, and Scott 2009). While the Court has a deep reservoir of diffuse support, frequent counter-majoritarian decisions could leave it at risk (Gibson, Caldeira, and Spence 2003, 365). By writing a clear opinion when ruling against public sentiment, though, justices can better inform the public *why* they so decided, and thereby manage any immediate loss of support they might suffer (or, perhaps more aptly, *think* they might suffer). Collectively, these results suggest that members of the public respond negatively to Court decisions they dislike. So, when justices issue decisions that contradict public opinion, they risk inciting a negative reaction among citizens.

When justices issue decisions that contradict public opinion, they also risk inciting a negative reaction among elected officials. Justices pay attention to public opinion because those who implement the Court's decisions follow public opinion. That is, although justices themselves do not face elections, they must contemplate whether external actors who *are* subject to elections will implement their decisions. As McGuire and Stimson (2004) explain: "The Court requires the cooperation of legislative and executive officials, many of whom are themselves careful auditors of mass opinion. For that reason, the members of the Court must reflect on how well their preferred outcomes will be received and supported by implementers" (1022). Hall (2014) likewise argues that public opinion constrains the Court because of justices' "fear of nonimplementation" (352). So, because justices must often rely on elected officials, public opinion indirectly influences them.

To be sure, important scholarship suggests the Court's legitimacy is solid and unlikely to be reduced seriously by a single "bad" decision (e.g., Gibson, Caldeira, and Spence 2003; Kritzer 2001). Yet, even that scholarship suggests that judicial carelessness with public opinion might diminish the Court's legitimacy. Indeed, Gibson, Caldeira, and Spence (2003) state: "A few rainless months do not seriously deplete a reservoir. A sustained drought, however, can exhaust the supply of water" (365). So, justices are likely to want to manage negative reactions. To prevent erosion of public confidence, they should want to take steps to justify and mitigate decisions against public opinion.

Perhaps more importantly, even if a single decision (or handful of decisions) does not *actually* reduce the Court's legitimacy, justices are likely to be concerned that it *might*. In other words, even if scholarship shows that public support for the Court is resilient, justices still are likely to fear backlash. Just as members of Congress are often "running scared" (Jacobson 1987) when they need not be, justices might worry about possible negative consequences of their opinions and try to manage them through opinion clarity. Indeed, Justice Stevens's dissent in *Bush v. Gore* (2000) highlights this dynamic. He stated: "Although we may never know with complete certainty the identity of the winner of this year's Presidential election, the identity of the loser is perfectly clear. It is the Nation's confidence in the judge as an impartial guardian of the rule of law."

Despite the possibility that others may not comply and that the Court may lose some support, justices do rule against public opinion. As many scholars have documented, judicial decisions reflect multiple considerations, such as legal constraints (e.g., Black and Owens 2009; Richards and Kritzer 2002), contextual factors (e.g., Maltzman, Spriggs, and Wahlbeck 2000), and justices' policy preferences (Segal and Spaeth 2002). Justices balance these considerations against the incentive to follow public opinion (e.g., Casillas, Enns, and Wohlfarth 2011). Sometimes, public opinion loses out. When that happens, justices will have greater concern about noncompliance and threats to its legitimacy (Hall 2014). To minimize the threat of these problems, justices will use opinion clarity.

We should pause to reiterate four things. First, it is not essential to our theory that the public actually reads the Court's opinions. All that matters is justices believe they might. Indeed, this fear of "getting caught with their pants down" motivates many a decision maker (Key 1961, 266; Arnold 1990, 68). In fact, one study quotes justices as saying (anonymously) that they are concerned with the public regardless of whether the public reads their opinions. One justice remarked: "We read the newspapers and see what is being said – probably more than most people do" (quoted in Clark 2009, 79). Another justice stated: "We know if there is a lot of public interest; we have to be careful not to reach too far …" (quoted in Clark 2009, 236). Second, the data show that the media often copy and paste passages directly from Court opinions, so it is likely that many members of the public are in fact exposed to, and read portions of, Court opinions. Third, even if the public does not read the Court's opinions, legal and political elites do – and the logic of our argument remains the same under this context. Fourth, even a dormant public can be alerted to counter-majoritarian High Court decision making, thereby inducing widespread public attention.

We now turn our attention to analyzing how justices alter opinion clarity when they expect greater public opposition to their decisions. We take a two-pronged empirical approach. First, we conduct an individual case-level analysis that uses issue-specific public opinion polls taken before corresponding Supreme Court decisions (Marshall 1989, 2008) to demonstrate how justices write clearer opinions when they rule against public opinion in specific cases. We then employ an aggregate time series analysis to examine how general changes in popular sentiment lead to changes in clarity. While we recognize public mood is broad, the approach we take is the best possible given existing data – and it is consistent with existing literature (e.g., Casillas, Enns, and Wohlfarth 2011; Flemming, Bohte, and Wood 1997; Giles, Blackstone, and Vining 2008; McGuire and Stimson 2004; Mishler and Sheehan 1993).

7.2   An individual-level analysis of opinion clarity and public opinion

Our goal is to determine whether the Court modifies the clarity of its opinions when disregarding prevailing public opinion. To pursue this goal, ideally we would want a measure of public opinion (i.e., a poll result) on a wide variety of issues corresponding to Court decisions among opinion polls taken just prior to the Court's decision. In reality, however, those data simply do not exist. Issue-specific (and temporally appropriate) public opinion data are scarce. Marshall (2008) put it best: "Unfortunately, no published index of scientific, nationwide polls that match Supreme Court decisions exists" (29).

Fortunately, Marshall performed an exhaustive search for polls that match public opinion with issues in Supreme Court cases (Marshall 1989, 2008). Marshall identified polls in sources by searching for key words such as "Supreme Court" or key words from the issues discussed in particular Court opinions. He scoured many sources to find these matches, including the Roper Archive of Polls, the published polls of Gallup Poll, "The Polls" section in *Public Opinion Quarterly*, and other various newspaper or magazine polls. If the case had multiple polls, Marshall selected the poll closest in time to the decision. All polls are national samples, with each poll having at least 600 respondents, though many have far larger sample sizes. For a complete discussion and list of his criteria and thorough explanations, see Marshall (2008, 29–33) and Marshall (1989, 75–77). For our individual case-level analysis, we use Marshall's poll question-case matches among polls that *preceded* relevant Court decisions.

We have 106 poll questions matched to specific issues decided in Supreme Court cases that span the 1946–2004 terms.[1] We select these terms based on the availability of Marshall's data. Importantly, these 106 observations involve a wide range of legal issue areas. There are 26 observations in criminal procedure, 23 observations in civil rights, 24 observations in First Amendment, 12 observations in privacy, and the remaining observations spread across issues such as due process, unions, economic activity, judicial power, and federalism. While the bulk of our observations come from cases that primarily involve issues of civil rights and liberties, we note the majority of the modern Court's docket also focused on those cases.

Supreme Court opinion clarity. Our dependent variable is the readability score of each Supreme Court majority opinion. We employ the composite readability index detailed in Chapter 3. They measure the difficulty a general reader (i.e., a member of the public or news reporter) is likely to encounter when reading a Court decision. Figure 7.1 presents a visual

---

[1] We exclude poll questions that were matched to denials of certiorari. The 106 observations in our dataset do include four *cases* that appear more than once because Marshall collected multiple poll questions for a case if a case addressed multiple issues. For example, *Planned Parenthood v. Casey* (1992) represents four observations in Marshall's original data because it discussed four issues: (1) informed consent; (2) husband notification; (3) one-parent consent for minors' abortions; and (4) 24-hour waiting rule. Our substantive findings do not differ, however, if we exclude those multiple observations for a single case.

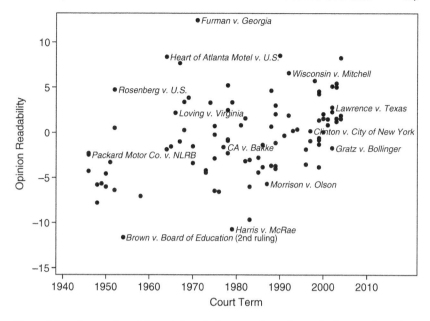

Figure 7.1:   Scatterplot of the opinion clarity score for each case in the sample and the Supreme Court term.

depiction of the readability scores among of our sample of cases. We highlight the case names associated with select data points.

Inconsistent with public opinion. Our main covariate of interest in this analysis measures whether the Court rules contrary to prevailing public opinion, as determined by Marshall's polls. We employ Marshall's measure of an "inconsistent decision," reflecting when a Court decision "disagreed in substance with a poll majority (or plurality)" (Marshall 2008, 31). Marshall's measure is appropriate because it captures the essence of our theoretical argument – the Court is concerned about the clarity of its opinions when it decides against an oppositional body that is larger than the supporting body. Therefore, we operationalize *Inconsistent With Public Opinion* as a dichotomous measure, with observations coded as 1 if there was more opposition than support for the Court's position; 0 otherwise (i.e., it is 0 when the Court rules consistent with public opinion or the poll margin was within the margin of error). We have no theoretical reason to expect the Court to consider the precise size of the opposition once it exceeds the majority of the public. That is, we have no reason to expect justices will write a clearer opinion with 70% opposition compared to, say, 60% opposition.

For an example, consider *Clinton v. City of New York* (1998), which struck down the line-item veto as unconstitutional. As Marshall (2008) reports: "Gallup Poll asked respondents: 'As you may know, Congress recently approved legislation called the line item veto, which for the first time allows the President to veto some items in a spending bill without vetoing the entire bill. Do you generally favor or oppose the line item veto' A 65-to-24% majority favored the line-item veto, [hence] *Clinton v. City of New York* was coded as 'inconsistent'" (Marshall 2008, 31).[2]

Control predictors. To ensure the robustness of our empirical test, we also include a number of control variables likely to influence the readability of Court opinions. We control for a change in the legal status quo by accounting for when the Court *Precedent Alteration*, coded as 1 if the Supreme Court Database so declares; 0 otherwise. We capture the ideological heterogeneity of the Supreme Court majority coalition in each case by including *Coalition Heterogeneity*, which is the standard deviation of the JCS scores for all justices in the majority coalition.

We also account for the presence of dissent in the lower court that heard the case. When a lower court judge dissents in a case, it often signifies that the case is complicated or otherwise ideologically charged. We suspect justices might write less clear opinions in such cases. So, we include a binary indicator called *Lower Court Dissent*, which measures whether a judge in the court that decided the case dissented. As in earlier chapters, we utilize amicus participation to measure *Case Complexity*, reflecting the total number of briefs in each case.[3] We also examine, consistent with earlier chapters, the effect of majority coalition size – *Majority Votes* – which continues to reflect the number of justices in the majority. As there is greater consensus among the justices on the Court, we expect opinions will be clearer. Next, we control for *Judicial Review* – cases where the Court's opinion struck down a federal or state statute, or local ordinance as unconstitutional. We code this variable as 1 if, according to the

---

[2] For the distribution of our 106 observations, we adapt Marshall's data, where 37 observations were labeled as "inconsistent" with public opinion, and 69 observations were labeled as either "unclear" or "consistent" with public opinion. We combine "unclear" with "consistent" because if there were unclear poll results, which usually meant multiple conflicting polls, then the Court could easily write an opinion as if the supporting body was larger than the opposition body.

[3] Alternatively, one could attempt to measure complexity with the number of legal issues in each case (using the maximum number of legal issues in a docket, as identified by the "caseIssuesId" variable in the Supreme Court Database). The subsequent empirical results are robust when specifying this alternative indicator of case complexity.

Supreme Court Database, the Court struck down a law as unconstitutional; 0 otherwise.[4]

Next, we account for the separation of powers dynamic, as greater ideological divergence between the Court and Congress might lead justices to obfuscate opinions (Owens, Wedeking, and Wohlfarth 2013). We measure *SOP Constraint* as the absolute value of the distance between the Court's median justice and the closest chamber median. When the median justice falls between the House and Senate chamber medians, *SOP Constraint* equals 0. When the median is more liberal or conservative than the House and Senate medians, *SOP Constraint* equals the absolute value of the distance between that justice and the closest pivot.[5]

We also account for variance in opinion clarity that might be due to shifts over time, different legal contexts and issue areas, or the idiosyncrasies of majority opinion authors (see, e.g., Owens and Wedeking 2011). Accordingly, we include a predictor reflecting the *Court Term* associated with each majority opinion, fixed effects to control for the primary *Issue Area* of each case, and fixed effects accounting for the identity of the *Majority Opinion Author* within each case. Finally, as we note earlier in the book, we also control for potential false full stops that might otherwise drive our measure of opinion clarity.

7.2.1 Methods and results

Because our dependent variable is continuous, we fit ordinary least squares linear regression models and used robust standard errors.[6] Our results appear in Table 7.1, and they support our hypothesis. Model 1 shows the bivariate relationship between ruling against public sentiment and opinion clarity. It is statistically significant and positively signed, indicating that when the Court issues a ruling inconsistent with public opinion, the Court delivers a significantly clearer opinion.

---

[4] Note that this parameterization differs from other chapters in this book, where we disaggregate when the Court invalidates federal versus state laws. We find no evidence of a difference between the two in this model (i.e., there is still no statistically significant relationship), so we opt for the more parsimonious measurement strategy given our relatively small sample size.
[5] The statistically significant impact of public opinion on opinion clarity is consistent if we use the median of the Court's majority coalition in each case and/or alternate legislative pivots to construct the *SOP Constraint* control predictor.
[6] Our substantive inferences are unchanged, however, if we use classical standard errors instead.

Table 7.1: *An individual-level view of the impact of public sentiment on Supreme Court majority opinion content*

	(1)	(2)	(3)
Inconsistent With Public Opinion	1.822**	1.467**	1.240*
	(0.815)	(0.812)	(0.913)
Precedent Alteration		−0.076	−0.881
		(0.992)	(1.618)
Coalition Heterogeneity		−16.219**	−20.349**
		(4.564)	(7.539)
Lower Court Dissent		−0.820	−0.548
		(0.725)	(1.020)
Case Complexity		0.027	−0.003
		(0.035)	(0.046)
Majority Votes		1.007**	0.918**
		(0.400)	(0.532)
Judicial Review		0.281	0.840
		(1.055)	(1.461)
SOP Constraint		5.043*	6.039
		(3.688)	(5.595)
Court Term		0.137**	0.233**
		(0.028)	(0.076)
False Full Stops		0.000	−0.001
		(0.002)	(0.002)
Constant	−1.014**	−275.259**	−459.544**
	(0.546)	(55.179)	(148.318)
Majority Opinion Writer Controls	No	No	Yes
Issue Area Controls	No	No	Yes
N	106	106	106
R^2	0.04	0.28	0.40
BIC	615.06	626.03	718.51

Note: Table entries are OLS regression estimates with robust standard errors in parentheses. * $p < 0.05$; * $p < 0.10$; (one-tailed). The dependent variable represents the Supreme Court majority opinion readability score for each case, with larger values reflecting greater clarity. The sample of Court cases and public opinion polls come from Marshall (1989, 2008), among those where polls temporally precede the Court's decision.

Models 2 and 3 check the robustness of this result by first including the control predictors (but without fixed effects), and then adding the issue area and majority opinion writer fixed effects, respectively. This last model allows us to control for the possibility that opinion clarity is driven by idiosyncratic factors – related to different legal issue contexts and justices' writing styles – unrelated to our theoretical argument. As the table reveals, the public opinion measure is resolute. It remains statistically significant across all models. Indeed, a Wald test reveals that even the apparent weakening that occurs between Model 1 and Model 3 is not statistically meaningful ($p = 0.53$).

To help understand the magnitude of the estimated relationship between *Inconsistent With Public Opinion* and the clarity of each majority opinion, we estimated predicted values using the empirical results from Model 1. Specifically, when the Court decides a case *consistent* with public opinion, its opinion readability is approximately -1.01. By contrast, when the Court makes a decision that is *inconsistent* with public sentiment, however, the readability of the opinion is approximately 0.81. This substantive difference – about a 1.82 unit change – is more than one-third of a standard deviation in the underlying population of Supreme Court majority opinions. In terms of percentiles, the comparison is between an opinion in the 40th percentile (consistent with public opinion) versus the 57th percentile (inconsistent with public opinion) of opinion clarity. Regardless of how one looks at the results, they are statistically and substantively important differences that link public sentiment with the Court's opinions.

Among the control predictors, the results in Model 2 suggest that opinions supported by heterogeneous coalitions result in less clear opinions than those written by homogeneous ones. Similarly, holding all else equal, larger coalitions tend to produce clearer opinions than those from smaller coalitions. When the Court is constrained it also, according to results from Model 2 (but not Model 3), tends to write clearer opinions than when it is unconstrained.[7] And, finally, the data suggest that the Court's opinions have also become clearer across time.

---

[7] Owens, Wedeking, and Wohlfarth (2013) find that the Court's opinions tend to be less readable when it is ideologically distant from Congress. The result we obtain here appears to be a function of this subset of cases. If we estimate our model on all decisions (necessarily excluding the public opinion variable due to a lack of data), then the *SOP Constraint* variable is negatively signed and statistically significant, which comports with the threesome's initial finding (i.e., the Court writes less clear opinions when faced with an ideologically opposed Congress).

7.3   An aggregate analysis of opinion clarity and public opinion

The previous empirical results suggested justices write clearer majority opinions when issuing decisions that contradict prevailing public opinion polling. The individual-level analysis' strength is that it utilizes existing issue-specific polling data to offer a precise match with the primary issue area of corresponding Supreme Court decisions. The scarcity of reliable opinion polling data, however, enable appropriate issue matches with only a small subset of the Court's decisions. To address this limitation, we now turn to an aggregate, over-time analysis of public opinion's impact on opinion clarity. We utilize an indicator of the general tenor of public opinion that enables us to examine majority opinions across the range of issues on the docket.

An aggregate focus offers several benefits. It enables us to connect our analysis to the predominant analytical strategy (and measures) used in prior research. That is, most literature on the Court-opinion relationship utilizes an aggregate indicator of the public's policy mood (Stimson 1991). This measure of public opinion (described below) only varies with respect to time, and thus is best suited for macro analyses predicting the term-level, net-content of Court decision making.[8] What is more, a macro analysis offers the best means to model the autocorrelation inherent in aggregate policy mood's variance and the potential for a dynamic effect of public opinion on the Court.

Consistent with the individual-level analysis, we test the argument that justices write clearer majority opinions when they anticipate public opposition to their decisions. We use data from the 1952–2011 Court terms. We begin the analysis in 1952 and end it in 2011 because it corresponds to the time period of the available *Public Mood* data.[9] We expect that as public opinion becomes more liberal, justices write clearer opinions among their conservative decisions. Similarly, as public opinion becomes more conservative, justices write clearer opinions among their liberal decisions. We construct two aggregate time series of the average clarity of the Court's majority opinions each term: one series examines the Court's conservative

---

[8] This analytical strategy necessarily holds individual-level factors constant. Though we have developed a micro-level theory to inform a macro analysis, we keep inferences in this section at the macro level. See Kramer (1983) for the classic account of the virtues of macro-level analysis (as it relates to the individual level) (see also, Erikson, MacKuen, and Stimson 2002).

[9] We use updated estimates of public mood (2/13/12 data release) retrieved from: www.unc .edu/~cogginse/Policy_Mood.html.

decisions over time; the other examines its liberal decisions.[10] We separate the Court's decisions into two time series models because that approach offers the most effective modeling strategy at the aggregate level to estimate how shifts in public opinion over time predict changes in the average level of opinion clarity (a variable without an inherent ideological dimension).[11]

Opinion clarity. The dependent variable – *Opinion Readability* – is the mean readability score of all the Court's majority opinions decided each term. This measure reflects the composite readability of each Supreme Court opinion using a host of individual readability indices. We simply calculate the mean of these scores per term. Recall that greater values indicate a more readable opinion.

Public mood. Our primary covariate is yearly public mood, as measured (and updated) by Stimson (1991, 1999).[12] Public mood is a longitudinal indicator of how the public's preference for "more" or "less" government shifts over time. It is an aggregate reflection of the general tenor of public opinion (and preference over desired public policy) on the standard liberal-conservative dimension. *Public Mood* is the most predominant indicator of public opinion in literature that examines public opinion and the Supreme Court (e.g., Casillas, Enns, and Wohlfarth 2011; Enns and Wohlfarth 2013; Epstein and Martin 2010; Giles, Blackstone, and Vining 2008; McGuire and Stimson 2004; Mishler and Sheehan 1993), and is currently the most reliable aggregate measure of the public's general political orientation. Larger values of *Public Mood* reflect a more liberal public while smaller values reflect a more conservative public.

We expect justices anticipate a greater prospect of public opposition to their conservative (liberal) decisions as public opinion becomes more

---

[10] We use the *decisionDirection* variable in the Supreme Court Database to identify liberal and conservative decisions.

[11] We examine the Court's opinions that involve constitutional or federal statutory provisions. We identify these cases using the *lawType* variable in the Supreme Court Database, aggregating those decisions where *lawType* is coded as 1, 2, or 3 among the Court's signed opinions and judgments (i.e., where the Database's *decisionType* variable is coded as 1 or 7). Thus, we include federal and state cases that involved federal legal issues, and omit cases involving "Court rules," "other" cases, cases involving "infrequently litigated statutes," cases that involved "state or local law or regulation," and cases with "no legal provision."

[12] Given that the public mood indictor is measured based on the calendar year, we match it with the corresponding Supreme Court term so there is a nine-month lag prior to the start of the term. This ensures changes in public opinion temporally precede the justice's decisions and opinion writing (see, e.g., Casillas, Enns, and Wohlfarth 2011).

liberal (conservative). Thus, we expect that, among their conservative decisions, justices will write clearer opinions as public opinion becomes more liberal. Conversely, among their liberal decisions, justices will write clearer opinions as public opinion becomes more conservative. That is, we expect a positive relationship between *Public Mood* and our dependent variable when analyzing the conservative decision time series, and a negative relationship when analyzing the liberal decision time series.

Average case complexity. We also include a control variable to account for the possibility that changes in the complexity of Supreme Court cases over time might lead to less clear opinions. If cases have become more complex, opinions may have become less readable. Consistent with previous analyses, we utilize amicus participation to measure case complexity (Collins 2008).[13] We measure *Average Case Complexity* by counting the total number of amicus curiae briefs filed in each Court term and dividing it by the total number of decisions issued by the justices during that term. For example, in the 2000 term, the Court issued 23 conservative decisions involving constitutional or statutory provisions and received a total of 145 amicus briefs among those cases. Thus, *Case Complexity* in the 2000 term would equal 6.30 for the conservative decision time series.

Civil liberties docket. We account for the potential that shifts in the issue composition of the Court's docket over time affect average opinion clarity. A greater proportion of (non-criminal procedure) civil liberties and rights cases on the docket may produce an average opinion clarity score that is less clear. We measure *Civil Liberties Docket* as the percentage of cases decided each term that primarily involve a civil liberties issue, excluding criminal procedure cases.[14] Consistent with the unit of analysis described earlier, we compute separate civil liberties time series among conservative and liberal decisions.

---

[13] We obtain data on amicus participation during the 1953–2001 Supreme Court terms from Collins (2008), and use Lexis to collect amicus data from 2002 to 2011. Alternatively, one could attempt to measure complexity with the average number of legal issues per case. The subsequent empirical results are robust when specifying this alternative indicator of case complexity.

[14] We utilize the *issueArea* variable in the Supreme Court Database and include all cases primarily involving an issue of civil rights, First Amendment, due process, or privacy. We exclude criminal procedure issues because Owens and Wedeking (2011) show that those opinions are systematically clearer than other civil liberties issues. However, the impact of public mood does not change when including criminal procedure issues in this control predictor.

Separation of powers constraint. We also account for the potential that greater ideological divergence between the Court and Congress might lead justices to obfuscate opinions (Owens, Wedeking, and Wohlfarth 2013). Using the JCS scores (Epstein et al. 2007), we include a predictor that accounts for the ideological divergence between the Court and Congress. When the median justice on the Court is more liberal or more conservative than both chamber medians in Congress, we measure *SOP Constraint* as the absolute value of the ideological distance between the Court and the closest of the two chamber medians. If the median justice falls ideologically between the House and Senate chamber medians, *SOP Constraint* equals 0.[15]

7.3.1   Methods and results

Prior to estimating our models, we "prewhitened" our time series predictors by filtering them with ARIMA(p,d,q) noise models so that all series (seemingly) reflect white noise (Box and Jenkins 1976). This step filters out the error aggregation process within each time series to ensure that our statistical results are not driven by serial correlation and each series' dependence on its own past values. That is, for each predictor, we first modeled the serial correlation inherent in the time series, extracted the residuals from that model, and then used those white-noise residuals as our (filtered) time series predictor in a standard regression model. Employing "prewhitened" time series predictors ensures that the data are *i.i.d.* and is necessary to protect against spurious association that could result from regressing nonstationary series. What is more, "prewhitened" filtering represents a conservative analytical approach in the time series literature (e.g., Clarke and Stewart 1994; Granger and Newbold 1974), and offers the most stringent statistical test in the present analysis. Indeed, as Box-Steffensmeir, Boef, and Lin (2004) state, a prewhitened series will actually "err on the side of null findings" (525). From a substantive perspective, our statistical models will enable us to examine specifically whether "innovations" in public opinion (that are not driven by its own prior values) have an impact on Supreme Court opinion clarity (see, e.g., MacKuen, Erikson, and Stimson 1989). See the appendix to Chapter 7 for more details on how we "prewhitened" the predictors.

---

[15] We note that our sample size is reduced for models that include the *SOP Constraint* variable due to missingness with the JCS scores in the last few terms of the sample that existed when we conducted these analyses.

With "prewhitened" time series in hand, we turn to our statistical models. We employ OLS and estimate three time series regression models. To examine the relationship between *Opinion Clarity* and *Public Mood* over time, we first present a baseline model that estimates the simple binary relationship. Next, we consider a second model specification that accounts for changes in the average case context by including the *Average Case Complexity* and *Civil Liberties Docket* control predictors. Lastly, the third model specification includes all control predictors by adding the *SOP Constraint* indicator.[16]

Table 7.2 presents our results. Across every model specification, *Public Mood* exhibits the expected impact on *Opinion Readability*. When looking at the time series of conservative decisions, the statistically significant, positive coefficients suggest the average opinion clarity increases when public opinion becomes more liberal. That is, when the Court is ruling against public opinion, it writes a clearer opinion to communicate its decision. This result is consistent across multiple specifications, including a simple baseline model and models that control for case complexity, docket composition, and SOP constraints over time.

Looking next at the time series of liberal decisions, *Public Mood* again displays the expected coefficients across all model specifications. As public opinion shifts in a conservative direction, the average liberal opinion becomes increasingly clear.[17]

What is more, the magnitude of *Public Mood's* effect on *Opinion Readability* suggests it is a substantively meaningful predictor of clarity. As Figure 7.2 shows, when viewing the conservative decision time series and statistical results from model 1(c), a shift from conservative to liberal public mood exhibits an expected change of about 1.8 units on the "prewhitened" opinion clarity scale.[18] That is, a shift in *Public Mood* can

---

[16] One might also estimate these model specifications while including a lagged dependent variable (LDV), thus enabling *Public Mood* to have a dynamic impact on opinion clarity (i.e., a change in public opinion at time t might affect opinion clarity across future time periods). The subsequent results and inferences are consistent when including the LDV.

[17] We also considered alternative modeling strategies to evaluate the robustness of our empirical results across both the conservative and liberal time series. These alternative models yield substantively consistent results. In particular, the empirical results are consistent when fractionally differencing the *Opinion Readability* dependent variable (see, e.g., Hosking 1981; Tsay and Chung 2000).

[18] Summary statistics for the "prewhitened" *Opinion Readability* measure are as follows. Conservative decisions: −0.01 (mean), −2.45 (minimum), 2.62 (maximum), and 1.23 (standard deviation). Liberal decisions: 0.01 (mean), −2.41 (minimum), 2.52 (maximum), and 1.13 (standard deviation).

Table 7.2: *The aggregate impact of public opinion on Supreme Court majority opinion clarity.*

	(1) Conservative Decisions			(2) Liberal Decisions		
	(a)	(b)	(c)	(a)	(b)	(c)
Public Mood	0.124**	0.121**	0.129**	−0.111**	−0.128**	−0.118**
	(0.061)	(0.062)	(0.066)	(0.057)	(0.057)	(0.062)
Average Case		0.069	0.105		−0.038	−0.051
Complexity		(0.099)	(0.124)		(0.079)	(0.123)
Civil Liberties		−0.880	−1.026		−2.194*	−1.809
Docket		(1.451)	(1.586)		(1.407)	(1.527)
SOP Constraint			−0.026			−1.604
			(2.127)			(1.959)
Constant	−0.044	−0.042	−0.088	0.014	0.052	0.037
	(0.148)	(0.149)	(0.161)	(0.138)	(0.139)	(0.152)
N	60	60	56	60	60	56
R^2	0.07	0.08	0.09	0.06	0.11	0.11
BIC	192.54	199.89	193.96	183.92	189.29	184.35

Note: Table entries are OLS coefficients with standard errors in parentheses. * $p < 0.10$ and ** $p < 0.05$ (one-tailed). The dependent variable represents the annual average Supreme Court majority opinion readability score each term (among decisions involving a constitutional provision or federal statute), 1952–2011, with larger values reflecting greater clarity. All variables have been "prewhitened" with ARIMA(p,d,q) filters to yield white noise time series (see chapter appendix for additional details).

generate a change in opinion clarity that exceeds 1.50 standard deviations. Likewise, when viewing the liberal decision time series (in model 2(c)), a shift from the minimum to maximum level of conservatism in *Public Mood* also yields a similar expected change of approximately 1.6 units on the clarity scale, which is equivalent to 1.4 standard deviations on that scale. When viewing the control predictors, the results suggest that, among the Court's liberal decisions, a greater proportion of (non-criminal procedure) civil liberties and rights cases on the docket leads to an average opinion clarity score that is less clear.

One further point bears emphasis. The reader might be concerned about the role of issue salience. Recall that the cases we examined in the

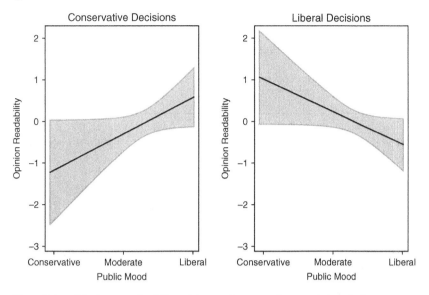

Figure 7.2:   The impact of public opinion on Supreme Court opinion clarity. Estimates reflect the predicted level of opinion clarity across the range of *Public Mood*, with larger readability scores representing greater readability. The gray shaded area in each plot denotes 95% confidence intervals. Predicted effects among conservative and liberal decisions are computed using regression results from Models 1(c) and 2(c), respectively. All differences across values are statistically significant.

individual-level analysis are among the most salient on the Court's docket. For instance, 89 of the 106 cases appeared on the front page of the *New York Times* (Epstein and Segal 2000); 76 of 106 appear on *Congressional Quarterly's* list of landmark cases. Because pollsters typically only ask questions on the salient issues of the day, we were limited by necessity to look only at predominantly salient cases in the individual-level analysis. Nevertheless, we split the aggregate time-series data into salient vs. non-salient cases. Though we do not have sufficient data to make inferences about salient cases – there are not enough liberally and conservatively decided salient cases to compute an aggregate each term – we do have enough data on non-salient cases. When we examine only non-salient cases, the results are substantively the same as what we present above, suggesting our results are not driven by salient cases.

7.4 Discussion

Scholars have paid considerable attention to the relationship between the Court and public opinion but the results have been mixed. Surprisingly, there has been little attention devoted to how public opinion influences the Court's opinion content. Our findings offer something new. They show public opinion does in fact influence the Supreme Court in systematic ways. In this capacity, the results have the potential to re-frame a recurring debate. Indeed, a dominant theory of judicial decision making argues justices are likely to respond to public opinion. Our results support that theoretical claim. While scholars have long examined various Court behaviors (e.g., voting) for evidence of the public's influence, perhaps we need to pay more attention to the content of the majority coalition's opinion language.

What is more, these results are stout. We employed both macro- and micro-level analyses. At the macro level, we observe that when the public becomes more liberal, the Court's conservative decisions become clearer. And when the public becomes more conservative, the Court's liberal decisions are clearer. This suggests justices respond to the threat of noncompliance, and possible repercussions to the Court's legitimacy by writing more clearly. The micro-level analysis reveals the same dynamic. By writing clearer opinions in the face of public opposition, justices aggressively seek out their goals. Writing clearer opinions becomes all the more important if the public perceives the Court in political terms (Bartels and Johnston 2013). And while opinion clarity will not give the justices freedom to do whatever they wish, it is something they seem to use to mitigate possible negative responses to their counter-majoritarian opinions.

The results are now in. The Court writes clearer opinions when it deals with ideologically scattered (and opposed) circuit courts. It writes clearer opinions when it rules against poor performing federal agencies. It writes clearer opinions when it decides cases involving citizen legislatures. And, it writes clearer opinions when it rules against the side favored by public opinion. Combined, these results suggest strong report for our theory that justices use opinion clarity to enhance compliance with their decisions and to manage public support for the Court.

While we certainly could end the story here, we wanted to go one step farther and examine whether the clarity of the Court's opinions actually has its intended effect. Surely, it is enough to recognize that justices believe clarity can enhance compliance and help the Court. But is there evidence that it actually does? Our next chapter, the final empirical chapter of this book, examines just that.

7.5   Appendix to Chapter 7

We filtered the *Opinion Readability* time series using an ARIMA(0,1,1) filter for the liberal series and an ARIMA(0,1,2) filter for the conservative series, as their error aggregation exhibits long-term temporal dependence best represented by an integrated process that requires first-differencing along with a moving average error component. The results of the Augmented Dickey Fuller (with various specified lag lengths), Phillips-Perron, and DF-GLS (across 10 lags) unit root tests all suggest that the series is nonstationary. And, the results of a KPSS stationarity test (across 10 lags) is consistent with this conclusion. What is more, the autocorrelation function (ACF) and partial autocorrelation function (PACF) both exhibit evidence consistent with this error diagnosis. The results of a Ljung-Box white noise test confirms that the *Opinion Readability* time series filtered with an ARIMA(0,1,1) noise model among liberal decisions, and an ARIMA(0,1,2) model among conservative decisions, yields white noise residuals.

Next, the error aggregation process of the *Public Mood* time series is best represented by a first-order autoregressive noise model to yield a white noise series (i.e., an AR(1) filter). Given the temporal increase inherent in amicus participation before the Supreme Court over time, the *Average Case Complexity* series is a trending, nonstationary series that requires first differencing to generate a white noise series. And, in the case of the *Case Complexity* series constructed using conservative decisions, it requires an additional MA(1) filter to "prewhiten" the series (i.e., an I(1) and ARIMA(0,1,1) filter for the liberal and conservative decision time series, respectively). The error aggregation process in the *Civil Liberties Docket* predictor is best filtered using an ARIMA(1,0,1) model, among both the liberal and conservative time series. Lastly, we filtered the *SOP Constraint* time series using an ARIMA(1,0,0) noise model.

The diagnosis of *Public Mood* with an AR(1), *Civil Liberties Docket* as an ARMA(1,1), *SOP Constraint* with an AR(1), and *Case Complexity* as an I(1) (among liberal decisions) and ARIMA(0,1,1) (among conservative decisions) error aggregation pattern is consistent with the visual evidence apparent in each series' ACF and PACF. And, a Ljung-Box white noise test confirms that each filtered time series is seemingly white noise.

8

Establishing compliance as a function of clarity

The thrust of this book focuses on how justices seek to enhance compliance with their decisions and manage negative responses to Court decisions by adapting the clarity of their opinions to fit the context. And, the results have been supportive. In this chapter, we do something different. Here, we seek to assure the reader that opinion clarity can actually enhance compliance.

While there are a number of ways to check whether clarity induces compliance, we perform two tests. First, we examine whether clearer Supreme Court opinions induce greater compliance among lower federal court judges. As we demonstrate in Chapter 4, Supreme Court justices alter the clarity of their precedent-setting opinions when they have greater reason to expect circuit court judges will produce legal conflicts and shirk precedents. In this chapter, we take this examination one step farther. We consider whether federal circuit courts are in fact more likely to comply with clearer Supreme Court opinions. Second, we perform a study in which we ask survey respondents to read excerpts of opinions and rate whether they or others would comply. These results, like our statistical model of actual lower court compliance, show that people are less likely to comply with unclear opinions.

8.1 Modeling lower court compliance as a function of opinion clarity

We began by drawing a random sample of more than 500 Supreme Court opinions decided between the 1953 and 2000 terms.[1] We choose these terms as bookends because 1953 corresponds to what scholars acknowledge as the beginning of the modern Supreme Court. We pick 2000 as the most recent term to ensure the opinions had sufficient opportunity to filter down to the lower courts and be treated by them. Next, to observe whether lower courts are more likely to treat (i.e., apply) clearer opinions

---

[1] We began with 550 random opinions but discarded 24 observations due to missing data.

positively than unclear opinions, we identify the approximately 9,500 federal circuit court cases that later applied those 500 Supreme Court precedents.

Our dependent variable accounts for whether the lower court positively treated the Supreme Court precedent, negatively treated it, or treated it neutrally.[2] More specifically, using the *Shepard's* categories, a decision that "followed" a Supreme Court precedent is a positive application. A decision that "explained" or "harmonized" a precedent reflects a neutral application. And, a decision that "overruled," "criticized," "questioned," "limited," "superseded," or "distinguished" a precedent represents a negative application. We code positive applications as 1, neutral applications as 0, and negative applications as -1.[3]

Opinion clarity. Our main covariate – *Opinion Readability* – is the readability score of the Supreme Court's precedent-setting opinion (the opinion that is later applied by the federal circuit courts). To measure the opinion's readability, we employ the same principal component measure that appears throughout this book, representing the shared variance of 28 readability indicators. The scale of the measure is such that larger scores represent greater readability while smaller scores represent less readability.

Circuit court-precedent distance. We account for the possibility that a circuit court, based on circuit judges' own policy preferences, will be less inclined to apply an ideologically distant precedent positively. We take three steps to measure the ideological distance between the Supreme Court precedent and the circuit court panel. First, to measure the ideological value of each precedent, we use the JCS score (Epstein et al. 2007) of the median justice in the majority coalition that created the precedent. Second, we measure the policy preferences of the circuit judges who applied the precedent. To do so, we identified the names and JCS scores of the judges who sat on the circuit panel that applied the precedent. We then determined, within each case, which circuit judges joined the lower court majority. We then coded the circuit panel's ideological preferences as the JCS score of the median circuit court judge in the majority coalition in each case. In a unanimous three-judge circuit court panel decision, circuit court ideology reflects the

---

[2] This trichotomy is standard in the literature (e.g., Hansford and Spriggs 2006; Westerland et al. 2010).

[3] Alternatively, one could drop the neutral treatment category and estimate a dichotomous logit model predicting only positive vs. negative treatments. The subsequent empirical results are robust to this alternative specification.

JCS score of the median judge on the panel. In cases with a dissent or a special concurrence, we used the midpoint between the two judges in the majority coalition. If the lower court decision was en banc, we code circuit court ideology as the median judge in the en banc majority. When district court judges sit by designation on the circuit panel, or when the appeal is from a three-judge district court panel, we follow Giles, Hettinger, and Peppers (2001) and use the common space scores of the home-state senators. Third, after we calculated those two scores, we simply determined the absolute value of the difference between them.

Supreme Court-precedent distance. We expect circuit courts are less likely to apply a precedent positively as the sitting Supreme Court becomes increasingly estranged ideologically from that precedent (Westerland et al. 2010). Lower court judges often interpret Supreme Court precedent by looking to the ideological composition of the current Supreme Court. Westerland et al. (2010) and Benesh and Reddick (2002) find circuit court judges who interpret precedent are more likely to look to the policy preferences of sitting Supreme Court justices than to the precedent-setting Court. Therefore, as the current Supreme Court becomes more ideologically distant from the precedent, lower court judges become less likely to follow that precedent. We take three steps to measure the ideological distance between the Supreme Court and the precedent under review. First, we continue to measure the ideological content of each precedent using the JCS score of the median member of its majority coalition. Second, to measure the ideological location of the reviewing (or sitting) Supreme Court, we follow Westerland et al. (2010) and calculate the JCS score of the median justice on the current Court. Third, we calculate the absolute value of the distance between those two values.

Precedent vitality. Recent empirical work shows the strength of Supreme Court precedent influences justices' application of it, as well as lower court compliance with those precedents (Hansford and Spriggs 2006). Following the general strategy of Hansford and Spriggs (2006), we measure *Positive Vitality* and *Negative Vitality* as the number of previous positive and negative Supreme Court interpretations of that precedent, respectively (up to, but not including, the year in which a case was decided). This measurement strategy enables us to capture the net positive and negative vitality of each precedent while also distinguishing between the number of times the Supreme Court has applied the precedent over time.[4]

---

[4] Our results remain the same if we simply use a "net positive" vitality score.

Precedent characteristics. We employ multiple control predictors to account for characteristics of the Supreme Court precedent that may affect subsequent compliance by a circuit court. First, we account for the potential that more complex cases might inhibit circuit judges' ability to comply faithfully with a precedent, thereby generating more negative treatments. We attempt to capture this effect with amici presence in each case, as greater participation from external parties in the Court's decision-making process often signifies greater case complexity (Collins 2008). We measure *Case Complexity* by counting the number of amicus curiae briefs filed in the precedent-setting case. We obtain amicus participation from the 1953–2001 Supreme Court terms from Collins (2008) and collect amicus data from 2002–2007 using Lexis. We also examine the size of the majority coalition as an indicator of internal (dis)agreement on the precedent-setting Court. One might expect that greater internal disagreement (i.e., smaller majority size) within a Court decision will lead to less compliance. We code *Majority Votes* as the member of justices joining the precedent-setting majority coalition in the case.[5]

We next control for whether the Supreme Court opinion being applied altered prior precedent, as lower court judges are less compliant when the Supreme Court alters its own precedent (Benesh and Reddick 2002). We code *Precedent Alteration* as 1 if, according to the Supreme Court Database, the precedent-setting Court majority formally altered an existing precedent; 0 otherwise.[6] Next, we account for precedent-setting opinions that struck down either a federal law or state action as unconstitutional. When the Supreme Court takes the major step of nullifying an act of the elected branches, it is likely to engender less faithful compliance and more negative treatments by future lower court judges. We code *Federal Judicial Review* as 1 if, according to the Supreme Court Database, the Court struck down an act of Congress; 0 otherwise. And, we measure *State Judicial Review* using a dichotomous indicator to reflect when the justices constitutionally nullified a state's law, regulation, or constitutional provision, as identified by the Supreme Court Database.[7] We also control for the age of the Supreme Court precedent under review. *Precedent Age*

---

[5] We use the *majVotes* variable in the Supreme Court Database to identify the size of the majority coalition.
[6] We utilize the *precedentAlteration* variable in the Supreme Court Database to identify decisions that formally altered prior precedent.
[7] We utilize the *declarationUncon* variable in the Supreme Court Database. Specifically, *Federal Judicial Review* and *State Judicial Review* take on a value of 1 when *declarationUncon* equals 2 and 3, respectively.

reflects the number of years the precedent has survived up to its application in a case. Lastly, we account for variance in lower court compliance that might be due to different issue areas. We include fixed effects for the primary issue area of the precedent-setting Supreme Court case.[8]

8.1.1 Methods and results

Because the dependent variable represents a trichotomous, ordered outcome, we estimate an ordered logit regression model. A standard (or proportional odds) ordered logit model specification is inappropriate, however, because the data violate the parallel regression assumption, as several predictors display significantly different effects across the ordered configuration of the dependent variable.[9] As a result, we utilize a partial proportional odds, ordered logistic regression model (Williams 2006). This approach is flexible (and maximally efficient) in that it only estimates a separate parameter for variables that violate the parallel regression assumption (cf. a multinomial model, which would always estimate a separate parameter). Parameter estimates for this model are reported in Table 8.1.[10]

The columns in the table report the effect of each independent variable on observing the outcome specified in the column title. Thus, "Neutral or Positive" reports how each independent variable is related to observing a non-negative treatment outcome. Positive values indicate that an increase in a variable increases the chances of non-negative interpretation. Negative values mean the opposite. Similarly, the third column ("Positive") reports what impact each variable has on observing positive – as opposed to either neutral or negative – treatment. An example illustrates: the data suggest that whether a cited case has formally altered precedent has no systematic impact on non-negative treatment ($p = 0.77$), but it

---

[8] We follow the broad "issueArea" indicator in the Supreme Court Database to specify these fixed effects.

[9] The results of a likelihood-ratio test of the proportionality of odds across the outcome categories confirms this conclusion for the following predictors: *Positive Vitality, Case Complexity, Precedent Age, Precedent Alteration, State Judicial Review*, and three issue categories ($p < 0.05$).

[10] Our standard errors are robust and clustered on the application year to account for the possibility of correlated errors within each application year. The results for the impact of opinion clarity on the likelihood of a positive treatment are consistent when estimating classical (i.e., non-robust) standard errors, or using a multinomial logistic regression model (with a positive treatment as the baseline category) instead of treating the dependent variable as an ordered outcome.

Table 8.1: *The impact of opinion clarity on lower court compliance with Supreme Court precedent.*

	Neutral or Positive	Positive
Opinon Readability	0.017**	0.017**
	(0.008)	(0.008)
Circuit-Precedent Distance	−0.239**	−0.239**
	(0.122)	(0.122)
Supreme Court-Precedent Distance	−1.253**	−1.253**
	(0.225)	(0.225)
Positive Vitality	0.136**	0.184**
	(0.029)	(0.029)
Negative Vitality	−0.098**	−0.098**
	(0.041)	(0.041)
Case Complexity	0.001	0.030**
	(0.014)	(0.013)
Majority Votes	0.025*	0.025*
	(0.017)	(0.017)
Precedent Alteration	0.056	−0.598**
	(0.188)	(0.185)
Federal Judicial Review	−1.951**	−1.951**
	(0.453)	(0.453)
State Judicial Review	−0.264**	−0.463**
	(0.134)	(0.131)
Precedent Age	−0.013**	−0.005
	(0.005)	(0.005)
False Full Stops	−0.000	−0.000
	(0.000)	(0.000)
Constant	1.275**	0.378**
	(0.144)	(0.134)
Issue Area Controls	Yes	
N	9534	
Pseudo-R^2	0.03	

Note: Table entries are coefficients from a partial proportional odds, ordered logistic regression model with clustered standard errors (on the application year) in parentheses. * $p < 0.10$, ** $p < 0.05$ (one-tailed). Model estimated via the gologit2 command in Stata 14 (Williams 2006). The dependent variable represents each individual circuit court application of Supreme Court precedent ($1 =$ positive; $0 =$ neutral; $−1 =$ negative).

does decrease the likelihood that such a precedent is specifically treated positively as opposed to neutrally or negatively.

Fortunately, there is no systematic evidence that *Opinion Readability*, our main covariate of interest, violates the parallel regression assumption ($p > 0.10$). Accordingly, the model estimates a single parameter for this variable, which, as expected, is positively signed and statistically significant. Clearer opinions induce heightened compliance among the circuit courts. Figure 8.1 displays the predicted probability of a positive circuit court application when varying the level of opinion clarity. As an opinion articulating a precedent shifts across the observed range of the readability scale, the probability the lower court will apply the precedent positively increases by as much as 0.11, shifting from an expected 0.51 to a 0.62 probability – a relative increase of approximately 22%. The data thus suggest clearer opinion text induces a greater probability of future positive applications. In other words, lower court compliance suffers when the Supreme Court chooses to craft opinions that employ unclear language.

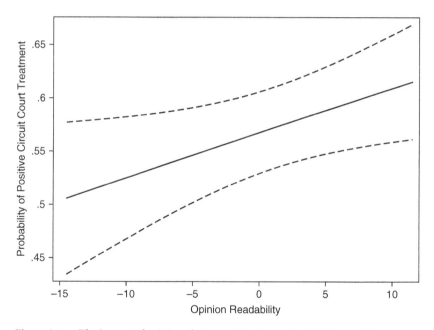

Figure 8.1: The impact of opinion clarity on circuit court applications of Supreme Court precedent. Estimates reflect the predicted probability (with 95% confidence intervals) of a positive circuit court application, generated from Table 8.1 using the mgen command as implemented in Stata 14 by Long and Freese (2014).

As expected, the results also show the sitting Supreme Court's ideological preferences significantly affect lower court applications. As the High Court increasingly diverges from the precedent, circuit courts are less likely to apply the precedent positively. Increasing the ideological distance between the precedent-setting and sitting Supreme Court by one standard deviation yields an approximate 0.04 decrease in the probability of a positive circuit court application. The direction and magnitude of this effect accords with previous studies showing that lower courts take cues from the political composition of the sitting Supreme Court (Westerland et al. 2010).

What is more, enhanced opinion clarity can help mitigate the negative effects of ideological distance. Figure 8.2 illustrates the additive effects of opinion clarity and the Supreme Court-Precedent ideological distance measure. Low and high readability are, respectively, the sample minimum

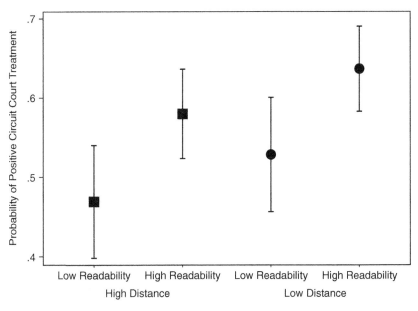

Figure 8.2:   The additive effects of opinion clarity and ideological distance on circuit court applications of Supreme Court precedent. Estimates reflect the predicted probability (with 95% confidence intervals) of a positive circuit court application, generated from Table 8.1. High and low ideological distance (between the precedent-setting and sitting Supreme Courts) are the 75th and 25th percentile values, respectively. Low and high readability are the sample minimum and maximum.

and maximum values. For ideological distance, we use the 25th and 75th percentile values. A highly readable but ideologically distant opinion is actually more likely to be treated positively than an unreadable but close opinion.[11] Thus, the positive effect of a move from less to more clarity more than offsets the negative impact of ideological distance. Clarity can, in short, help to balance the countervailing impact of ideological divergence from a precedent. Taken together, the meaningful effect of opinion readability on future circuit court compliance underscores the importance of opinion language as a tool Supreme Court justices may use to influence how audiences respond to their decisions.

The data also display several statistically significant effects among the control variables. First, a circuit court panel is less likely to apply a precedent positively as it diverges ideologically from the precedent. Furthermore, a circuit court panel is more likely to apply a precedent positively when it applies a precedent with greater vitality. A precedent that has received more previous positive (negative) applications by the Supreme Court is more (less) likely to be treated positively by future circuit courts. Among the numerous characteristics of the original precedent, a more complex precedent (measured as the degree of amicus participation) can enhance the expectation of a positive application. On the other hand, older precedents, those that overturned an act of Congress or state government, and those formally altering a prior Supreme Court precedent generate an expected decrease in the likelihood of a positive application.

8.2 A study of non-elite compliance as a function of opinion clarity

We sought further evidence to support our claim that actors will be more likely to comply with clearer opinions. Here we report the results of two such studies. The first study was actually one described previously in Chapter 3 as part of the validation of our measure of opinion clarity. We asked a total of seventy-two undergraduate students to each read eight excerpts from Supreme Court majority opinions. The excerpts varied between 170 and 300 words in length, with an average of 222 words. We varied these excerpts on a number of dimensions such as issue area and

---

[11] We estimate a 58% chance of positive treatment for a precedent of high ideological distance and high clarity. The chances of positive treatment for an ideologically proximate but unclear opinion is 53%.

salience, but the most important difference among these excerpts was their readability, which was either difficult or easy.

After being presented with the excerpt, the raters were asked a series of objective and subjective questions about the text. The objective, factual questions formed the basis for our comprehension measure and, as we noted in Chapter 3, we find strong evidence that our computer-generated measure predicts whether actual readers comprehend a legal text – a foundational result that is the basis for the rest of what we examine in this book.

Beyond those objective questions, we also asked our raters a series of subjective questions about the excerpts. Of primary importance for the goal of this chapter is an item where respondents were asked to assess, on a seven-point scale, how likely people would be to comply with the Court's decision in the case. We then regressed these responses on the readability of the opinion excerpt (and a number of controls – see Table 3.1 in Chapter 3). Our results show a statistically and substantively significant relationship between clarity and predicted compliance, with unclear opinions being much less likely to elicit compliance than their more clear counterparts. Using an ordered logistic regression model, we estimate a 0.65 probability that a rater assigns the highest compliance score for an opinion that is very clear. Replace that opinion with one that is very *un*clear and that probability plummets to just 0.08.

Intrigued by this finding, we sought to expand it with a more comprehensive and nuanced approach to measuring compliance. To that end, we performed a survey experiment where approximately 212 undergraduate students were randomly assigned excerpts from two Supreme Court decisions involving First Amendment protection of speech that criticized judges. Following the approach of Chapter 3, one excerpt was very readable and the other was very unreadable. After being presented with the excerpt, we measured each subject's comprehension and attitudes towards those opinions.

Comprehension was measured using the same approach described in Chapter 3. In particular, we asked a number of multiple choice questions about the opinions excerpt and combined these responses with information about how long each subject took to complete the task and how difficult the subject perceived the text to be. As before, we estimate an exploratory factor analysis with these variables and use those factor loadings to generate an overall *Comprehension* score for each subject. The score has a mean and standard deviation of 0.00 and 0.89, respectively and ranges between -1.94 and 2.69, with larger values indicating higher comprehension.

In terms of compliance, we asked three questions: (1) Based on what you understand from the opinion above, how strongly would you rate the likelihood of people complying with the decision? (seven-point scale); (2) Thinking about the reasoning of the opinion text you just read, how persuasive was it in terms of making you want to comply with the Court's ruling? (four-point scale); and (3) In the case you just read about, imagine that the side who lost in the case decided they were going to disobey with the Court's ruling. How justified do you believe they would be in not following the Court's opinion? (five-point scale).

In creating these questions we sought to explore potentially distinct aspects of compliance. The data suggest we accomplished that goal. The average inter-item correlation is just 0.26. Similarly, the Cronbach's alpha for these three items is just 0.50, which is well below the cutoff that is frequently used for creating an index (i.e., 0.70). And, an exploratory factor analysis fails to return even a single factor with an eigenvalue above one. Thus, for what follows, we treat these items as distinct.

An additional enhancement of our second study was that we also measured the pre-existing attitudes of each subject towards the case excerpt subject matter. This follows the design of other survey experiments about opinion content (e.g., Zink, Spriggs, and Scott 2009). We did this via two questions. First, we asked how important each respondent thought it was "to live in a country where the media can report the news without censorship?" Second, we asked how important a respondent thought it was "to live in a country where you can openly say what you think and criticize judges." Available answer choices for both questions consisted of a four-point scale ranging from "Not at all important" to "Very important."[12]

We begin by verifying our key result from Chapter 3: do our computer-generated clarity scores actually predict how humans perceive legal texts? Starting with a pooled analysis, the average comprehension score for individuals assigned to clear opinions is 0.11 compared to an average of -0.10 for individuals assigned to unclear opinions ($p < 0.05$, one-tailed test). Thus, individuals who read clearer opinions had systematically higher comprehension levels than those assigned to unclear opinion. As we note above, however, we are also able to examine whether this effect is stronger for some individuals.

Of particular substantive interest are those whose initial policy attitudes are *inconsistent* with the Court's ruling in a case. Indeed, this is precisely

---

[12] In practice, however, the responses broke into two categories with approximately 70% saying "Very important" to each question and 25% saying "Somewhat important."

Table 8.2: *Average comprehension scores, conditional on ex ante policy opposition and opinion segment clarity.*

	Opinion Readability		
	Low	High	Difference
High Opposition	−0.24	0.43	0.70**
Medium Opposition	−0.17	0.12	0.29*
Low Opposition	−0.04	−0.01	0.02

$^*\,p < 0.10$ and $^{**}\,p < 0.05$ (one-tailed test).

the audience justices are attempting to reach and subsequently persuade in their writing. To that end, we group individuals into three levels of opposition: low, medium, and high.[13] Table 8.2 reports average comprehension scores for each of these three groups, split by the clarity of the opinion excerpt they read (i.e., clear vs. unclear).

Starting with high opposition individuals, we see a statistically and substantively compelling effect caused by opinion clarity. Among those who the Court is most interested in convincing, opinion clarity has a strong impact on whether the content is actually comprehended. Respondents presented with an unclear excerpt typically ended up with comprehension scores in approximately the 44th percentile. Being assigned to a clear opinion boosted average comprehension scores to the 70th percentile, however. As the table illustrates, when the level of policy opposition decreases, so too does the impact of clarity on comprehension. If the Court is able to get its foot in the door and write for a partially sympathetic audience, clarity still matters, but its impact is less than half of what it is for those who are more opposed to the underlying policy content. And, finally, when there is full buy-in to the policy outcome, the packaging of the message ceases to affect whether a reader understands it.

Next, we sought to gain leverage on the linkage between comprehension and compliance. To that end, we regressed – through an ordered logistic regression model – the compliance ratings obtained above on our comprehension scores. We also controlled for a subject's policy

---

[13] "Low" individuals were those who answered "Very important" (the strongest response available) to *both* of the predisposition questions we asked. 57% of respondents fell into this category. "High" individuals were those who provided a response weaker than "Very important" to both questions (15% of respondents). And, finally, respondents with mixed responses (e.g., "Very important" for one question but not the other) were classified as having a "Medium" level of opposition (28% of respondents).

opposition, as measured by the same three categories utilized before, treating low opposition as the omitted baseline category. Table 8.3 reports the results of these regression models. Each column corresponds to one of the three distinct compliance measures.

Table 8.3: *The impact of opinion comprehension on compliance.*

	Compliance Measure (see table note)		
	(A) Others	(B) Yourself	(C) Disobedience
Comprehension	0.631**	0.937**	0.487**
	(0.147)	(0.167)	(0.150)
High Opposition	−0.490*	0.792**	−0.821**
	(0.347)	(0.376)	(0.376)
Medium Opposition	−0.336	−0.083	−0.976**
	(0.286)	(0.293)	(0.298)
κ_1	−5.678**	−1.627**	−4.298**
	(1.012)	(0.222)	(0.482)
κ_2	−2.694**	0.396**	−2.204**
	(0.281)	(0.193)	(0.244)
κ_3	−1.456**	3.246**	0.003
	(0.208)	(0.340)	(0.182)
κ_4	−0.052		1.753**
	(0.182)		(0.234)
κ_5	1.635**		
	(0.220)		
κ_6	3.534**		
	(0.429)		
Observations	212	212	212
Pseudo-R^2	0.03	0.08	0.04

Note: Table entries are ordered logistic regression coefficients. * $p < 0.10$ and ** $p < 0.05$ (one-tailed). κ_n denotes the nth cut-point. Each column corresponds to responses to the following compliance questions: (A) Based on what you understand from the opinion above, how strongly would you rate the likelihood of people complying with the decision? (B) Thinking about the reasoning of the opinion text you just read, how persuasive was it in terms of making you want to comply with the Court's ruling? (C) In the case you just read about, imagine that the side who lost in the case decided they were going to disobey with the Court's ruling. How justified do you believe they would be in not following the Court's opinion?

As the top result line of the table makes clear, regardless of the specific compliance measure used, we find a positive and statistically significant relationship between comprehension and a subject's response. When individuals understand what they are reading, they are more likely to (1) believe that others will comply with the decision, (2) comply with it themselves, and (3) believe that people who do *not* comply with the decision are unjustified in doing so.

Beyond mere statistical significance, the substantive significance is also noteworthy. Using Long and Freese (2014)'s mgen command, we computed a series of predicted probabilities from our models, which we display in Table 8.4. Each of the three rows correspond to the three unique compliance questions we asked our respondents. The two columns – low and high – denote whether a respondent had low or high comprehension, which we calculated as the sample minimum and maximum, respectively. Cell values for the first two rows (i.e., "Others ..." and "You Will ...") indicate whether a respondent gave a pro-compliance response to each question. Cell values for the third row ("Disobedience Justified") indicate whether a respondent agreed that someone would be justified disobeying with the Court's ruling in a case.

As the table values makes clear, comprehension yields impressive substantive effects. When a subject has low comprehension of the Court's opinion, we estimate only a 5% chance that she will indicate a strong

Table 8.4: *Substantive impact of comprehension on compliance attitudes.*

	Comprehension	
	Low	High
Others Will Comply	0.05	0.52
You Will Comply	0.01	0.33
Disobedience Justified	0.22	0.03

Cell values are the probability of a high-compliance response, which we generated using the results from Table 8.3 and the mgen command as implemented in Stata 14 by Long and Freese (2014). "Others Will Comply" and "Disobedience Justified" report the probability that a respondent gave one of the two highest values (out of seven and five, respectively) to the questions. "You Will Comply" reports the probability the respondent gave the highest (out of four) responses to the question.

likelihood that other people will comply with the Court's decision. Even more telling, we estimate just a 1% chance that she herself will find the opinion persuasive in terms of making her want to comply with the Court's decision. And there's nearly a one-in-four chance that a respondent would believe that someone would be at least somewhat justified in disobeying the Court's ruling. By contrast, when someone understands the Court's ruling, we find the polar opposite. Someone is more than ten times as likely to believe that others will comply with the Court's ruling and more than thirty times as likely to find the opinion highly persuasive themselves. Further, we see that knowledge and understanding all but eliminate the foundation of support for those who would potentially disobey the Court's edict.

8.3   Discussion

This chapter makes a number of crucial contributions to our argument. First, a primary linchpin of our theoretical argument is that the Court manages and manipulates the clarity of its opinions based on audience characteristics and their anticipated reaction. Up until this chapter it was taken on faith that opinion clarity was linked to compliance. The results of this chapter show that opinion clarity, as the main explanatory variable, is significantly related to how lower courts comply with its decisions.

Second, we bolster these observational data with an additional survey experiment that probes the causal mechanism by which compliance arises. At the same time, we show that, at least when it comes to a non-elite but reasonably educated audience, there is important heterogeneity in how that audience is affected by opinion clarity. In particular, clarity tends to matter the most when the would-be target of persuasion is opposed to the underlying policy content contained in the opinion. Clearer opinions beget comprehension. Unclear opinions hinder it. What is more, comprehension is the glue that links compliance and clarity together. If someone cannot understand the content of a directive, then it is difficult to expect them to comply with it.

9

Conclusion

In his influential book, *Judges and Their Audiences*, Larry Baum argued: "the vantage point of audience can enhance our capacity to understand [judicial] choices" (Baum 2006, xii). We agree. Baum focused on how personal audiences could influence judges' behavior. Would judges who valued the adoration of lawyers change their behavior when the lawyerly class opposed overturning a precedent? Would judges who value the respect of interest groups render more conservative or liberal decisions than they otherwise might in order to retain those groups' support? Would judges who value professional advancement change their behavior so as to get elevated? According to Baum, such personal features influence the choices judges make.

Whereas Baum focused on how personal audiences influence judicial behavior, we focused on how audiences might influence justices for instrumental reasons. We focused on whether those audiences influence the clarity of High Court opinions. Our goal was to determine whether justices alter the clarity of their opinions to adapt to their audiences and enhance compliance with their decisions. Our theory was that justices are goal-driven actors who want to see their decisions implemented faithfully, and that they will do what they must to enhance compliance and manage public support. In our context, this involved writing clearer opinions. Why? Because clearer opinions can remove the discretion of audiences to shirk, make it easier for others to spot and alert the Court of noncompliance, better assist those actors who are inclined to comply with the Court's directives, and improve or maintain the Court's standing among the mass public.

The results across a wide range of analyses support our theory. We looked, first, at the conditions under which lower courts might influence Supreme Court opinion clarity. We argued that legal and ideological goals would affect how justices write their opinions. For starters, we argued the heterogeneity of the circuits is important to justices because one of the High Court's legal obligations is to ensure (relative) interpretive uniformity across the circuits. Indeed, one of the primary purposes of having one "supreme" court is to resolve conflicts as a sovereign. And, justices take this obligation seriously.

Our data showed that when the circuits are ideologically disparate from one another – and therefore more likely to conflict with each other over the proper interpretation of law – justices writer clearer opinions. Additionally, we argued the ideologies of lower court judges is important to justices as well. Research tells us justices want to etch their policy preferences into law. They are likely to be concerned, then, about how lower court judges – especially those who are ideologically distant from them – will treat those opinions. Chapter 4 showed that when the circuits become increasingly scattered from one another, the High Court writes clearer opinions. It does so, we argued, to limit the amount of conflict among the circuits on a going forward basis. What is more, when the circuits become more distant from the Supreme Court, justices write clearer opinions. In short, the interpreting audience (i.e., lower courts) influence justices' legal and policy goals, and matters to justices in ways we predict.

Next, we looked at how the characteristics of different implementing audiences – federal agencies and states – might influence opinion clarity. We hypothesized that the characteristics of these entities would influence the clarity of the Court's opinions – and that things like competence would matter. The data concur. Looking, first, at the Court's interaction with federal agencies, we used recent data on agency performance. Our argument was that justices would have some general sense of which agencies were stronger performers than others, and that this general awareness would manifest itself in the clarity of the Court's opinions. It did. Justices write clearer opinions when they rule against a lower quality agency. The data also showed the Court writes clearer opinions as states become more resource capable. Based on existing research and data, we identified which state legislatures and governors were the most professionalized. We argued justices would write clearer opinions when they dealt with less professionalized state actors. The results supported this belief. Justices write clearer opinions when dealing with citizen legislatures versus professionalized legislatures. And this effect is exacerbated when the Court faces a politically unified state. In short, when justices have the most reason to expect the least compliance, they write clearer opinions.

We next examined how the secondary audience (i.e., public opinion) could influence the clarity of the High Court's opinions. Because the Court depends on legitimacy for its survival, justices should take steps to manage that legitimacy. With little formal institutional capability to enforce the Court's decisions and to compel the elected branches to respect its judgments, scholars commonly argue justices often act strategically in their opinion writing, adjusting to shifts in public opinion to ensure the efficacy of their decisions (Casillas, Enns, and Wohlfarth 2011; Epstein and Knight 1998; McGuire and Stimson 2004; Mishler and Sheehan 1993, 1996; Murphy 1964).

When the Court does rule against prevailing sentiment, it should state so clearly and concisely. And this is precisely what we find. The Court writes increasingly readable opinions when it rules against public opinion. These findings support our argument that justices strategically craft the language of majority opinions when they have reason to expect a greater chance of noncompliance by external actors, and further highlights the importance of public opinion as a constraint on opinion content.

Additionally, we spent time ensuring the validity of our measures and checking their robustness. Lower court judges are more likely to comply with increasingly readable opinions. Moreover, survey respondents believed clearer opinions generated more compliance. Both of these results suggest our focus on readability is appropriate.

We recognize some readers may still question whether justices strategically use opinion clarity to overcome noncompliance or manage public support. Some may argue justices simply use opinion clarity to make good law. We certainly think making good law or following legal norms are goals for justices (see, e.g., Black and Owens 2009) – and there is some evidence in Chapter 4 that justices want to ensure legal uniformity (which is a legal goal). The weight of the evidence supports our inference that justices are being strategic as they work toward their goals (whatever they may be). All of our findings line up behind each other; they all point in the same direction; and they all suggest justices use opinion clarity strategically.

***

The thought that an audience can and will influence the content of a speaker's message goes back to the dawn of knowledge. Writing about persuasion, Aristotle once claimed that speakers could use three "artistic proofs" to persuade their audiences (logos, ethos, and pathos). First, they could make arguments based on logic and reason (logos). Second, they could make appeals based on their personal credibility (ethos) because "we believe good men more fully and readily than others" (Penn translation, p.8). Third, and most important for our purposes, they could persuade listeners by putting them into a certain frame of mind (pathos).

That is, speakers could appeal to the *shared common ground* between the listener and speaker and thereby help listeners *want* to believe the speaker. Pathos, in short, links the audience and speaker.

Others throughout history have tailored their messages to their audiences. Consider how early Christians crafted the Gospel. All four books of the Gospel (Matthew, Mark, Luke, and John) tell essentially the same story: the birth of Jesus and his resurrection. Yet, they tell the stories in very different ways – and they did so because of their different audiences. The book of Matthew was written to persuade Jews. It therefore casually refers often to Old Testament prophesies and Jewish customs. The book of Mark, on the other hand, was written for Romans in an effort to convert them. Not surprisingly, it is written quite differently than Matthew. It is fast-paced and contains more action, something that would appeal to the Roman reader. Once again, the identity of the audience influenced the speaker.

Members of Congress also understand the role of audience. As Fenno (1977) notes, when members of Congress travel home to their districts, they adopt a certain "homestyle" to enhance their political success. Importantly, this "homestyle" differs considerably from their behavior in Washington D.C., where they have a different audience. By picking these home styles, members can gain trust from their constituents that will help them stay in office and accumulate power. Their styles and messages are influenced by whether they address their geographic, reelection, primary, and personal constituencies.

The Supreme Court, in short, follows a long line of actors and institutions that consider how their audiences will respond to their messages.

What effects do these results hold for future research? We can think of many. One approach would be to examine how the Court's opinion clarity has changed in response to its institutional powers. Today, the Court is powerful and can afford at times to dare Congress and the president. But this was not always so. Scholars should consider examining the Court's clarity historically. It would be particularly interesting to see when the Court used clarity (or ambiguity) to evade challenges to its power, when those attempts worked and when they did not work.

We also wonder how judicial institutions lead to heightened opinion clarity. Is it the case that common law systems are clearer than civil law systems? Are there features specific to a judicial system, such as lengthy tenure or no higher court review, that lead to heightened or diminished clarity of opinions?

We also would like to see scholars look at how audiences influence some justices more than others. Our approach to this was to look at how audiences interact with the Court on more or less an institutional level. But it seems to us – and there is evidence to support this claim (Baum 2006) – that some audiences are more likely to matter to some justices some of the time. How do these personal audiences influence opinion clarity and other behaviors?

These and other research questions await exploration. Our hope is future scholars build off our initial findings and discover more about the role of audience and how audiences influence judicial behavior.

REFERENCES

Alt, James E. and David Dreyer Lassen. 2003. "The Political Economy Of Institutions and Corruption in American States." *Journal of Theoretical Politics* 15(3):341–365.

Arnold, R. Douglas. 1990. *The Logic of Congressional Action.* New Haven: Yale University Press.

Bailey, Michael and Forrest Maltzman. 2011. *The Constrained Court: Law, Politics, and the Decisions Justices Make.* Princeton University Press.

Bartels, Brandon L. and Christopher D. Johnston. 2013. "On the Ideological Foundations of Supreme Court Legitimacy in the American Public." *American Journal of Political Science* 57(1):184–199.

Bass, Jack. 1981. *Unlikely Heroes: The Dramatic Story of the Southern Judges of the Fifth Circuit Who Translated the Supreme Court's Brown Decision into a Revolution for Equality.* New York: Simon and Schuster.

Baum, Lawrence. 1976. "Implementation of Judicial Decisions: An Organizational Analysis." *American Politics Quarterly* 4(1):86–114.

1978. "Lower-Court Response to Supreme Court Decisions: Reconsidering a Negative Picture." *Justice System Journal* 3:208–219.

1980. "Responses of Federal District Judges to Court of Appeals Policies: An Exploration." *Western Political Quarterly* 33(2):217–224.

2006. *Judges and Their Audiences: A Perspective on Judicial Behavior.* Princeton University Press.

Bawn, Kathleen. 1995. "Political Control versus Expertise: Congressional Choices about Administrative Procedures." *American Political Science Review* 89:62–73.

1997. "Choosing Strategies to Control the Bureaucracy: Statutory Constraints, Oversight, and the Committee System." *Journal of Law, Economics and Organization* 13:101–126.

Bell, Derrick A. 1982. "Civil Rights Lawyers on the Bench." *The Yale Law Journal* 91(4):814–826.

Benesh, Sara C. 2002a. *The U.S. Court of Appeals and the Law of Confessions: Perspectives on the Hierarchy of Justice.* El Paso: LFB Scholarly Publishing.

2002b. *The U.S. Courts of Appeals and the Law of Confessions: Perspectives on the Hierarchy of Justice.* El Paso: LFB Scholarly Publishing.

Benesh, Sara C. and Malia Reddick. 2002. "Overruled: An Event History Analysis of Lower Court Reaction to Supreme Court Alteration of Precedent." *Journal of Politics* 64(2):534–550.

Benesh, Sara C. and Wendy L. Martinek. 2002. "State Court Decision Making in Confession Cases." *Justice System Journal* 23(1):109–133.

Benson, Robert W. and Joan B. Kessler. 1987. "Legalese v. Plain Langauge: An Empirical Study of Persuasion and Credibility in Appellate Brief Writing." *Loyola of Los Angeles Law Review* 20:301–322.

Berkman, Michael B. 2001. "Legislative Professionalism and the Demand for Groups: The Institutional Context of Interest Population Density." *Legislative Studies Quarterly* 26(4):661–679.

Berry, William D., Michael B. Berkman and Stuart Schneiderman. 2000. "Legislative Professionalism and Incumbent Reelection: The Development of Institutional Boundaries." *American Political Science Review* 94(4):859–874.

Beyle, Thad L. 1983. *Being Governor.* Duke University Press chapter Governors' Offices: Varations on Common Themes.

1990. *Politics in the American States.* Little, Brown chapter Governors.

Birkby, Robert H. 1966. "The Supreme Court and the Bible Belt: Tennessee Reaction to the 'Schempp' Decision." *Midwest Journal of Political Science* 10(3): 304–319.

Black, Ryan C., Anthony J. Madonna, Ryan J. Owens and Michael S. Lynch. 2007. "Adding Recess Appointments to the President's 'Tool Chest' of Unilateral Powers." *Political Research Quarterly* 60(4):645–654.

Black, Ryan C. and James F. Spriggs, II. 2008. "An Empirical Analysis of the Length of U.S. Supreme Court Opinions." *Houston Law Review* 45(3):621–683.

Black, Ryan C. and Ryan J. Owens. 2009. "Agenda-Setting in the Supreme Court: The Collision of Policy and Jurisprudence." *Journal of Politics* 71(3): 1062–1075.

2011a. "Solicitor General Influence and Agenda Setting on the U.S. Supreme Court." *Political Research Quarterly* 64(4):765–778.

2011b. "Consider the Source (and the Message): Supreme Court Justices and Strategic Audits of Lower Court Decisions." *Political Research Quarterly* 64(4):765–778.

2012a. "Looking Back to Move Forward: Quantifying Policy Predictions in Political Decision Making." *American Journal of Political Science* 56(4): 802–816.

2012b. *The Solicitor General and the United States Supreme Court: Executive Influence and Judicial Decisions.* Cambridge University Press.

Black, Ryan C., Ryan J. Owens and Jennifer L. Brookhart. 2014. "We Are the World: The U.S. Supreme Court's Use of Foreign Sources of Law." *British Journal of Political Science* . FirstView Article found at: http://dx.doi.org/10.1017/S0007123414000490.

Blanchard, Lloyd A. 2008. *Performance Management and Budgeting: How Governments Can Learn from Experience*. M.E. Sharpe, Inc. chapter PART and Performance Budgeting Effectiveness, pp. 67–91.

Bowman, Ann O'M., Neal D. Woods and Milton R. Stark. 2010. "Governors Turn Pro: Separation of Powers and the Institutionalization of the American Governorship." *Political Research Quarterly* 63(2):304–315.

Box, George E. P. and Gwilym M. Jenkins. 1976. *Time Series Analysis: Forecasting and Control*. San Francisco: Holden-Day.

Box-Steffensmeir, Janet M., Suzanna De Boef and Tse-Min Lin. 2004. "The Dynamics of the Partisan Gender Gap." *American Political Science Review* 98(3): 515–528.

Brent, James. 2003. "A Principal-Agent Analysis of U.S. Courts of Appeals Responses to Boerne v. Flores." *American Politics Research* 31(5):557–570.

Calabresi, Guido. 1985. *A Common Law for the Age of Statutes*. Cambridge, MA: Harvard University Press.

Caldeira, Gregory A. 1986. "Neither the Purse Nor the Sword: Dynamics of Public Confidence in the Supreme Court." *American Political Science Review* 80(4):1209–1226.

Caldeira, Gregory A. and John R. Wright. 1988. "Organized Interests and Agenda Setting in the U.S. Supreme Court." *American Political Science Review* 82(4):1109–1127.

Cameron, Charles M., Jeffrey A. Segal and Donald Songer. 2000. "Strategic Auditing in a Political Hierarchy: An Informational Model of the Supreme Court's Certiorari Decisions." *American Political Science Review* 94(1): 101–116.

Cameron, Charles M. and Lewis A. Kornhauser. 2005. "Decision Rules in a Judicial Hierarchy." *Journal of Institutional and Theoretical Economics* 161:264–292.

Caminker, Evan H. 1994a. "Precedent and Prediction: The Forward-Looking Aspects of Inferior Court Decisionmaking." *Texas Law Review* 73:1–82.

1994b. "Why Must Inferior Courts Obey Superior Court Precedents?" *Stanford Law Review* 46(4):817–873.

Canon, Bradley C. 1991. "Courts and Policy: Compliance, Implementation, and Impact." In *The American Courts: A Critical Assessment*, ed. Gates and Johnson. Washington, D.C.: CQ Press.

Canon, Bradley C. and Charles A. Johnson. 1999. *Judicial Policies: Implementation and Impact*. Washington, D.C.: CQ Press.

Carey, John M. 1998. *Term Limits and Legislative Representation*. Cambridge University Press.

Carey, John M., Richard G. Niemi and Lynda W. Powell. 2000a. "Incumbency and the Probability of Reelection in State Legislative Elections." *Journal of Politics* 62:671–700.

2000*b. Term Limits in State Legislatures.* University Of Michigan Press.

Carlsen, William. 1996. "Frontier Justice." *San Francisco Chronicle* October 6:1,5.

Casillas, Christopher J., Peter K. Enns and Patrick C. Wohlfarth. 2011. "How Public Opinion Constrains the U.S. Supreme Court." *American Journal of Political Science* 55(1):74–88.

Casper, Jonathan D., Tom Tyler and Bonnie Fisher. 1988. "Procedural Justice in Felony Cases." *Law and Society Review* 22(3):483–508.

Chebat, Jean-Charles, Claire Gelinas-Chebat, Sabrina Hombourger and Arch G. Woodside. 2003. "Testing Consumers' Motivation and Linguistic Ability as Moderators of Advertising Readability." *Psychology & Marketing* 20: 599–624.

Clark, Tom S. 2009. "The Separation of Powers, Court-Curbing and Judicial Legitimacy." *American Journal of Political Science* 53(4):971–989.

Clarke, Harold D. and Marianne C. Stewart. 1994. "Prospections, Retrospections and Rationality: The 'Bankers' Model of Presidential Approval Reconsidered." *American Journal of Political Science* 38:1104–1123.

Clinton, Joshua D., Anthony Bertelli, Christian R. Grose, David E. Lewis and David C. Nixon. 2012. "Separated Powers in the United States: The Ideology of Agencies, Presidents, and Congress." *American Journal Of Political Science* 56(2):341–354.

Clinton, Joshua D. and David E. Lewis. 2008. "Expert Opinion, Agency Characteristics, and Agency Preferences." *Political Analysis* 16(1):3–16.

Clynch, Edward J. and Thomas P. Lauth. 1991. *Governors, Legislatures, and Budgets: Diversity across the American States.* Greenwood Press.

Coleman, Brady. 2001. "Lord Denning and Justice Cardozo: The Judge as Poet-Philosopher." *Rutgers Law Journal* 32:485–518.

Coleman, Brady and Quy Phung. 2010. "The Language of Supreme Court Briefs: A Large-Scale Quantitative Investigation." *The Journal of Appellate Practice and Process* 11:75–103.

Collins, Jr., Paul M. 2008. "Amici Curiae and Dissensus on the U.S. Supreme Court." *Journal of Empirical Legal Studies* 5(1):143–170.

Comparato, Scott A. and Scott D. McClurg. 2007. "A Neo-Institutional Explanation of State Supreme Court Responses in Search and Seizure Cases." *American Politics Research* 35(5):726–754.

Corley, Pamela C. 2009. "Uncertain Precedent: Circuit Court Responses to Supreme Court Plurality Opinions." *American Politics Research* 37(1):30–49.

Corley, Pamela C. and Justin Wedeking. 2014. "The (Dis)Advatnage of Certainty: The Importance of Certainty in Language." *Law and Society Review* 48(1): 35–62.

Corley, Pamela C., Paul M. Collins, Jr. and Bryan Calvin. 2011. "Lower Court Influence on U.S. Supreme Court Opinion Content." *Journal of Politics* 73(1):31–44.

Corley, Pamela C., Robert M. Howard and David C. Nixon. 2005. "The Supreme Court and Opinion Content: The Use of the Federalist Papers." *Political Research Quarterly* 58(2):329–340.

Cross, Frank. 2005. "Appellate Adherence to Precedent." *Journal of Empirical Legal Studies* 2(2):369–405.

Cross, Frank B. and Emerson H. Tiller. 1998. "Judicial Partisanship and Obedience to Legal Doctrine: Whistleblowing on the Federal Courts of Appeals." *Yale Law Journal* 107(7):2155–2176.

de Tocqueville, Alexis. 2010. *Democracy in America*. Indianapolis: Liberty Fund.

Dilger, Robert Jay, George A. Krause and Randolph R. Moffett. 1995. "State Legislative Professionalism and Gubernatorial Effectiveness." *Legislative Studies Quarterly* 20(4):553–571.

Dolbeare, Kenneth and Phillip E. Hammond. 1971. *The School Prayer Decisions: From Court Policy to Local Practice*. University of Chicago Press.

DuBay, William H. 2004. *The Principles of Readability*. Impact Information.

Durr, Robert H., Andrew D. Martin and Christina Wolbrecht. 2000. "Ideological Divergence and Public Support for the Supreme Court." *American Journal of Political Science* 44(4):768–776.

Dworkin, Ronald. 1978. *Taking Rights Seriously*. Cambridge, MA: Harvard University Press.

1985. *A Matter of Principle*. Cambridge, MA: Harvard University Press.

1986. *Law's Empire*. Cambridge, MA: Harvard University Press.

Easton, David. 1965. *A Systems Analysis of Political Life*. Hoboken, NJ: John Wiley and Sons, Inc.

1975. "A Re-Assessment of the Concept of Political Support." *British Journal of Political Science* 5:435–457.

Ellickson, Mark C. and Donald E. Whistler. 2001. "Explaining State Legislators' Casework and Public Resource Allocations." *Political Research Quarterly* 54(3):553–569.

Enns, Peter K. and Patrick C. Wohlfarth. 2013. "The Swing Justice." *Journal of Politics* 75(4):1089–1107.

Epstein, David and Sharyn O'Halloran. 1994. "Administrative Procedures, Information, and Agency Discretion." *American Journal of Political Science* 38:697–722.

Epstein, Lee and Andrew D. Martin. 2010. "Does Public Opinion Influence the Supreme Court? Possibly Yes (But We're Not Sure Why)." *University of Pennsylvania Journal of Constitutional Law* 13:263–281.

Epstein, Lee, Andrew D. Martin, Jeffrey A. Segal and Chad Westerland. 2007. "The Judicial Common Space." *Journal of Law, Economics, & Organization* 23(2):303–325.

Epstein, Lee and Jack Knight. 1998. *The Choices Justices Make*. Washington, D.C.: CQ Press.

Epstein, Lee and Jeffrey A. Segal. 2000. "Measuring Issue Salience." *American Journal of Political Science* 44(1):66–83.

Epstein, Lee, Jeffrey A. Segal and Jennifer Nicoll Victor. 2002. "Dynamic Agenda Setting on the U.S. Supreme Court: An Empirical Assessment." *Harvard Journal on Legislation* 39(2):395–433.

Erikson, Robert S., Michael B. MacKuen and James A. Stimson. 2002. *The Macro Polity*. New York: Cambridge University Press.

Eskridge, Jr., William N. 1986. "Dynamic Statutory Interpretation." *University of Pennsylvania Law Review* 135:1479.

Estreicher, Samuel and Richard L. Revesz. 1989. "Nonacquiescence by Federal Administrative Agencies." *Yale Law Journal* 98(4):679–772.

Fenno, Jr., Richard F. 1977. "U.S. House Members in Their Constituencies: An Exploration." *American Political Science Review* 71(3):883–917.

Ferguson, Margaret R. 2003. "Chief Executive Success in the Legislative Arena." *State Politics and Policy Quarterly* 3(2):158–182.

Ferguson, Margaret R. and Jay Barth. 2002. "Governors in the Legislative Arena: The Importance of Personality in Shaping Success." *Political Psychology* 23(4):787–808.

Fisher, Patrick and David Nice. 2005. *The Book of the States, 2005*. Council of State Governments chapter Staffing the Governor's Office: A Comparative Analysis.

Flemming, Roy B. and B. Dan Wood. 1997. "The Public and the Supreme Court: Individual Justice Responsiveness to American Policy Moods." *American Journal of Political Science* 41(2):468–498.

Flemming, Roy B., John Bohte and B. Dan Wood. 1997. "One Voice Among Many: The Supreme Court's Influence on Attentiveness to Issues in the United States, 1947–92." *American Journal of Political Science* 41(4):1224–1250.

Friedersdorf, Conor. 2013. "Why Clarence Thomas Uses Simple Words in His Opinions." *The Atlantic* February 20, 2013: Available at: www.theatlantic .com/national/archive/2013/02/why–clarence–thomas–uses–simple–words– in–his–opinions/273326/.

Friedman, Joel William. 2009. *Champion of Civil Rights: Judge John Minor Wisdom*. Baton Rouge: Louisiana State University Press.

Fuller, Lon. 1964. *The Morality of Law*. New Haven: Yale University Press.

Galanter, Marc. 1974. "Why the 'Haves' Come out Ahead: Speculation on the Limits of Legal Changes." *Law & Society Review* 9(1):95–160.

Gao, Yuan. 2012. "Investigating Supreme Court Impact on Federal Agency Efficiency in Procurement and Contracting." Available at: https://appam .confex.com/data/extendedabstract/appam/2012/Paper_1484_extendedabstr act_255_0.pdf.

Gely, Rafael and Pablo T. Spiller. 1990. "A Rational Choice Theory of Supreme Court Statutory Decisions with Applications to the *State Farm* and *Grove City* Cases." *Journal of Law, Economics, & Organization* 6(2):263–300.

Gentzkow, Matthew, Edward L. Glaeser and Claudia Goldin. 2006. *Corruption and Reform: Lessons from America's Economic History*. University of Chicago Press chapter The Rise of the Fourth Estate How Newspapers Became Informative and Why It Mattered, pp. 187–230.

Gibson, James L. and Gregory A. Caldeira. 2009. *Citizens, Courts, and Confirmations: Positivity Theory and the Judgments of the American People*. Princeton University Press.

2011. "Has Legal Realism Damaged the Legitimacy of the U.S. Supreme Court?" *Law and Society Review* 45(1):195–219.

Gibson, James L., Gregory A. Caldeira and Lester Kenyatta Spence. 2003. "The Supreme Court and the U.S. Presidential Election of 2000: Wounds, Self-Inflicted or Otherwise?" *British Journal of Political Science* 33(4): 535–556.

Gibson, James L., Gregory A. Caldeira and Vanessa A. Baird. 1998. "On the Legitimacy of National High Courts." *American Political Science Review* 92(2): 343–358.

Gibson, James L. and Michael J. Nelson. 2015. "Is the U.S. Supreme Court's Legitimacy Grounded in Performance Satisfaction and Ideology?" *American Journal of Political Science* 59(1):162–174.

Gigerenzer, Gerd and Wolfgang Gaissmaier. 2011. "Heuristic Decision Making." *Annual Review of Psychology* 62:451–482.

Giles, Michael W., Bethany Blackstone and Richard L. Vining. 2008. "The Supreme Court in American Democracy: Unreavling the Linkages between Public Opinion and Judicial Decision Making." *Journal of Politics* 70(2):293–306.

Giles, Michael W., Virginia A. Hettinger and Todd Peppers. 2001. "Picking Federal Judges: A Note on Policy and Partisan Selection Agendas." *Political Research Quarterly* 54(3):623–641.

Gilmour, John B. and David E. Lewis. 2006. "Political Appointees and the Competence of Federal Program Management." *American Politics Research* 34(1): 22–50.

Ginsburg, Ruth Bader. 1994. "Address to the Annual Dinner of the American Law Institute—May 19, 1994." *American Law Institute Proceedings* 71:324–331.

Ginsburg, Tom and Nuno Garoupa. 2009. "Judicial Audiences and Reputation: Perspectives from Comparative Law." *Columbia Journal of Transnational Law* 47:451–490.

Goelzhauser, Greg and Damon M. Cann. 2014. "Judicial Independence and Opinion Clarity on State Supreme Courts." *State Politics and Policy Quarterly* 14(2):123–141.

Granger, Clive W.J. and Paul Newbold. 1974. "Spurious Regressions in Econometrics." *Journal of Econometrics* 26:1045–1066.

Grossman, Stuart A., Steven Piantadosi and Charles Covahey. 1994. "Are Informed Consent Forms That Describe Clinical Oncology Research Protocols

Readable by Most Patients And Their Families?" *Journal of Clinical Oncology* 12(10):2211–2215.

Gruenfeld, Deborah H. 1995. "Status, Ideology, and Integrative Complexity on the U.S. Supreme Court: Rethinking the Politics of Political Decision Making." *Journal of Personality and Social Psychology* 68:5–20.

Gruenfeld, Deborah H. and Jared Preston. 2000. "Upending the Status Quo: Cognitive Complexity in U.S. Supreme Court Justices Who Overturn Legal Precedent." *Personality and Social Psychology Bulletin* 26:1013–1022.

Gruhl, John. 1980. "The Supreme Court's Impact on the Law of Libel: Compliance by Lower Federal Courts." *Western Political Quarterly* 33(4):502–519.

Hall, Matthew E.K. 2014. "The Semiconstrained Court: Public Opinion, the Separation of Powers, and the U.S. Supreme Court's Fear of Nonimplementation." *American Journal of Political Science* 58(2):352–366.

Hamilton, Alexander. 1788. "Federalist Number 78."

Hansford, Thomas G. and James F. Spriggs, II. 2006. *The Politics of Precedent on the U.S. Supreme Court*. Princeton: Princeton University Press.

Hart, H.L.A. 1961. *The Concept of Law*. Oxford University Press.

1963. *Law, Liberty, and Morality*. Stanford University Press.

Harvey, Anna and Michael Woodruff. 2013. "Confirmation Bias in the United States Supreme Court Judicial Database." *Journal Law, Economics, and Organization* 29(2):414–460.

Hellman, Arthur D. 1995. "By Precedent Unbound: The Nature and Extent of Unresolved Intercircuit Conflicts." *University of Pittsburgh Law Review* 56: 693–800.

Hettinger, Virginia A., Stefanie A. Lindquist and Wendy L. Martinek. 2003. "Separate Opinion Writing on the United States Courts of Appeals." *American Politics Research* 31(3):215–250.

Hinkle, Rachael K., Andrew D. Martin, Jonathan David Shaub and Emerson H. Tiller. 2012. "A Positive Theory And Empirical Analysis Of Strategic Word Choice In District Court Opinions." *Journal of Legal Analysis* 4(2): 407–444.

Hoekstra, Valerie. 2005. "Competing Constraints: State Court Responses to Supreme Court Decisions and Legislation on Wages and Hours." *Political Research Quarterly* 58(2):317–328.

Hogan, Robert E. n.d. "Factors Conditioning the Representational Activities of State Legislators." Presented at the Annual State Politics and Policy Conference at Rice University, Houston, TX, February 14, 16 2012.

Holbrook, Thomas M. and Charles M. Tidmarch. 1991. "Sophomore Surge in State Legislative Elections, 1968–1986." *Legislative Studies Quarterly* 16:49–63.

Hosking, Jonathan RM. 1981. "Fractional Differencing." *Biometrika* 68:165–176.

Huber, John D. and Charles R. Shipan. 2002. *Deliberate Discretion: The Institutional Foundations Of Bureaucratic Autonomy*. Cambridge University Press.

Huber, John D., Charles R. Shipan and Madelaine Pfahler. 2001. "Legislatures and Statutory Control of Bureaucracy." *American Journal of Political Science* 45(2):330–345.

Jacobson, Gary C. 1987. "The Marginals Never Vanished: Incumbency and Competition in Elections to the U.S. House of Representatives, 1952–1982." *American Journal of Political Science* 31(1):126–141.

Johnson, Charles A. 1979. "Lower Court Reactions to Supreme Court Decisions: A Quantitative Analysis." *American Journal of Political Science* 23(4): 792–8004.

　　1986. "Follow-Up Citations in the U.S. Supreme Court." *Western Political Quarterly* 39:538–547.

Johnson, Charles A. and Bradley C. Canon. 1984. *Judicial Policies: Implementation and Impact.* Washington, D.C.: CQ Press.

Johnson, Timothy R., James F. Spriggs, II and Paul J. Wahlbeck. 2005. "Passing and Strategic Voting on the U.S. Supreme Court." *Law & Society Review* 39(2):349–377.

Johnston, Christopher D. and Brandon L. Bartels. 2010. "Sensationalism and Sobriety Differential Media Exposure and Attitudes Toward American Courts." *Public Opinion Quarterly* 74(2):260–285.

Jones, Douglas, Edward Gibson, Wade Shen, Neil Granoien, Martha Herzog, Douglas Reynolds and Clifford Weinstein. 2005. Measuring Human Readability of Machine Generated Text: Three Case Studies in Speech Recognition and Machine Translation. IEEE International Conference on Acoustics, Speech, and Signal Processing (ICASSP2005).

Ka, Sangjoon and Paul Teske. 2002. "Ideology and Professionalism: Electricity Regulation and Deregulation Over Time in the American States." *American Politics Research* 30(3):323–343.

Kassow, Benjamin J., Donald R. Songer and Michael P. Fix. 2012. "The Influence of Precedent on State Supreme Courts." *Political Research Quarterly* 65(2): 372–384.

Kennedy, Anthony. 2013. "Statement of Justice Anthony Kennedy Associate Justice of the Supreme Court of the United States Before the Subcommittee on Financial Services and General Government of the House Committee on Appropriations." March 14.

Key, Vladimir Orlando. 1961. *Public Opinion and American Democracy.* New York: Alfred A. Knopf.

King, David C., Richard J. Zeckhauser and Mark T. Kim. 2004. "The Mangement Performance of the U.S. States." KSG Working Paper No. RWP04-028. Available at SSRN: http://ssrn.com/abstract=571821 or http://dx.doi.org/10.2139/ssrn.571821.

King, James D. 2000. "Changes in Professionalism in U.S. State Legislatures." *Legislative Studies Quarterly* 25(2):327–343.

Korobkin, Russell B. 2000. "Behavioral Analysis and Legal Form: Rules vs. Standards Revisited." *Oregon Law Review* 79:23.

Kramer, Gerald H. 1983. "The Ecological Fallacy Revisited: Aggregate- versus Individual-Level Findings on Economics and Elections, and Sociotropic Voting." *American Political Science Review* 77:92–111.

Kritzer, Herbert M. 2001. "The Impact of *Bush v. Gore* on Public Perceptions and Knowledge of the Supreme Court." *Judicature* 32:35–37.

Lau, Richard R. and David P. Redlawsk. 2001. "Advantages and Disadvantages of Cognitive Heuristics in Political Decision Making." *American Journal of Political Science* 45(4):951–971.

Law, David S. and David Zaring. 2010. "Law versus Ideology: The Supreme Court and the Use of Legislative History." *William and Mary Law Review* 51(5): 1–62.

Leben, Steve. 2011. "An Expectation of Empathy." *Washburn Law Journal* 51: 49–59.

Lewis, David E. 2003. *Presidents and the Politics of Agency Design: Political Insulation in the United States Government Bureaucracy, 1946–1997.* Stanford University Press.

　　2008. *The Politics of Presidential Appointments: Political Control and Bureaucratic Performance.* Princeton: Princeton University Press.

Lindquist, Stefanie A. and David E. Klein. 2006. "The Influence of Jurisprudential Considerations on Supreme Court Decisionmaking: A Study of Conflict Cases." *Law & Society Review* 40(1):135–162.

Lindquist, Stefanie A., Susan B. Haire and Donald R. Songer. 2007. "Supreme Court Auditing of the U.S. Courts of Appeals: An Organizational Perspective." *Journal of Public Administration Research and Theory* 17: 607–624.

Long, J. Scott and Jeremy Freese. 2014. *Regression Models for Categorical Dependent Variables Using Stata.* 3rd ed. College Station, TX: Stata Press.

MacKuen, Michael B., Robert S. Erikson and James A. Stimson. 1989. "Macropartisanship." *American Political Science Review* 83:1125–1142.

Maestas, Cherie. 2000. "Professional Legislatures and Ambitious Politicians: Policy Responsiveness of State Institutions." *Legislative Studies Quarterly* 25(4): 663–690.

Malhotra, Neil. 2008. "Disentangling the Relationship between Legislative Professionalism and Government Spending." *Legislative Studies Quarterly* 33(3): 1–28.

Maltzman, Forrest, James F. Spriggs, II and Paul J. Wahlbeck. 2000. *Crafting Law on the Supreme Court: The Collegial Game.* New York: Cambridge University Press.

Manwaring, David R. 1968. *The Supreme Court as a Policy Maker.* Public Affairs Research Bureau, Southern Illinois University at Carbondale.

Manwaring, David R., Donald R. Reich and Stephen L. Wasby. 1972. *The Supreme Court as Policy-Maker: Three Studies on the Impact of Judicial Decisions.* Public Affairs Research Bureau, Southern Illinois University at Carbondale.

Marshall, Thomas R. 1989. *Public Opinion and the Supreme Court.* Crows Nest, New South Wales: Unwin Hyman.

2008. *Public Opinion and the Rehnquist Court.* Albany: State University of New York Press.

Martin, Andrew D. and Kevin M. Quinn. 2002. "Dynamic Ideal Point Estimation via Markov Chain Monte Carlo for the U.S. Supreme Court, 1953–1999." *Political Analysis* 10(2):134–153.

McCubbins, Mathew D. and Thomas Schwartz. 1984. "Congressional Oversight Overlooked: Police Patrols versus Fire Alarms." *American Journal of Political Science* 28(1):165–179.

McCubbins, Mathew, Roger Noll and Barry Weingast. 1987. "Administrative Procedures as Instruments of Political Control." *Journal of Law, Economics, and Organization* 3:243–277.

McGuire, Kevin T. 2009. "Public Schools, Religious Establishments, and the U.S. Supreme Court: An Examination of Policy Compliance." *American Politics Research* 37(1):50–74.

McGuire, Kevin T. and James A. Stimson. 2004. "The Least Dangerous Branch Revisited: New Evidence on Supreme Court Responsiveness to Public Preferences." *Journal of Politics* 66(4):1018–1035.

McKay, Robert B. 1956. "With All Deliberate Speed: A Study of School Desegregation." *New York University Law Review* 31:991–1090.

McNollgast. 1994. "Politics and Courts: A Positive Theory of Judicial Doctrine and the Rule of Law." *Southern California Law Review* 68:1631–83.

Milner, Neal A. 1971. *The Court and Local Law Enforcement: The Impact of Miranda.* Thousand Oaks, CA: Sage Publications.

Mishler, William and Reginald S. Sheehan. 1993. "The Supreme Court as a Counter-majoritarian Institution? The Impact of Public Opinion on Supreme Court Decisions." *American Political Science Review* 87:87–101.

1994. "Popular Influence on Supreme Court Decisions." *American Political Science Review* 88(3):716–724.

1996. "Public Opinion, the Attitudinal Model, and Supreme Court Decision Making: A Micro-Analytic Perspective." *The Journal of Politics* 58:169–200.

Moe, Terry M. 1985. "Control and Feedback in Economic Regulation: The Case of the NLRB." *American Political Science Review* 79(4):1094–1116.

1987. "Interests, Institutions, and Positive Theory: The Politics of the NLRB." *Studies in American Political Development* 2:236–299.

Monahan, John and Laurens Walker. 2009. *Social Science in Law.* Eagan, MN: Foundation Press.

Moncrief, Gary F., Joel A. Thompson, Michael Haddon and Robert Hoyer. 1992. "For Whom the Bell Tolls: Term Limits and State Legislatures." *Legislative Studies Quarterly* 17(1):37–47.

Moncrief, Gary, Richard Niemi and Lynda Powell. 2004. "Time, Term Limits, and Turnover: Membership Stability in U.S. State Legislatures." *Legislative Studies Quarterly* 31:37–47.

Mooney, Christopher Z. 1995. "Citiizens, Structures, and Sister States: Influences on State Legislative Professionalism." *Legislative Studies Quarterly* 20: 47–67.

Mosher, Frederick. 1982. *Democracy and the Public Service*. 2nd ed. New York: Oxford University Press.

Murphy, Walter F. 1959. "Lower Court Checks on Supreme Court Power." *American Political Science Review* 53(4):1017–1031.

1964. *Elements of Judicial Strategy*. University of Chicago Press.

Nelson, Michael J. n.d. "Elections and Explanations: Judicial Elections and the Readability of Judicial Opinions." Unpublished paper available at: http://mjnelson.org/papers/NelsonReadabilityAugust2013.pdf.

Niskanen, William. 1971. *Bureaucracy and Representative Government*. New York: Aldine-Atherton.

Norcross, Eileen and Joseph Adamson. n.d. "An Analysis of the Office of Mangement and Budget's Program Assessment Rating Tool (PART) for Fiscal Year 2008." Paper available at: http://mercatus.org/sites/default/files/publication/20070725_Analysis_of_PART_for_FY_2008.pdf.

Novak, Linda. 1980. "The Precedential Value of Supreme Court Plurality Decisions." *Columbia Law Review* 80(4):756–781.

O'Brien, David M. 2008. *Storm Center: The Supreme Court in American Politics*. New York, NY: W. W. Norton & Company.

Owens, Ryan J. and David A. Simon. 2012. "Explaining the Supreme Court's Docket Size." *William and Mary Law Review*.

Owens, Ryan J. and Justin P. Wedeking. 2011. "Justices and Legal Clarity: Analyzing the Complexity of Supreme Court Opinions." *Law and Society Review* 45(4):1027–1061.

2012. "Predicting Drift on Politically Insulated Institutions: A Study of Ideological Drift on the U.S. Supreme Court." *Journal of Politics* 74:487–500.

Owens, Ryan J., Justin P. Wedeking and Patrick C. Wohlfarth. 2013. "How the Supreme Court Alters Opinion Language to Evade Congressional Review." *Journal of Law and Courts* 1(1):35–59.

Owens, Ryan J. and Patrick C. Wohlfarth. 2014. "State Solicitors General, Appellate Expertise, and State Success Before the U.S. Supreme Court." *Law and Society Review* 48(3):657–685.

Pacelle, Richard L. and Lawrence Baum. 1992. "Supreme Court Authority in the Judiciary: A Study of Remands." *American Politics Research* 20:169–191.

Paulsen, Michael Stokes. 1990. "Accusing Justice: Some Variations on the Themes of Robert M. Cover's Justice Accused." *Journal of Law and Religion* 7:33–97.

Peltason, J.W. 1971. *Fifty-Eight Lonely Men.* Urbana: University of Illinois Press.

Pennebaker, James W. and Thomas C. Lay. 2002. "Linguistic Styles: Langauge Use As." *Journal of Research in Personality* 36:271–282.

Pennebaker, James W., Richard B. Slachter and Cindy K. Chung. n.d. "Linguistic Markers of Psychological State through Media Interviews: John Kerry and John Edwards in 2004, Al Gore in 2000." Unpublished Technical Report.

Perry, Jr., H.W. 1991. *Deciding to Decide: Agenda Setting in the United States Supreme Court.* Cambridge, MA: Harvard University Press.

Posner, Richard A. 2008. *How Judges Think.* Cambridge, MA: Harvard University Press.

Priest, George L. and Benjamin Klein. 1984. "The Selection of Disputes for Litigation." *Journal of Legal Studies* 13(1):1–55.

Provost, Colin. 2003. "State Attorneys General, Entrepreneurship, and Consumer Protection in the New Federalism." *Publius: The Journal of Federalism* 33: 37–53.

——— 2006. "The Politics of Consumer Protection: Explaining State Attorney General Participation in Multi-State Lawsuits." *Political Research Quarterly* 59:609–618.

Quinn, Kevin M., Burt L. Monroe, Michael Colaresi, Michael H. Crespin and Dragomir R. Radev. 2010. "How to Analyze Political Attention with Minimal Assumptions and Costs." *American Journal of Political Science* 54(1):209–228. http://dx.doi.org/10.1111/j.1540-5907.2009.00427.x

Randazzo, Kirk A., Richard A. Waterman and Jeffrey A. Fine. 2006. "Checking the Federal Courts: The Impact of Congressional Statutes on Judicial Behavior." *Journal of Politics* 68(4):1006–1017.

Randazzo, Kirk A., Richard W. Waterman and Michael P. Fix. 2011. "State Supreme Courts and the Effects of Statutory Constraint: A Test of the Model of Contingent Discretion." *Political Research Quarterly* 64(4):779–789.

Riccucci, Norma M. 1995. *Unsung Heroes: Federal Execucrats Making a Difference.* Washington, D.C.: Georgetown University Press.

Richards, Mark J. and Herbert M. Kritzer. 2002. "Jurisprudential Regimes in Supreme Court Decision Making." *American Political Science Review* 96(2):305–320.

Richards, Mark J., Herbert M. Kritzer and Joseph L. Smith. 2006. "Does Chevron Matter?" *Law & Policy* 28:444–469.

Roberts, John. 2013. "2013 Year-End Report on the Federal Judiciary." Available at: www.supremecourt.gov/publicinfo/year–end/year–endreports.aspx.

Romans, Neil T. 1974. "The Role of State Supreme Courts in Judicical Policy Making: Escobedo, Miranda and the Use of Judicial Impact Analysis." *Western Political Quarterly* 27(1):38–59.

Rosenberg, Gerald N. 1991. *The Hollow Hope: Can Courts Bring about Social Change?* University of Chicago Press.

Rosenthal, Alan. 1996. "State Legislative Devlopment: Observations from Three Perspectives." *Legislative Studies Quarterly* 21:169–198.

Ross, William G. 2002. "Attacks on the Warren Court by State Officials: A Case Study of Why Court-Curbing Movements Fail." *Buffalo Law Review* 50: 483–612.

Schwartz, Bernard. 1986. *Swann's Way.* Oxford University Press.

Segal, Jeffrey A. and Harold J. Spaeth. 2002. *The Supreme Court and the Attitudinal Model Revisited.* New York: Cambridge University Press.

Shanahan, Frank E. 1963. "Proposed Constitutional Amendments: They Will Strengthen Federal-State Relations." *American Bar Association Journal* 49:631–636.

Shapiro, Martin. 1968. *The Supreme Court and Administrative Agencies.* New York: The Free Press.

Shipan, Charles R. 2004. "Regulatory Regimes, Agency Action, and the Conditional Nature of Congressional Influence." *American Political Science Review* 98(3):467–480.

Shipan, Charles R. and Craig Volden. 2006. "Bottom-Up Federalism: The Diffusion of Antismoking Policies from U.S. Cities to States." *American Journal of Political Science* 50(4):825–843.

Smith, Joseph L. and Emerson H. Tiller. 2002. "The Strategy of Judging: Evidence from Administrative Law." *The Journal of Legal Studies* 31(1):61–82.

Songer, Donald R. 1987. "The Impact of the Supreme Court on Trends in Economic Policy Making in the United States Courts of Appeals." *Journal of Politics* 49(3):830–841.

Songer, Donald R., Ashlyn Kuersten and Erin Kaheny. 2000. "Why the Haves Don't Always Come out Ahead: Repeat Players Meet Amici Curiae for the Disadvantaged." *Political Research Quarterly* 53(3):537–556.

Songer, Donald R., Jeffrey A. Segal and Charles M. Cameron. 1994. "The Hierarchy of Justice: Testing a Principal-Agent Model of Supreme Court-Circuit Court Interactions." *American Journal of Political Science* 38(3):673–696.

Songer, Donald R. and Reginald S. Sheehan. 1990. "Supreme Court Impact on Compliance and Outcomes: Miranda and New York Times in the United States Courts of Appeals." *Western Political Quarterly* 43(2):297–316.

Songer, Donald R., Reginald S. Sheehan and Susan Brodie Haire. 1999. "Do the 'Haves' Come out Ahead over Time? Applying Galanter's Framework to Decisions of the U.S. Courts of Appeals, 1925-1988." *Law & Society Review* 33(4):811–832.

Songer, Donald R. and Susan Haire. 1992. "Integrating Alternative Approaches to the Study of Judicial Voting: Obscenity Cases in the U.S. Courts of Appeals." *American Journal of Political Science* 36(4):963–982.

Spriggs, II, James F. 1996. "The Supreme Court and Federal Administrative Agencies: A Resource-Based Theory and Analysis of Judicial Impact." *American Journal of Political Science* 40(4):1122–1151.

1997. "Explaining Federal Bureaucratic Compliance with Supreme Court Opinions." *Political Research Quarterly* 50(3):567–593.

Spriggs, II, James F. and Thomas G. Hansford. 2001. "Explaining the Overruling of U.S. Supreme Court Precedent." *Journal of Politics* 63(4):1091–1111.

Squire, Peverill. 1988. "Politics and Personal Factors in Retirement from the United States Supreme Court." *Political Behavior* 10(2):180–190.

1993. "Professionalization and Public Opinion of State Legislatures." *Journal of Politics* 55:479–491.

1998. "Membership Turnover and the Efficient Processing of Legislation." *Legislative Studies Quarterly* 23(1):23–32.

2007. "Measuring State Legislative Professionalism: The Squire Index Revisited." *State Politics and Policy Quarterly* 7:211–227.

Stalebrink, Odd J. and Velda Frisco. 2011. "PART in Retrospect: An Examination of Legislators' Attitudes Toward PART." *Public Budgeting and Finance* 31(2): 1–21.

Staton, Jeffrey K. and Georg Vanberg. 2008. "The Value of Vagueness, Delegation, Defiance, and Judicial Opinions." *American Journal of Political Science* 52(3):504–519.

Staudt, Nancy C. 2004. "Agenda Setting in Supreme Court Tax Cases: Lessons from the Blackmun Papers." *Buffalo Law Review* 52(3):889–922.

Staudt, Nancy, Barry Friedman and Lee Epstein. 2008. "On the Role of Ideological Homogeneity in Generating Consequential Constitutional Decisions." *University of Pennsylvania Journal of Constitutional Law* 10(2):361–386.

Stern, Robert L., Eugene Gressman, Stephen M. Shapiro and Kenneth S. Geller. 2002. *Supreme Court Practice*. 8th ed. Washington, D.C.: The Bureau of National Affairs.

Stidham, Ronald and Robert A. Carp. 1982. "Trial Courts' Responses to Supreme Court Policy Changes: Three Case Studies." *Law and Policy* 4(2):215–234.

Stimson, James A. 1991. *Public Opinion in America: Moods, Cycles, and Swings*. Boulder: Westview Press.

1999. *Public Opinion in America: Moods, Cycles, and Swings*, 2nd ed. Boulder: Westview Press.

Stimson, James A., Michael B. Mackuen and Robert S. Erikson. 1995. "Dynamic Representation." *American Political Science Review* 89(3):543–565.

Suedfeld, Peter and A. Dennis Rank. 1976. "Revolutionary Leaders: Long-Term Success as a Function of Changes in Conceptual Complexity." *Journal of Personality and Social Psychology* 34:169–178.

Sunshine, Jason and Tom R. Tyler. 2003. "The Role of Procedural Justice and Legitimacy in Shaping Public Support for Policing." *Law and Society Review* 37(3):513–548.

Tarr, George Alan. 1977. *Judicial Impact and State Supreme Courts.* Lexington Books.

Tetlock, Philip E. 1981*a.* "Personality and Isolationaism: Content Analysis of Senatorial Speeches." *Journal of Personality and Social Psychology* 41:737–743.

1981*b.* "Pre- To Post-Election Shifts In Presidential Rhetoric: Impression Management Or Cognitive Adjustment?" *Journal of Personality and Social Psychology* 41:207–212.

1984. "Cognitive Style and Political Belief Systems in the British House of Commons." *Journal of Personality and Social Psychology* 46:365–375.

Tetlock, Philip E., Jane Bernzweig and Jack L. Gallant. 1985. "Supreme Court Decision Making: Cognitive Style as a Predictor of Ideological Consistency of Voting." *Journal of Personality and Social Psychology* 48:1227–1239.

Thompson, Joel A. 1986. "State Legislative Reform: Another Look, One More Time, Again." *Polity* 19(1):27–41.

Tsay, Wen-Jay and Ching-Fan Chung. 2000. "The Spurious Regression of Fractional Integrated Processes." *Journal of Econometrics* 96:155–182.

Ura, Joseph Daniel. 2014. "Backlash and Legitimation: Macro Political Responses to Supreme Court Decisions." *American Journal of Political Science* 58: 110–126.

Ura, Joseph Daniel and Patrick C. Wohlfarth. 2010. "An Appeal to the People: Public Opinion and Congressional Support for the Supreme Court." *Journal of Politics* 72(4):939–956.

Vickrey, William C., Douglas G. Denton and Wallace B. Jefferson. 2012. "Opinions as the Voice of the Court: How State Supreme Courts Can Communicate Effectively and Promote Procedural Fairness." *Court Review: The Journal of the American Judges Association* 48(3):74–85.

Vines, Kenneth N. 1963. "The Role Of Circuit Courts Of Appeal In The Federal Judicial Process: A Case Study." *Midwest Journal of Political Science* 7(4): 305–319.

Wahlbeck, Paul J. 1998. "The Development of a Legal Rule: The Federal Common Law of Public Nuisance." *Law & Society Review* 32(3):613–637.

Wahlbeck, Paul J., James F. Spriggs and Forrest Maltzman. 2009. "The Burger Court Opinion Writing Database." http://supremecourtopinions.wustl.edu/.

Wahlbeck, Paul J., James F. Spriggs, II and Lee Sigelman. 2002. "Ghostwriters on the Court? A Stylistic Analysis of U.S. Supreme Court Draft Opinions." *American Politics Research* 30(2):166–192.

Wasby, Stephan. 1993. *The Supreme Court in the Federal System.* Chicago: Nelson-Hall Publishers.

Wedeking, Justin P. 2010. "Supreme Court Litigants and Strategic Framing." *American Journal of Political Science* 54(3):617–631.

Weingast, Barry R. and Mark J. Moran. 1983. "Bureaucratic Discretion or Congressional Control: Regulatory Policymaking by the FTC." *Journal of Political Economy* 91:765–800.

Westerland, Chad, Jeffrey A. Segal, Lee Epstein, Charles Cameron and Scott Comparato. 2010. "Strategic Defiance and Compliance in the U.S. Courts of Appeals." *American Journal of Political Science* 54(4):891–905.

Wheeler, Darren A. 2006. "Implementing *INS v. Chadha*: Communication Breakdown?" *Wayne Law Review* 52:1185–1221.

Wildavsky, Aaron. 1992. *The New Politics of the Budgetary Process*, 2nd ed. New York: Harper Collins.

William Ker Muir, Jr. 1967. *Prayer in the Public Schools*. University of Chicago Press.

Williams, Richard. 2006. "Generalized Ordered Logit-Partial Proportional Odds Models for Ordinal Dependent Variables." *The Stata Journal* 6:58–82.

Wilson, James Q. 1989. *Bureaucracy: What Government Agencies Do and Why They Do It*. New York: Basic Books.

Wood, B. Dan and James E. Anderson. 1993. "The Politics of U.S. Antitrust Regulation." *American Journal of Political Science* 37(1):1–39.

Wood, B. Dan and Richard W. Waterman. 1994. *Bureaucratic Dynamics: The Role of Bureaucracy in a Democracy*. Boulder: Westview Press.

Woods, Neal D. and Michael Baranowski. 2006. "Legislative Professionalism and Influence on State Agencies: The Effects of Resources and Careerism." *Legislative Studies Quarterly* 31(4):585–609.

Zilis, Michael. n.d. "I Respectfully Dissent: Coverage of High Salience Supreme Court Decisions in the *New York Times*, 1981–2008." Unpublished paper available at: http://tinyurl.com/zillisPaper.

Zink, James R., James F. Spriggs, II and John T. Scott. 2009. "Courting the Public: The Influence of Decision Attributes on Individuals' Views of Court Opinions." *Journal of Politics* 71(3):909–925.

INDEX

Adamson, Joseph, 86
Adarand Constructors, Inc. v. Peña
(1995), 8
Alexander v. Choate (1985), 97–8
Alt, James E., 105
Anderson, James E., 19
Arnold, R. Douglas, 38, 125
Attorney General, 11, 84
audience attention
Supreme Court's desire for, 3
types of, 3–4
groups, 5–10
obstacles, 10–11
audience type
interpreting, 5–7
consuming, 5–6, 8–9
implementing, 5–6, 8
secondary, 5–6, 9

Baker v. Carr (1962), 105
Bartels, Brandon L., 30, 123, 139
Barth, Jay, 118
Bailey, Michael, 123
Baird, Vanessa A., 9, 28
Baranowski, Michael, 104
Bass, Jack, 17
Baum, Lawrence, 3, 14, 24, 27, 29, 38,
60, 87, 156, 160
Bawn, Kathleen, 21, 42n3
Bell, Derrick A., 17
Benesh, Sara C., 7n6, 19n9, 20, 22, 23,
42n2, 72, 143, 144
Benson, Robert W., 30, 47
Berkman, Michael B., 101–3, 108
Bernzweig, Jane, 45, 46
Berry, William D., 102, 105, 108
Bertelli, Anthony, 20

Beyle, Thad L., 106, 109, 110
Birkby, Robert H., 19
Black, Hugo, 122
Black, Ryan C., 11, 14, 28, 31, 42, 63,
65, 91, 101, 158
Blackstone, Bethany, 9, 125, 133
Blanchard, Lloyd A., 86
Bohte, John, 9, 125
Bowman, Ann O.M., 110
Box, George E.P., 135
Box-Steffensmeir, Janet M., 135
Brennan, William, 2, 32–4, 36–7
Brent, James, 11, 28, 101
Brockington v. Rhodes (1969), 34–5
Brookhart, Jennifer L., 31
Brown v. Board of Education (1954), 1,
4, 7n8, 9, 20–1, 51–2
Brown v. Board of Education II (1955),
52
Burger Court, 69
Burger, Warren, 1–2, 32–33, 48, 69
Bush v. Gore (2000), 26, 124

Calabresi, Guido, 80
Caldeira, Gregory A., 9, 13, 28, 29, 30,
32, 123, 124
*California Human Resources Dept v.
Java* (1971), 32
Calvin, Bryan, 13
Cameron, Charles M., 18n6, 19n9, 20,
27, 29, 65, 100, 142, 143, 148
Caminker, Evan H., 7, 18n6, 29
Cann, Damon M., 14, 48
Cannon, Bradley C., 5, 6, 8, 9, 17,
20–21, 26, 87, 119
Cardozo, Benjamin, 48
Carey, John M., 102, 108

Carlsen, William, 7
Carp, Robert A., 19
Casillas, Christopher J., 9, 13, 29, 37, 123–5, 133, 158
Cervantes v. Guerra (1981), 17
Chebat, Jean-Charles, 47, 48
Chevron U.S.A., Inc. v. Natural Resources Defense Council, Inc. (1984), 42–3, 80
Chung, Ching-Fan, 136
Chung, Cindy K., 45n7
circuit courts. *See* courts of appeals
Clark, Tom, 122, 125
Clarke, Howard D., 135
Clinton, Joshua D., 20
Clinton v. City of New York (1998), 127–8
Clynch, Edward J., 104
Colaresi, Michael, 44n6
Coleman, Brady, 14, 46, 48
Collins, Jr., Paul M., 13, 73, 92, 112, 134, 144
Communication between justices, 32–5, 37
Comparato, Scott A., 18n6, 20, 142, 143, 148
Congress
  as audience for Supreme Court opinions, 36, 38, 42, 48, 82
Corley, Pamela C., 13, 22, 23, 24, 27, 41
courts of appeals
  District of Columbia Circuit, 60
  Fourth Circuit, 17–8, 60
  Fifth Circuit, 17
  Ninth Circuit, 60
  Second Circuit, 80
  noncompliance, 18
Covahey, Charles, 46
Crespin, Michael H., 44n6
criminal procedure, 78, 96, 100, 118
Cross, Frank, 7, 10, 28, 61, 66, 101

Davis v. Davis (1981), 17–8
DeBoef, Suzanna, 135
Denning, Lord Alfred Thompson, 48
Denton, Douglas G., 30, 31, 47
deTocqueville, Alexis, 80
Diliger, Robert Jay, 109, 118

Dolbeare, Kenneth, 7, 19
DuBay, William H., 14
due process, 96
Durr, Robert H., 13–14
Dworkin, Ronald, 62n3

Easton, David, 28
Eighth Amendment, 18
Ellickson, Mark C., 102–4, 108
Enns, Peter K., 9, 13, 29, 37, 123–5, 133, 158
Environmental Protection Agency, 84–6
EPA. *See* Environmental Protection Agency
Epstein, Lee, 13, 18n6, 26, 26n14, 29, 41, 42n3, 53, 67, 112, 132, 133, 135, 138, 142, 158
Equal Protection Clause, 17
Erikson, Robert S., 9–10, 132, 135
Escobedo v. Illinois (1964), 20, 26, 100
Eskridge, Jr., William N., 18n6
Estreicher, Samuel, 19n8
Executive branch
  as audience for Supreme Court opinions, 8, 82, 100, 106, 107, 110
Ex Parte McCardle (1869), 9n10

FCC. *See* Federal Communications Commission
Federal agencies
  as audience for Supreme Court opinions, 43, 80–1, 83, 87, 91, 96, 120, 157
  competencies, 81
  compliance with Supreme Court decisions, 21, 79–81, 88, 157
  fixed terms, 91–2, 94
  independence of, 81, 91–5
  involvement in cases before the Supreme Court, 80, 83–6
  opinion clarity, 21, 88, 96
  partisan balance requirements, 91
  performance, 86–7, 91, 95
  professionalism of, 81, 91, 93–5
Federal Communications Commission, 84–6

Federal Power Commission, 85–6
Federal Rehabilitation Act of 1973,
    97–8
Federal Trade Commission, 84–6, 90
Fenno, Jr., Richard F., 159
Ferguson, Margaret R., 118
Fine, Jeffrey A., 42, 100
First Amendment, 53, 55–6, 78
*First National Bank of Arizona v. Cities
    Service Co.* (1968), 52–3
Fisher, Patrick, 106
Fix, Michael P., 20, 22, 42, 100
Flemming, Roy B., 9, 125
Fourth Amendment, 8
FPC. *See* Federal Power Commission
Freese, Jeremy, 147, 154
Friedersdorf, Conor, 4
Friedman, Barry, 41
Friedman, Joel William, 17
FTC. *See* Federal Trade Commission
Fuller, Lon, 62

Gaissmaier, Wolfgang, 23
Galanter, Marc, 24
Gallant, Jack L., 45, 46
Garoupa, Nuno, 3, 4
Gelinas-Chebat, Claire, 47, 48
Geller, Kenneth S., 63n4
Gentzkow, Matthew, 105
Gibson, Edward, 56
Gibson, James L, 9, 13, 28, 30, 32, 123,
    124
Gigerenzer, Gerd, 23
Giles, Michael W., 9, 67, 125, 133, 143
Gilmour, John B., 86, 89, 90
Ginsburg, Ruth Bader, 63
Ginsburg, Tom, 3, 4
GIP. *See* Governor's Institutional
    Powers score
Glaeser, Edward L., 105
Glona v. American Guarantee Co.
    (1968), 52
Goelzhauser, Greg, 14, 48
Golden, Claudia, 105
Governors
    gubernatorial power, 98, 108–9,
        117–8

compliance with Supreme Court
    decisions, 106, 157
    see also Governor's Institutional
        Powers score
Governor's Institutional Powers score,
    109–10
Granger, Clive W.J., 135
Granoien, Neil, 56
Gressman, Eugene, 63n4
Grose, Christian R., 20
Grossman, Stuart A., 46
Gruenfeld, Deborah H., 44, 45
Gruhl, John, 19n9, 43

Haddon, Michael, 102
Haire, Susan B., 19n9, 20, 24, 65
Halbig v. Burwell (2014), 60
Hall, Matthew E.K., 10, 124
Hamilton, Alexander, 9
Hammond, Phillip E., 7, 19
Hansford, Thomas G., 12, 22, 22n10,
    142, 144
Harlan, John Marshall, 34–5
Hart, H.L.A., 62n3
Harvey, Anna, 44
Healy v. James (1972), 18
Hellman, Arthur D., 61, 61n2
Herzog, Martha, 56
Hettinger, Virginia A., 20, 67, 143
Hinkle, Rachel K., 42n4
Hoekstra, Valerie, 19n9
Hogan, Robert E., 102, 104
Holbrook, Thomas M., 102
Hombourger, Sabrina, 47, 48
Hosking, Jonathan R.M., 136n17
Hoyer, Robert, 102
Huber, John D., 20, 42n3, 100, 104
Hutto v. Davis (1982), 18, 18n5

ICC. *See* Interstate Commerce
    Commission
ideological difference
    between the Supreme Court and the
        lower courts, 72, 74–7, 157
ideological dispersion of Courts over
    time, compared to Supreme
    Court, 70

INS v. Chadha (1983), 5, 80
intercircuit uncertainty, 67–9, 74–6
interest groups
  as audience for Supreme Court, 6,
    11–2, 28, 38, 82, 100, 101, 102, 156
Internal Revenue Service, 84–6
Interstate Commerce Commission,
  84–5
IRS. *See* Internal Revenue Service

Jacobson, Gary C., 124
Jefferson, Wallace B., 30, 31, 47
Jenkins, Gwilym M., 135
Johnson, Charles A., 5, 6, 8, 9, 17, 19n9,
  20–21, 22, 25, 26, 41, 42n2, 43, 119
Johnson, Timothy R., 69
Johnston, Christopher D., 30, 123, 139
Jones, Douglas, 56
Judgment Day, 47
Judicial Common Space scores, 67–8,
  70–1, 88, 111, 128, 135, 142–3
judicial hierarchy, 18, 29, 60, 78–9, 119

Ka, Sangioon, 104
Kaheny, Erin, 24
Kassow, Benjamin J., 20, 22
Kennedy, Anthony, 71–2
Kessler, Joan B., 30, 47
Key, V.O., 36, 125
Kim, Mark T., 24, 102, 104, 118
King, David C., 24, 102, 104, 118
King, James D., 108
Klein, Benjamin, 62
Klein, David E., 60
Knight, Jack, 13, 26, 158
Korematsu v. United States (1944), 122
Kornhauser, Lewis A., 29
Korobkin, Russell B., 62
Kramer, Gerald H., 132n8
Krause, George A., 109, 118
Kritzer, Herbert M., 41, 43, 124
Kuersten, Ashlyn, 24

Lassen, David Dreyer, 105
Lau, Richard R., 23n11
Lauth, Thomas P., 104
Law, David S., 49

Lay, Thomas C., 45n7
legitimacy
  of Supreme Court opinions, 28–9,
    66, 123–4
  relationship with public opinion,
    29–31, 123
  see also opinion clarity
Levitt v. Committee for Public Ed
  (1973), 32
Lewis, David E., 20, 21, 86, 89, 90, 91,
  92
Lin, Tse-Min, 135
Lindquist, Stefanie A., 20, 60, 65, 108
Long, J. Scott, 147, 154
lower courts
  as audience for Supreme Court
    decisions, 2, 6–8, 10, 20, 42, 61,
    72, 78–9, 143, 157
  opinion clarity, 24, 28, 60, 64 65–6,
    141, 145–7, 156
  compliance, 20, 22–3, 43, 65–6, 72,
    79, 100, 141, 143–4, 146–7, 155,
    157
Lynch, Michael S., 91

Mackuen, Michael B., 9–10, 132n8, 135
Madonna, Anthony J., 91
Maestas, Cherie, 102, 108
majority coalition
  size, 40–2, 45, 57, 79, 92, 118
majority opinion draft, 1, 36, 97–8
Malholtra, Neil, 108
Maltzman, Forrest, 2, 12, 32, 34, 35, 98,
  123, 124
Manwaring, David R., 7, 19
Mapp v. Ohio (1961), 122
Marshall, Thomas R., 125–8
Marshall, Thurgood, 97
Marshall's poll questions, 126
Martin, Andrew D., 13–14, 29, 67, 92,
  112, 133, 135, 142
Martin v. Hunter's Lessee (1816), 61n2
Martinek, Wendy L., 19n9, 20
Massachusetts v. EPA (2007), 80
McClurg, Scott D., 20
McCubbins, Mathew D., 21, 25n12, 28
McGuire, Kevin T., 9, 19, 20, 29, 123,
  125, 133, 158

McKay, Robert B., 19
McNollgast, 27
Medicaid, 97
Milliken v. Bradley (1974), 53
Milner, Neal A., 7, 19, 87
Miranda v. Arizona (1966), 26, 100
Mishler, William, 9, 29, 125, 133, 158
Moe, Terry M., 21, 106
Moffett, Randolph B., 109, 118
Monahan, John, 9
Moncrief, Gary F., 102, 108
Monell v. Department of Social Services
    (1978), 32
Monroe, Burt L., 44n
Mooney, Christopher Z., 108
Moran, Mark J., 21, 36
Mosher, Frederick, 106
Murphy, Walter F., 5, 7, 19, 22, 26n14,
    42n4, 60, 158

National Labor Relations Board, 84–5,
    106
Nelson, Michael J., 30, 31, 48, 119, 123
Newbold, Paul, 135
Nice, David, 106
Niemi, Richard G., 102, 108
Niskanen, William, 21, 96
Nixon, David C., 20
NLRB. *See* National Labor Relations
    Board
Noll, Roger, 21, 25n12
nonimplementation of Supreme Court
    decisions, 124
Norcross, Eileen, 86
Novak, Linda, 27

O'Brien, David M., 122
O'Connor, Sandra Day, 98
Office of Management and Budget, 86,
    89–90
O'Halloran, Sharyn, 42n3
OMB. *See* Office of Management and
    Budget
opinion clarity
    and complexity, 23, 134
    and compliance, 26, 141
    and discretion, 10, 26–7, 61, 82, 99

and instructions, 11, 29, 61, 82, 99
and judicial legitimacy, 3, 11, 13–4,
    28–32, 122, 157
and positive treatment of Supreme
    Court precedent, 142, 154–5
and whistle-blowing, 10, 27–9, 61,
    82, 100, 105
cognitive clarity, 41, 44–6
definition, 40
doctrinal clarity, 41, 43–4
measures of, 41–3
overturning precedent, 22–3, 29–30
previous attempts to measure, 40–46
reason for, 4–5
rhetorical clarity, 41
roll of media, 37–8
see also textual readability
Owens, Ryan J., 11, 14, 28, 31, 41, 45,
    45n8, 46, 49, 62, 63, 65, 73, 74, 78,
    83, 91, 92, 101, 112, 113, 119, 129,
    131, 134, 158

Pacelle, Richard L., 27
PART. *See* Program Assessment Rating
    Tool
Paulsen, Michael Stokes, 7
Peltason, J.W., 7, 119
Pennebaker, James W., 45n7
Peppers, Todd, 67, 143
Perry, Jr., H.W., 26n14, 60, 62, 63
Pfahler, Madelaine, 20, 100, 104
Piantadosi, Steven, 46
Planned Parenthood v. Casey (1992), 53,
    126
Poole and Rosenthal Common Space
    scores, 67
Posner, Richard A., 22
Powell, Lewis, 12, 32, 97–98
Powell, Lynda W., 102, 108
precedent, 22–26, 45, 72, 75–76, 112,
    114, 116, 128, 130, 141–149
Preston, Jared, 45
Priest, George L., 62
principal-agent relationship, 79
privacy, 96
procedural fairness, 31
Program Assessment Rating Tool, 86,
    88–91

Provost, Colin, 119
Pruneyard Shipping Center v. Robbins (1980), 12
Public Mood data, 9, 125, 136–8, 141
public opinion
  as audience for Supreme Court decisions, 2, 4, 9, 15, 26, 82, 122–3, 125, 135, 157
  see also public support
public support
  as a source of legitimacy for the Supreme Court, 122
  influence on opinion clarity, 122, 124–127, 131–3, 135–6, 138–9
  the "secondary population," 112
  when the Supreme Court rules against, 129–131, 157–8

Quinn, Kevin M., 44n6, 67, 92

Radev, Dragomir R., 44n6
Randazzo, Kirk A., 42, 100
Rank, A. Dennis, 45n7
reading comprehension, 150, 152–4
Reddick, Malia, 19n9, 22, 23, 42n2, 72, 143, 144
Redlawsk, David P., 23n11
Rehnquist, William, 36–7, 69, 98
Reich, Donald R., 7
Reinhardt, Stephen, 7, 36, 60
responsive compliance
  and ideological congruence, 20–1
  and opinion coalitions, 21–3
  and case characteristics, 21–3
  and audience resources, 23–4
  and opinion clarity, 24–9
review
  allocation of docket space, 65
  on ideologically disagreeable lower court decisions, 65–6
Revesz, Richard L., 19n8
Reynolds, Douglas, 56
Riccucci, Norma M., 105
Richards, Mark J., 41, 43, 124
Roberts, John G., 72
Romans, Neil T., 10, 20, 26, 27, 61, 100

Rosenthall, Alan, 108
Ross, William G., 104, 105

Santa Fe v. Doe (2000), 54–5
Schneiderman, Stuart, 102, 105, 108
Schwartz, Thomas, 1, 28
Scott, John T., 22, 29–30, 123, 151
SEC. *See* Securities and Exchange Commission
Securities and Exchange Commission, 105
Segal, Jeffrey A., 18n6, 19n9, 20, 26n14, 27, 53, 65, 67, 100, 112, 124, 135, 138, 142, 143, 148
Separation of powers, 73, 92, 112, 129, 135
Shanahan, Frank E., 105
Shapiro, Martin, 21, 87
Shapiro, Stephen M., 63n4
Shaub, Jonathan David, 42n4
Sheehan, Reginald S., 9, 19n9, 24, 29, 125, 133, 158
Shen, Wade, 56
Shipan, Charles R., 20, 42n3, 100, 102, 104, 108
Sigelman, Lee, 4
Simon, David A., 83
Slachter, Richard B., 45n7
Smith, Joseph L., 26n14, 41, 43
Solicitor General, 11, 28, 49, 61, 63, 101
Songer, Donald, 19n9, 20, 22, 24, 65, 100
Spaeth, Harold J., 124
Spence, Lester Kenyatta, 30, 32, 123, 124
Spriggs II, James F., 2, 4, 8, 12, 21, 22, 22n10, 25, 27, 29–30, 32, 34, 35, 42, 43, 80, 87, 88, 98, 101,123, 124, 142, 144, 151
Squire, Peverill, 102, 103, 108
Stalebrink, Odd J., 86, 89
stare decisis, 29
Stark, Milton R., 110
State Department, 90
state legislatures
  as audience for Supreme Court opinions, 98–120, 157
  citizen legislatures, 102–4, 106

state legislatures (cont.)
  compliance with Supreme Court
    decisions, 99, 101–2, 106, 157
  obstruction, 104
  opinion clarity, 20–2, 98–9, 107, 119
  professionalism of institutions, 98,
    100–3, 106, 108, 113–117
Staton, Jeffrey K., 10, 27, 27n15, 87, 101
Staudt, Nancy, 24, 41
Stell v. Savannah-Chatham County
  Board of Education (1963), 21
Stenberg v. Carhart (2000), 53
Stern, Robert L., 63n4
Stevens, John Paul, 34, 124
Steward, Potter, 32
Stewart, Marianne C., 135
Stidham, Ronald, 19
Stimson, James A., 9, 10, 29, 123, 125,
    132, 133, 135, 158
Stone, Harlan Fiske, 122
Story, Joseph, 61
strategic opinion writing
  why use,, 12–14
Sudenfeld, Peter, 45n7
Sunshine, Jason, 31
Supreme Court Database, 72, 84, 88n8,
    91n11, 93n13, 111–113, 128,
    132n9, 133n10, 134n13, 144,
    145n8
Supreme Court Rule 10, 62
Swann v. Charlotte-Mecklenburg Board
  of Education (1971), 1

Teske, Paul, 104
Tetlock, Phillip E., 45, 45n7, 46
textual readability, 14, 40–1, 46–59,
    67, 88
  and lower courts, 67–8
  and federal agencies, 88–96
  previous work, 47–49
  available tools, 49–51
  measurement process, 49–51
  validation of measure, 53–8
Thomas, Clarence, 4, 31, 39
Thompson, Joel A., 102, 103
Thompson v. Keohane (1995), 63
Tidmarch, Charles M., 102

Tiller, Emerson H., 10, 26n14, 28, 42n4,
    61, 66, 101
Tocqueville, Alexis de, 80
Tsay, Wen-Jay, 136n17
Tyler, Tom R., 31

Uniformity of law
  and agenda-setting, 61–3
  and Court power relative to the other
    branches, 66
  and merits, 62–4
  see also Opinion implementation
United Airlines Inc. v. McDonald (1997),
    36
Upjohn Co v. United States (1981), 36
Ura, Joseph Daniel, 13, 28

Vanberg Georg, 10, 27, 27n15, 87, 101
Vickrey, William C., 30, 31, 47
Victor, Jennifer Nicoll, 26n14
Vines, Kenneth N., 19
Vining, Richard L, 9, 125, 133
Volden, Craig, 102, 104, 108

Wahlbeck, Paul J., 2, 4, 12, 19n9, 25, 32,
    34, 35, 98, 124
Walker, Laurens, 9
Wardius v. Oregon (1973), 98
Warren Court, 19, 69
Warren, Earl, 122
Wasby, Stephen L, 7, 24
Waterman, Richard W., 20, 42, 100
Wedeking, Justin, 11, 14, 22, 23, 24, 38,
    41, 45, 45n8, 46, 62, 73, 74, 78, 92,
    112, 113, 129, 131, 134
Weingast, Barry, 21, 25n12, 36
Weinstein, Clifford, 56
Westerland, Chad, 18n6, 67, 112, 134,
    142, 143, 148
Wheeler, Darren, 5
White, Byron, 32, 34
Wildavsky, Aaron, 20, 96
William Ker Muir, Jr., 19
Williams, Richard, 145

Wilson, James Q., 20, 96
Wohlfarth, Patrick C., 9, 13, 14, 29, 37, 73, 78, 92, 112, 119, 123–5, 129, 131, 133, 135, 158
Wolbrecht, Christina, 13–14
Wood, B. Dan, 9, 19, 21, 125
Woodruff, Michael, 44
Woods, Neal D., 104, 110

Woodside, Arch G., 47, 48
Wright, John R., 28

Zaring, David, 49
Zeckhauser, Richard J., 24, 102, 104, 118
Zillis, Michael, 38
Zink, James R., 22, 29–30, 123, 151

CPSIA information can be obtained at www.ICGtesting.com
Printed in the USA
BVOW06*1857310316

442509BV00003B/4/P

9 781107 137141